BORDER KIBBUTZ

MICHAEL GORKIN

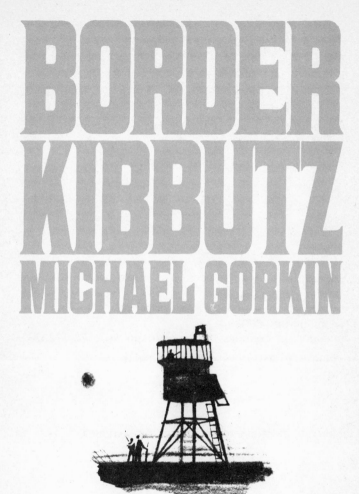

HART PUBLISHING COMPANY, INC.   NEW YORK

Acknowledgements
*I would like to thank my typist, Karen Sue Peters;
my father Jess Gorkin;
and above all, my friend Margaret Cutler.*

ISBN : 0--448--00686-3
LIBRARY OF CONGRESS CATALOG CARD NO. : 73-172023

PUBLISHED SIMULTANEOUSLY IN CANADA.

PRINTED IN THE UNITED STATES OF AMERICA.

For my grandfather
William Kleinberg

This book is based on incidents that actually happened. The names of the kibbutz and of the characters have been changed in order to protect the privacy of the individuals and the integrity of their confidential relationship with the author.

M. G.

Contents

Arrival

range-blossom smell hanging heavy in the spring night air.

The plane door had swung open, and standing there in front of the line, I smelled the remembered smell. Good reception, I thought . . . Almost too good.

"Watch your step as you go down," cautioned the *El Al* stewardess.

I stepped out of the jet, still carrying my overcoat (it had been snowing when we left New York), and headed towards the airport terminal building. A stewardess directed me to the passport control section. It was almost midnight. The terminal was empty.

I walked over to a white Formica desk and plunked down my passport. "I don't want it stamped," I told the officer. "Let me have the white card."

Once before I had made the mistake of having my passport validated with the Israeli entrance stamp, and I was not able to get into Arab countries until I obtained a new one.

"Here you go," said the officer. He did not look up.

The driveway in front of the airport was deserted except for a small fleet of black Chevrolet taxis and a cluster of drivers. The drivers were talking. As I stood there with two suitcases and a camera bag, one of them came hustling over.

1

"Where you going, sir?" he asked in English. He had black slicked-back hair, and I couldn't tell whether he was a Jew or an Arab.

"To Tel Aviv," I answered disinterestedly. I was planning to take the bus.

"Good. I take you."

"How much?"

"Six pounds. That is our fare."

"*Yoter m' dai*," I said in Hebrew. "It's too much."

"All right, five pounds for you." Now he was speaking in Hebrew, too. "My lowest price."

"I'll go by bus."

He shrugged and I left.

When the Tel Aviv bus finally arrived, the driver — a man of thirty, wearing short pants and sandals — hopped off and disappeared, leaving the front door open. An old man and two soldiers carrying Uzi submachine guns got on. They sat in front and I went to the rear, where it was dark. It was hot and stuffy, just like the New York subways. I opened the window, and putting my head as far out as I could, I smelled it again. The orange blossoms . . . Jesus, it's good though.

"*Carteesim, carteesim!*" The bus driver had returned. "*Nu*, come get your ticket!" he repeated in Hebrew, still not moving from the driver's seat.

I didn't get up. He was being rude. Or just Israeli.

"Teekets," he yelled, this time in near-English. "You need you teeket."

"You're the driver," I shouted back in English. "Why must *I* move?"

He stared at me a moment, shook his head, and started walking slowly towards me. I met him mid-way, and to my surprise he started smiling — a large, toothy smile that came out from under his black handle-bar mustache.

"This is not America," he said, pressing a ticket into my hand. "We all friends here." He slapped my back, and returned to the driver's seat, saying something on the way that made the two soldiers laugh.

About forty-five minutes later, we arrived at the usually madhouse

Tel Aviv bus station, but at this hour there was little traffic. Across the street several outdoor cafes were still lit up, and people, mostly men, were sitting under the awnings and drinking. It must have been eighty degrees outside.

Since the rear door didn't open, I lugged my bags to the front, where the bus driver, gathering his tickets and money, flashed me another toothy smile. "Enjoy you vacation, my friend," he said.

"*Todah rabah.* Thanks for the advice."

"*Chaver*, wait a minute," he called after me in Hebrew. "You're not in a hurry, are you?"

I turned around.

"Good. Let's go have a beer."

I was about to refuse, but he was already down the steps, running in the direction of a lit-up office. "Be right back. Wait here for me!"

When he returned, he grabbed the two suitcases from my hands, and led me around the corner to a cafe — a dingy looking place, with two or three metal tables, and a noisy fan. The driver greeted two men at a rear table, and then motioned me to a seat.

"Shlomo," he said, holding out his hand.

"*Shalom*," I answered.

"No . . . Shlomo. My name, Shlomo Amrani."

"Yes, of course. Michael Gorkin."

He gave my hand a thorough pumping and his face lit up. "You are Jewish, no? Russian Jew?"

"My grandparents were. I'm American."

He called to the waitress for two Goldstar beers. "So what brings you here to Israel, to the Old Country? You are on a little vacation?"

"I'm a journalist."

"A journalist!" Again the toothy smile. "*Life? Look?* Wait, don't tell me. I know, I can tell by the cameras. *Playboy!*"

I laughed hard, though I was a bit surprised. "You don't mean to tell me you get *Playboy* here?"

"What? You think we're an underdeveloped country? Of course, we get *Playboy*. Every issue."

The waitress was there now with the beers. Shlomo watched her pour, and when she turned back to the kitchen he followed her with his eyes.

"Yes, sure we get every issue," he resumed. "You didn't see the latest issue? 'Girls from Israel' — that was the feature. Their best issue yet. But between you and me, they must have chosen the first fannies they saw. I've got better looking ones going in and out of the bus every day. Even in cheap little restaurants you can find better if you look." He glanced again towards the kitchen, and smacked his lips. "Believe me, very sweet. Tell me, you're not from *Playboy* are you? No, of course not. You're here to interview Golda. Maybe Moshe, too?"

"No, I'm going to write about a kibbutz."

His smile collapsed. "A *kibbutz*? What's there to write about a kibbutz? Everybody knows about kibbutzim. They are tired of it. Write about something interesting like the Air Force. Or *Al Fatah* — how they can't fight worth a damn. *That* is something to write about."

"I am writing about a border kibbutz."

"What kibbutz?"

"Bilat."

"I have heard of it." Shlomo's voice had lost its excitement. "How do you know this kibbutz?"

"I've been there before."

"That is how you know Hebrew."

"No, I lived a half-year in another kibbutz — Hazorea — about eight years ago. I learned Hebrew there. I visited Bilat last year and wrote an article about it. This time, I'm doing a book."

"Well, I wish you luck." He slapped me on the shoulder.

"Thank you."

"And whatever you write, be sure it is good. I do not like kibbutzim so much myself, but if you like them, good. Just be sure you make a good impression for us. Americans are our friends."

My beer was gone now, and Shlomo swigged his down, leaving a white foam on his mustache which he wiped on his forearm. He slapped three coins down on the table and said: "My pleasure. I must go quickly, my woman is waiting for me. You know how to find your hotel?"

"Yes, I've been there before."

"Good. *Shalom*." And he was out the door.

I took a cab to the small hotel by the sea where I had stayed the year before. It was, I remembered, a cheap and clean place, and on the door of room 17 was a sign stating that Menachem Begin, leader of the *Irgun*, the underground organization during the British occupation, had once lived there for two months. I did not like Menachem Begin, who now led the Israeli rightist party, *Herut*, but I liked the idea that he had lived there. Besides, I liked the hotel, and it was a good place to stay for the night

I woke up late, around noon. The hot sun was pouring through the open window, and you could hear the Mediterranean slapping up against the shore. You could also hear the cleaning lady slapping her mop against the walls outside in the hall. It was time to get moving. They were expecting me at the kibbutz sometime that day, and if I remembered the bus — rather the buses — it would take four hours, even if I made good connections.

I had first made this trip the previous summer. At the time, I was on assignment to spend about ten days in a border kibbutz, and to write a short piece on what I saw. It had not been so easy to make this arrangement, because several of the fifteen or so kibbutzim on the Jordan border — where the heaviest action was — refused to accept journalists who would be staying overnight; unless, of course, they were willing to come as volunteers, remain at least one month, and work full-time. Bilat, however, after some prodding from the secretary of their kibbutz movement office in Tel Aviv, invited me to stay a week, provided I worked half days. I agreed, and wound up spending nine days there picking olives in the morning and interviewing in the afternoon. In the end, I was told that I could come back and pick olives anytime I wanted.

In February, I decided to do just that. I also decided to write something longer, and hopefully deeper, about Bilat. I was never really satisfied that I understood what was going on there or what the war had done to them. But there was also something else, something far more important to me. Even after my three visits to Israel over the past seven years, I still hadn't settled how I felt about kibbutzim or about Israel. And for some reason, I had to do this. I wasn't sure why I had to do it. My disaffection with America? The fact that I was born *Jewish*? A general malaise? I couldn't say why. But I had to do it.

It was sweltering. The 2:00 P.M. bus that went from Tel Aviv to Tiberias was already filled and still they kept coming: soldiers with rifles and submachine guns, Sephardic ladies in flower-print dresses and bags of groceries, kids in those goofy pail hats, and religious ones in the black outfits. They kept coming, and when it was almost impossible to breathe, the driver finally decided it was time to go.

The ride was uneventful. It was too hot to talk and it was too hot to read, but I did notice on the front page of the newspaper on my lap an announcement that the country was having its worst heat wave — for this time of year — in 43 years. I was grateful for my seat by the window but I did not pay much attention to the landscape until we reached the hills just above Tiberias and the Sea of Galilee. Then I perked up.

This view of the Sea and the northern Jordan Valley is the best view in Israel. You have the large blue puddle of Galilee below the brown baked Golan Heights, and if you catch it right, the sky is an endless blue above. Large patches of green are on the southern shore of the Sea — date palms, citrus and bananas — and if you know the place, you know that these are the first kibbutzim. Further south is the Jordan rift, where the Golan Heights dip and rise again as the Gilead Heights of Jordan. Bilat was there beneath the Gilead, but I could not make it out. It was a bit too far and there was a thin haze over the Sea and the Valley.

In Tiberias, we spilled out of the bus like refugees. I was lucky. Another bus was about to leave for Bilat, and in a half-hour I was there. Well, almost there. It was another half-mile from the road to the central kibbutz buildings. And while this was normally a beautiful walk along a narrow, asphalt driveway through olive and datepalm orchards, it was a hell of a hike with two heavy suitcases and a camera bag. Particularly in this heat. Fortunately, a pick-up truck turned into the driveway, and stopped.

"Better rent a camel," the driver shouted, motioning for me to put my luggage in back.

"*Todah rabah*," I said, and put the suitcases alongside the boxes of tomatoes and sacks of grain. I hopped in front with the driver — a slightly built man about thirty years old. "You were here last year, no?" he asked.

"Right. I'm surprised you recognize me."

"So am I!" He laughed.

The truck bucked forward, seemed just about to stall, but then charged on. "Come on, you old mother you," he swore in Hebrew. "Don't stall on me now." He glanced over at me and smiled. "A real stubborn old lady, this one. Name's Golda."

We laughed hard together.

"I remember you from guard duty. You came by with Ben-Saadiah. We were on duty together and he was taking you around."

We pulled into a bumpy dirt parking area behind the dining hall and kitchen. He held out his hand, told me his name was Rafael, and said he was sorry he couldn't help me with my bags. Did I know how to find my way?

"Yes, sort of . . . . But you don't happen to know where Orna lives, do you?"

"On the other side of the dining hall. The apartment house behind shelter 20. Bottom floor, last room on your right. Can't miss it."

"Good. *L'hitraot.*"

"*L' hitraot.*"

A bare-chested man with shaving cream on one-half of his face came to the screen door. It was Shmulik, Orna's husband.

"You must be Michael."

"Yes."

"Come in." With his razor, he pointed me into the living room. "Orna will be right out." Then, yelling in the direction of the bathroom where the shower was running: "Orna, the American is here."

"Tell him I will be right there," she shouted back.

"She'll be right there," Shmulik said. "Excuse me for a minute, I must finish shaving." He went back to the sink in the pantry, leaving me to enjoy the air-conditioning in the small, neatly kept three-room apartment. Very modest, and quite comfortable.

Orna came out of the bathroom, wearing a yellow low-cut dress, and still towelling her short-cropped hair. At forty-four she was the oldest child born in Bilat, and though she had four children (one of whom was about my age, twenty-seven), she moved like a teenager, and was still very attractive.

"Good to see you again, Michael," she said smiling broadly. "Tell me, you didn't swim all the way did you?" She moved over to finger the sopping-wet shirt that clung to my chest.

"I wish."

She laughed and sat on the sofa to wipe her feet. "Well, good that you made it. I was beginning to wonder whether you were going to get here today."

"I slept late."

"Enjoying your last days of luxury, right? Well, I hate to rush you, but it's almost time for dinner. Why don't I take you to your room. I arranged for you to have a room by yourself. You can shower, and meet us in the dining hall as soon as you're ready. *B'seder?*"

"*B'seder gamoor.*"

Orna slipped on her sandals and took one of my suitcases. I protested, but she immediately shook me off. ("Never mind the chivalry, Michael.") She held the screen door open, led me down the staircase, and we walked around the dining hall. The sun was just going down, and the datepalm and avocado trees threw long shadows across the lawn. On the far side of the dining hall and adjacent to it, an enormous underground shelter was being constructed. Further ahead, where the children's houses were located, cement bunkers had been covered over by boulders, making them look like huge gray igloos.

Orna must have noticed the surprise on my face. "We've been doing some remodeling."

"I see."

"It's all new. The boulders are from Syria — the Golan, rather. The Syrian houses up there were made out of them. They hold up well, we found out. So . . . so, let's say, we borrowed them." She shrugged that Israeli what-can-you-do shrug.

We continued to walk silently, behind the children's houses toward two rows of motel-like apartments; with five or six apartments in each row. They were for volunteers. The rooms were comfortable, I recalled, with a bed, a closet, a table and chairs, a fan, a coffee pot, and — if you were lucky — an armchair and curtains. In the center of the building was a communal washroom.

"Yours is this last one on the left," Orna said as we entered the second building. "There's a good table in it, and an armchair, too.

And you can do what you want with these naked girls on the wall. The last boy, a Jew from France who went into the Army on Monday, was a bit of a . . . a collector. You can do what you want with them."

I nodded.

"And remember, I don't want to rush you, but. . . . Not too late, *b'seder?*"

The dining hall was almost empty when I arrived. A long, badly lit room with about seventy Formica tables, it had the capacity to seat all of Bilat's three hundred members as well as any volunteers, visitors or army reservists who happened to be around. On the average, I had been told, some fifty of these extras were generally there. Eating arrangements were informal, and in the evenings you could come as late as 8:00 P.M. and the tables would still have the tomatoes and cucumbers on them, and the kibbutznik wheeling around the eggs, herring and olives would still be there. By the time I arrived, the clean-up crew was already closing in on the last occupied tables. Orna and Shmulik were sitting there impatiently, their heads turned towards the door. I took a seat, apologizing for my tardiness.

"Here, take these," said Orna. She passed me a cucumber, an egg, and two lumpy tomatoes, she had saved for me. "They're not the best, but they won't kill you."

I began dicing up the vegetables and the hard-boiled egg into a salad — that celebrated kibbutz salad which you ate every breakfast and dinner as long as you were there, and which somehow should have become boring, and it did, but not so much as you expected. In fact, once you put the oil and vinegar on it, and mixed in a few olives and onions, it was pretty damned good.

I ate quickly, barely looking up from my soup plate, very grateful that kibbutz manners were what they were. Shmulik and Orna sat there in silence. Just as I was polishing off the last bits of salad, Orna jumped up and waved someone over.

"I want you to meet him," she said softly to me. "You're going to be working with him. He's also going to be your kibbutz father."

I had not had a "kibbutz father" the last time I was there, but it was a practice to assign long-term volunteers to a family. The man coming toward us was stocky, in his sixties, and he walked with his chest thrust forward, his hands swinging freely at his sides. He wore rumpled tan pants, a short-sleeve shirt, and his thick gray hair lay like steel wool over a massive head. His eyes, set deep, were looking at me. I thought he was smiling.

"Bierman," Orna said to me, "I would like you to meet Bierman."

Fathers and Sons

"I am Bierman," he said, choosing personally to introduce himself. Then to Orna: "Is this the American? He speaks Hebrew, doesn't he?"

"*Nayeem l'haceer otcha*," I interrupted. "A pleasure to meet you."

Bierman turned abruptly back to me, his face at full smile. "A Hebrew scholar! So I'm going to have a scholar with me!" He gave my hand another bone-crushing shake. "That *is* wonderful . . . But don't let me interrupt your dinner. Please sit down."

"I'm finished," I said, taking a last swallow of iced-tea. "I'm anxious to see where I'll be working."

Next to the *Masceeroot* (the main offices which housed Orna, the kibbutz chairman, economic manager, work manager, accountant, and other kibbutz functionaries), was a long, flat, single-story structure. Two large ventilators hummed on the roof, and a warm thick unfamiliar smell blew down on us. Bierman was fumbling with a ring that held at least twenty-five keys. Finally he opened the door.

"Welcome to the incubators," he boomed, throwing out his hand as if he were Moses first entering Canaan. "Well, what do you think? They're beautiful, aren't they?" he said. We walked over to one of the dozen polished wood lockers, and he patted it a few times. "Eighteen years old, these incubators, and they still look like new."

He raised the black curtain over the small window on the incubator and told me to look inside. I put my head under the curtain and saw eggs, hundreds of them, neatly arranged in dozens of trays.

"Six more days and they'll all be chicks."

"Really?"

"Ten thousand of them. You will see. Next week is a big week. Tell me, you've never worked in hatcheries or chicken houses before? Well, you will learn. It is not difficult work. You don't need bulging muscles to work with chickens, but you must have it up here." Bierman pointed to his massive head. "In the *kopf* . . . You do speak Yiddish, don't you, Michael?"

"No, but I know that *kopf* means 'head.'"

"Right. With a good *kopf* there is no problem. Don't worry, you are a scholar. You will learn quickly. I will teach you."

We made a quick tour around the room and inspected a few more incubators. Bierman described how the heating and watering system worked, and how the alarm went off in case there was a power failure. He was surprised I had never heard of these incubators, because they came from a company in Colorado, and if I ever got to Colorado, I had to stop in and say hello to the manager (who Bierman said he knew), and tell him that Bierman was still happy with his incubators.

When we left the incubator room, Bierman asked me to come to his apartment, and his wife would fix me something cold to drink. "It's not every day we have an American journalist come to work in the *Lool*. Besides, now you're one of my family, you know."

On the other side of the dining hall, was another group of two-story motel-like apartment houses. There was a well-worn path across the lawn in front of Bierman's house, but we took the stone walk that went the long way around. Bierman lived on the bottom floor, and under his window were several red and yellow rose bushes and a cactus as tall as my chin. The window was open and a woman with glasses was seated inside, knitting. We went in.

"Hannah, I want you to meet the American journalist, Michael."

"Welcome," she said. She used the Hebrew expression, "*Baruch ha ba'a*," which literally means, "Blessed be the comer."

Bierman motioned for me to sit down in a well-padded armchair, and Hannah immediately offered to go fix something to drink.

"She makes the best iced-coffee in the kibbutz," said Bierman, beaming at Hannah.

Hannah went off to the pantry. "I'll bring you some, too,

Bierman," she called out. She called him "Bierman," too. I asked about this.

"Pinchas is my first name. But everyone calls me Bierman. It's a long story. Or rather, it's a short story within a long story."

"I'd like to hear it."

"Bierman telling another of his stories?" Hannah asked, mockingly, as she returned with two glasses of coffee that had ice cream hanging over the edges. "Just say the word! He's the best story-teller in the kibbutz."

"It goes back to the time when I was in the training farm in Poland. That's where I met Hannah. We were all training to come as pioneers to Israel and it seemed that every other man was named Pinchas. I never knew if they were calling me or someone else. So, I decided to call myself by my last name — Bierman. Hannah and I were just friends then. We were only about eighteen, and there was no time for love — only love for Palestine. So, like everybody else, she called me Bierman. Later, when we came as a group to Palestine, and went to Kibbutz Yagur, Hannah and I decided to get married."

"By then I had gotten used to calling him Bierman," Hannah added. "So of course, everyone else has followed along. Even our two daughters. And the grandchildren, they all call him grandfather Bierman."

Bierman took a long swallow of iced-coffee and put the glass off to the side. He scratched lightly, contemplatively, at the gray tufts of hair just over his ears.

"You wouldn't know by looking at me, Michael, but I was once a Hasid, with long side-curls, black hats and coats that you see when you go to Mea Shearim, the religious section in Jerusalem. Yes, I was once one of them.

"That is when we lived in Lvov, in the Ukraine. At that time — in the twenties — it was part of Poland. We were a family of twelve — six boys and six girls. We lived in a small house in the center of town, and my father had his shop nearby. He was a wood merchant. Being a Hasid, he wanted me — since I was the one who did the best in school — to be a rabbi. After my *Bar Mitzvah*, he sent me to the yeshiva and I stayed there for three years. I was not a very enthusiastic student. Often I would skip school and go to the movies or traipse around with the girls. I'd tell the rabbi I wasn't feeling well, and then I'd take off. If by chance the rabbi ran into my father he'd naturally ask how I was feeling, if I had gotten over my upset stomach or whatever it was. Then I was in for it. I was always getting whacked.

"The worst arguments between my father and me, and what eventually led to my coming to Palestine, was the reading I did on the side. It began the third year I was in the yeshiva. A friend of mine had a book on Greek and Roman mythology and he gave it to me to read. Suddenly I realized that there were other people who had different gods and different reasons for believing in them. I didn't know what to make of it. I started to read books on other religions, those of China, Japan and India. Then history and novels. For a year I carried on like this, finding books and hiding them under my mattress.

"Finally, my father caught me reading a novel by Shalom Asch called *The Sanctification of the Name*, about the Inquisition in Spain. In one passage there is a description of a naked woman — her breasts, her lips, her backside — all described in great detail. As it happened, I was exactly on this section when my father came into my room. He grabbed the book from my hands, looked at the title, hit me and took the book away.

"He spent the whole night reading the book, from beginning to end. In the morning he came into my room. He looked me in the eyes and admitted that it was a very well-written book. He had never read Shalom Asch; he knew only that he was an *apikoros*, a heretic. It was a good book, yes, but in places it was filthy. He didn't want me to read such things. I argued, but it was to no avail. I saw that I could never convince him.

"I was not the first in the family to have arguments like this with my father. My brother, who was two and a half years older, also had problems with him. He was very interested in music and poetry, and he used to write lots of poems, especially to one very beautiful *shiksa* who never fell for him, and who later died of tuberculosis. For this, my father considered my brother a fool and a *goy*. They quarreled all the time, and my brother wound up leaving home and going to Paris, just about the time when I went to the yeshiva. But, every once in awhile he would come back, and he used to talk with me and take me places. Once I went with him to hear *Tosca*. To this day, whenever I hear *Tosca* I think back to that time. It was against Hasidic law to go to the opera. So I got dressed in regular clothes, not my Hasidic outfit, and I wrapped my side-curls around my chin and covered them with a cloth to pretend I had a toothache. It was wonderful, and on this occasion, my father didn't catch me.

"But, besides these problems with my father, and the fact that my brother had already left home, there was the general climate of anti-Semitism in Poland. In 1924, just when I was doing all the reading, there was a particularly bad outbreak. It came as a result of an assassination attempt on the President. A bomb was thrown at his carriage. Nothing happened to him, but several in the crowd were killed. A Jew was accused of the crime, and when this was announced, young Poles, especially students, ran through the streets with sticks in their hands, beating Jews — women with their children, old men, everyone. The situation was very difficult for us all through the trial, and then, right near the end of it when it looked like he was going to be convicted, Ukranian nationalists admitted it was they who had thrown the bomb. And what do you think happened? The Jew was released, and again there was a pogrom, this time because the students claimed the rich Jews had fixed the trial.

"Well, for me that was the final step. I knew there was no future for us in Poland, and that I would have to leave. I also knew that I would go to Palestine and break with Hasidism. Hasids, you see, thought the work being done in Palestine was futile; worse, that it was sacrilegious. Jews would have their state in Palestine when the Messiah came, and not until then. To go to Palestine and try to build a Jewish state was to become an *apikoros*.

"When I made the decision to go to Palestine, I went to the *Hechalutz* [Pioneering] movement office and told them I wanted to take my training to become a farmer. They looked at me, with my black Hasidic outfit and sidecurls, and asked me why I couldn't wait for the Messiah; didn't I think he was coming? Anyway, they decided to give me a chance.

"So one Saturday after dinner when my father dozed off, I went into the bathroom and cut off my sidecurls." Bierman made a scissors of two fingers of his left hand, and then clicking his tongue, he snipped first at the left temple, and next at the right. "It was over.

The sidecurls were gone, and I changed quickly into my Ukrainian blouse and my baggy pants with the thick belt — a real *goyische* peasant dress — and I took my luggage. My grandmother happened to come by while I was doing all this and she broke down in tears. 'You're becoming a *goy*, a *goy*,' she sobbed. There was no time for explanations, my father might have awakened. And so I left.

"I found out two years later — when I came back from my training — that my father had screamed in anger, berating himself: 'What have I done that my sons run off?' He was uncontrollable, they said, until a friend, also a Hasid, consoled him by saying: 'You are worrying over nothing. Your son who went off to Paris will wind up a human being; a Jew he'll never be, but a human being, yes. As for this one who's gone off to become a pioneer and work in the dirt, a human being he'll never be; but he'll stay a Jew. So between the two of them, you'll have everything — a human being and a Jew.' It seemed to satisfy my father, because he calmed down, and didn't say another word.

"That is, not until I returned from the training and told him I was leaving shortly for Palestine. He got all upset. For several days he wouldn't speak to me, and then one evening — a day or so before I left — he came into my room and said he had a question for me. 'Do you believe in God?' he asked. His voice was shaking, and I was shaking too. But I managed to tell him 'yes'; at that time, I still did. But, I also said to him that I didn't think it mattered to God if we followed all the intricacies of Hasidic law; if, for instance, we ate meat six hours after we drank milk, or only five. God was interested in the spirit, not the letter of the religious law.

"He wanted to know what I had done in my training. I told him about the work: how we raised crops — cucumbers, tomatoes, and especially cabbage — and how we had our own chickens, milk-cows, and horses. He was no longer very angry, but neither was he very impressed. In fact, he summed it all up by saying: 'To saddle horses, to feed cows and shovel manure, a ten-year-old *goy* knows how to do. Is this what *you* want to do with your life? Is this what *you* want to be?' It was the last question he ever asked me. But there was no answer to give him."

Bierman paused, shaking his head slowly. Then looking out of the window, he said: "I never saw him again. I might have, but . . . .

Well, it never worked out. You see, once Hitler came to power, even my father was convinced that it was time to go to Palestine. But, it didn't work out. It was too late. He and the rest of my family were wiped out."

A Day of Work

Rat-tat-tat-tat-tat-tat. Silence. Rat-tat-tat-tat-tat-tat. No alarm clock needed this morning, I thought. It was 4:30 A.M. and I recognized the noise as machine-gun fire coming from the valley below, from the direction of the banana fields that grew right up to the Yarmuk River, the border with Jordan. It was nothing to worry about, not if you were in the main kibbutz area. I had learned that last time.

I had also learned that since late '67, every morning at 4:00 A.M., army units with mine-detecting equipment drove along this border checking for infiltrators. There were three abandoned villages on the Arab side of the Yarmuk, and *Al Fatah* would hide out there and take pot-shots at the army patrols. They were lousy shots, according to the soldiers and kibbutzniks, but no matter how many of them you killed, they kept coming back. If you didn't stay down there and kill them, they would come across the River, snip the double row of barbed wire, try to make it through your mine-fields, and then plant mines in your banana groves. That is what they had done before the patrols started to go out, and in the kibbutz next door, four men had been blown up on their truck. It had taken five hours to find enough of them to bury, and when they did, they buried them out there where it happened and left the truck out there with the men's names written on it.

There were other incidents in the first few months after the Six-Day War, and the kibbutzniks, shocked because they had enjoyed a quiet border since the Independence War in 1948, prepared for the worst. They reinforced the old shelters, began building new gas-proof shelters, ripped up the lawns and dug out trenches, beefed up their night guard from two to eight, moved the hundred or so pre-teenage children into shelters at night, built reinforced-concrete rooms onto each apartment, bought three armored tractors to work the border fields, and laid asphalt roads to these fields. The government paid for all these adjustments, or most of them anyhow, and — if you were a visiting journalist — the kibbutzniks told you that they had become used to the changes and that they were secure and happy. If I stayed a few months, I would see what they meant: I would learn to sleep through the morning machine-gun fire.

That first morning, however, I didn't sleep through it. I lay in bed for a while listening to it spurt on and off, and then as the sun came over the Gilead Heights, it stopped. It was time to get up. At 6:00 A.M. I was due at the *Lool*, and since Bierman was apt to take my punctuality as a sign of my enthusiasm, I decided to get there early.

It was a quarter to six when I arrived for work and found the door open. A huge penguin-shaped woman in blue overalls and a long-sleeve gray shirt, was vigorously sweeping dust and feathers into a neat pile near the door. She stopped as I approached.

"You must be Michael." She thrust out her large fleshy hand, and welcomed me inside. "Bierman isn't here yet. He'll be along any minute. I'm Zelda." She suggested we go into the rear room, the office, and have a cup of coffee.

The coffee, a thick muddy brew, took several minutes to prepare. Meanwhile, Zelda marched in and out — first leaving to clean some glasses in the outside sink, then going to check on one of the incubators, and finally rushing to the door as someone entered. With all this heft and movement, she reminded me of a catcher on a woman's softball team.

"So, how are you this morning?" Bierman greeted me, as he stepped into the office, and took *his* seat at the wooden desk. Zelda sat to his side, secretary-like. "You slept well, I hope?"

"Not bad," I answered. "except for the machine-gun fire this morning."

Bierman laughed and slapped me hard on the knee. "It's nothing, my friend. You'll get used to it. You get used to everything after a while, believe me."

"Bierman's right," parroted Zelda. "You get used to everything."

I nodded. "Maybe I'll even get used to waking at 5:30 A.M."

"Of course you will," said Bierman. "You're about to learn a new profession. You're about to become a *Loolan*, a chicken man. Believe me, you'll *want* to get up early in the morning. With the roosters." I wasn't sure he was altogether joking.

When we finished our coffee, Bierman announced that he had a very easy job for me. Zelda smiled knowingly. Until breakfast, he said, he needed me to make cartons — the small cardboard kind which were used for sending newborn chicks to market. He needed about a hundred, and it would only take a couple of hours once he showed me how to do it. Then, I should go off to breakfast. "Of course, you don't *have* to go," he said straight-faced. "You can stay here with Zelda and me. We never go. Haven't in all the twenty-five years we've worked in the *Lool*, have we Zelda?"

Zelda grinned girlishly. "Come on, Bierman, don't be silly. Can't you see he's a growing boy? He needs his breakfast."

"Not exactly growing," I said. "But I am used to breakfast."

"Of course," agreed Bierman. "So you'll go to breakfast, and when you come back, then I'll take you over to the egg section. They'll need some help there later. All right?"

"Fine."

The boxes took about two hours to make, and then I headed for breakfast. It was only 8:30, but already the green velvet lawn in front of the dining hall was sending up heat waves. A family of lizards, that was sitting on the path, scampered out of the way as I crossed over to the rear of the dining hall, where there was a line of kibbutzniks standing in front of two small sinks. Nobody talked. They just stood there silently, reading their morning newspapers (each kibbutznik received his own newspaper), and when their turn came, they slopped some cold water over their hands and face, dried themselves on the communal towel, and then chugged into the dining hall to fuel up.

I couldn't see a damn thing when I first entered the dining hall. The combination of glare from the outside, and the fact that — to save electricity — the dining hall was never lit in the morning, made it difficult to see. However, I eventually located the egg-herring-olive man heading towards the last empty tables. I began walking over there, when someone caught hold of my arm and started shaking my hand. "So what brings you back?" he said loudly.

I stared at him for a long moment, before recognizing him. It was Edo — the tall, red-haired guy from the banana groves, who had been very helpful to me the first time I was here. While never very confiding, Edo had told me a great deal about the political and military situation of the kibbutz and country. He was extremely shrewd (Orna claimed he was the one genius in the kibbutz), and as long as I never asked about *his* role and *his* feelings, he was willing to talk.

"May I sit down?" I asked. There was an empty seat on Edo's right.

"Sure, just go get yourself some eggs from the cart. He's already been here."

I went and got a hard-boiled egg. I actually preferred soft-boiled eggs, but the odds were 1-in-3 of getting a genuine soft and not a runny-hard. With the real hard you at least could make a salad. I sat down and began dicing up the vegetables.

For several minutes, Edo was involved in a conversation with two men about the banana groves. Then he turned back to me and we talked, first about small things, and soon about politics. He asked whether I had noticed the various changes in the kibbutz: the new shelters and trenches as well as the reinforcement of old shelters. Bilat, he said, was preparing for a difficult summer. Just a few days back, Dayan had issued a warning to all border kibbutzim in the Jordan Valley, suggesting that they prepare for the worst, possibly even an out-and-out war if things continued to go as they were on the Canal.

This surprised me. Judging from the newspapers, Israeli jets had been bombing Egyptian artillery emplacements along the Canal almost at will. And moreover, there seemed to be no possibility that Egypt — even with the help of the Soviets — would try to cross the Canal.

"A very American view," Edo said matter-of-factly. "Very American, and very naive. What you fail to understand is that something has changed since Russia invaded Czechoslovakia. You see, ever since then it has been obvious to us that they no longer care about world opinion. No, the Russians have the power and they use it where they want. It is only a matter of time until they make things hard for us on the Canal.

"The situation cannot remain like it is," he went on. "The Russians have whetted their appetites, and" — he flashed me an exasperated look — "the Americans have not told them how much they can eat. The Russians will try to defend the Egyptian artillery on the Canal. That is the immediate goal. My guess is that they will not try to move missiles right into the Canal zone; it's too hazardous for them. We could bomb them out in a minute. I don't even think they'll try to fly their own Migs over the area — not yet. First, they'll start flying over the major cities. Then they'll move into the Canal zone. That's when the trouble will begin.

"Ultimately, of course, they would like to take over the entire Middle East. But the Americans cannot let them do this, so the question is how far they can push. At the very least, I think they will try to re-open the Canal. They are very eager to regain use of the Canal because it gives them access to the East — the Persian Gulf oil, the east coast of Africa, and the Far East. Remember, the Russians have been waiting 250 years, ever since Peter the Great, to get into the Mediterranean. Now that they are there, they must be able to sail out of it — eastward. Keep in mind, too, that the Russians haven't just been building Sputniks for the past fifteen years: they've been building a giant flotilla, and to use it properly, they now need to open the Canal.

"How will they open it?"

"As I said, they will try to defend the Egyptian artillery so that we cannot bomb them with our planes. In time, the unimpeded artillery would weaken us, and they — the Egyptians alone, or the Russians, too — could cross the Canal and establish a beachhead. Then they might try to get the U.N. to alter the cease-fire lines, or even try to push us further back into Sinai."

"Israel can't let this happen, of course."

"Of course not. There will be war. There could be war at any step along this path. That's how the Sinai War began and that's how the Six-Day War began. The pressure along the Egyptian front became unbearable for us, and we had to alleviate it. We're moving along that same path again."

It was not a very happy note on which to return to the incubators. I went out of the dining hall alone, and began walking slowly back to work. Already it's coming at you, I thought. You just got here and already they're hitting you with it. It's going to be a long summer. And what if that other thing happens, what if you get to like the place; really like it. I blocked the thought from my mind. Edo had made too much sense for me to try to refute him, and I didn't want to start thinking right away about what I would do if he were right.

"Ah hah! Look who's here," said Bierman, as I came in. I had taken almost an hour, instead of the usual thirty minutes.

"I'm sorry I'm late. I got into a discussion with Edo."

"Ah, no wonder! Smart fellow, that Edo. Little sad and down in the mouth sometimes, but a smart fellow." Bierman stopped short and reached over to the transistor radio on his desk and turned it up. "The news. Just take a minute."

" . . . In heavy fighting along the northern sector of the Canal last night," the announcer was saying, "one Israeli soldier was killed and two were wounded. The accident occurred shortly before midnight, when the vehicle in which they were traveling was fired on by Egyptian artillery . . . ." Bierman began shaking his head, and thrust his hands deep into his pockets. " . . . Army units in the area returned the fire, and this morning Israeli jets attacked Egyptian artillery positions in both the northern and central sectors of the Canal. All Israeli planes returned safely to base . . . ."

Bierman turned off the radio; he had heard enough. Then, without saying a word about the news, he began telling me what a fine job I had done with the cartons. Now he wanted to take me over to the egg section, where there was as much work to be done "as there were laws in the Talmud."

The egg section was located a couple of hundred yards away, near the cowsheds. It consisted of five long, flat buildings where the chickens were kept, and a central room where the eggs were brought to be cleaned, sorted and refrigerated. According to Bierman, the entire *Lool* operation earned some 350,000 Israeli pounds per year, or ten per cent of the kibbutz income. He was particularly proud of this because almost all of the ten workers in the *Lool* were *vateekim* (oldtimers), who were no longer able to work outdoors, but who were able to produce just as much by working in the *Lool*.

When we entered the central room of the egg section, Bierman introduced me to the two sorters and the two cleaners. He then turned me over to a younger man named Dodik, who appeared to be the supervisor. He was also the only one there, except for Bierman, who moved around easily, un-arthritically.

"I'll take care of him," Dodik assured Bierman, his large head bobbing up and down. Then he added something I didn't catch, something in Yiddish, and Bierman and the others in the room laughed.

"No, I'm sure he doesn't mind cleaning eggs," Bierman answered in Hebrew. "Do you, Michael?"

When Bierman left, Dodik handed me a wet rag which he took from a pail of dirty water, and instructed me how to clean the "dirt" from the eggs. Zvi, who was now cleaning the eggs, had to go to the infirmary in ten minutes — he had something wrong with his hands — and I was to take his place. There was nothing to it, Dodik said. Avram would send the eggs through the cleaning machine, and the ones that were still spotted, I would clean off and stack with the others in the egg trays. When I had a stack of six trays, I would bring them over to the sorters, Sarah and Sadie.

I worked like this for the rest of the morning. There was hardly any conversation. Avram was a quiet, shy man, and Sarah never said a word. The egg collectors who came in at 10:30 A.M. with a load of eggs, and then again at 11:30 A.M., drank a glass of water or tea in silence, and then left. The only one who talked was Sadie, and she made up for every one. She talked almost constantly, mostly in Sarah's direction, though if you passed by her, she was sure to direct it at you. Rarely, did anyone answer, and so the effect was one of a monologue, full of sound and fury, signifying loneliness. I was glad when Dodik came along at noon and told me I could go for lunch and that I was off for the afternoon.

I didn't do much that afternoon. It was still too hot. In fact, it was what the Israelis call *chamseen*, an Arabic word that literally means "fifty," and in this case it meant you could expect about fifty hot, dry days like this in a year. It was not an ordinary heat, this *chamseen*. It was a desert heat that stuck like dust in your nostrils and was so thick you felt you could lie back on it. You could not work in it, unless you and probably several generations before you had been born in it; and when it came, especially in the summer, the kibbutz took a siesta from about noon to three.

I lay most of the afternoon on my bed, dozing on and off, as the noisy fan blew the warm air onto me. When the sun went down, about seven, I took a shower and dressed to go over to Lea Sharett's. It was Friday night. At lunch Lea had invited me to join her for *Erev Shabat*. I had asked if she thought Bierman would be offended, and she said no, but I should be sure to tell him beforehand. I did, and he invited me to come to his house some other night — though he was sorry I would not be spending my first *Erev Shabat* with my "family."

In a way, though, Lea had been my family when I was here the previous summer. I had visited her three or four times and met her seventeen-year-old daughter, Neeli. But I never did meet her husband who she said came around regularly even though they had been separated about fifteen years. Frankly, I did not understand Lea. The separation from her husband and the fact that she said he still came around often, were not so puzzling ("We've done it for Neeli."), but there was some rift in her character that I couldn't figure out. She came from Germany in 1933, and had spent almost all her adult life — she was now in her fifties — in a kibbutz: first one which was about twenty miles to the south, and then here. She spoke enthusiastically about the simplicity of kibbutz life, the social justice of it, and the education of the children. Yet, she freely admitted that she received monthly checks from a wealthy sister in New York, that she "couldn't really get by" without these checks, and what is more, she thought the kids had been spoiled by too much progress, and she was not surprised that her two sons had left the kibbutz. I could not put all these admissions and assertions together. Nor could I understand why Lea seemed at once a dignified woman, and also somewhat of a gossip.

"Well, look who's here!" Lea called, as she came rushing to the screen door. She was smiling a deep, welcoming smile, and had evidently just finished washing her hair. Her face was red and wet. "Come in. *Do* come in. But you must excuse me. I haven't quite straightened out the apartment."

She escorted me inside, and quickly arranged two cushioned chairs next to a glass-topped coffee table.

"Your apartment looks as lovely as I remembered it," I told her. It really did. The curtains were hand-made with a lovely orange and yellow flower pattern. There were two bouquets of kibbutz-grown flowers, roses on the book-case, and jacaranda sprigs on a wooden table which also had framed pictures of her two sons and Neeli. The bookcase was neatly stacked with old German volumes, several art books and novels in English, and two long rows of books in Hebrew. The total impression was one of taste and order.

"Thank you for the compliment," she said, "but no, it doesn't look like it should. You see this room back here. . . ." She opened a door behind her and I could see chunks of plaster and several paint cans on the floor. "They were supposed to have it done by Passover, but they informed me today that it is impossible. By the end of the month, they now say."

I asked her if this was the new "security" room they had recently added to all apartments.

"Right. We are the last. The rest, almost all of them, have been done ages ago. But anyway, once they finish, it will be worth it. Twenty centimeters thick they have built these walls, and with *beten*, reinforced concrete. It would take a direct hit from a *Katyusha* rocket to pierce it. Otherwise we are safe."

It seemed strange to hear Lea, who was about my mother's age, describe the explosive potential of *Katyusha* rockets.

"As for ordinary cannon fire," she went on, "there's no possibility that it could penetrate. Or so they tell me . . . ." She stopped short, as the screen door opened, and a tall, fleshy girl — Neeli — and a gentlemanly-looking fellow with white hair, entered. Lea promptly introduced me to Moshe, and he shook my hand delicately.

"Moshe is a teacher in the kibbutz high school. I don't believe you got to visit the school last time, did you, Michael?"

"No. I was meaning to, but I didn't have the chance. Perhaps this time."

"Well, Moshe is the one to speak to," Lea announced. "Go ahead, don't be bashful."

She took Neeli by the hand and led her into the pantry, "to fix some snacks for the men." Moshe and I sat down and began discussing the possibilities of my visit. He thought it was a good idea, he said, but first he would have to discuss it with his "comrades"; he could not — even though he was principal of the school — make an "arbitrary decision." That wasn't the way things were done in the kibbutz.

"Peach cake!" announced Lea, as she and Neeli came back into the living room, carrying a large serving tray of refreshments. "Your favorite, right? Didn't think I'd remember, did you? Well, Neeli baked it today especially for you. On the Suzy Homemaker oven, remember?"

I nodded. She had told me about the Suzy Homemaker oven the year before. Most families didn't have such luxuries, the standard being a coffee pot and a hot plate, but Lea liked to bake and there was the money from her sister in New York for these things that she liked. ("But don't you go putting *that* in your magazine article," she had told me. "Not that it's such a big secret, but still it's better not to go publicizing it, right?")

Lea dished out the peach cake, and Moshe — who declined the cake "for dietary reasons" — went over to the bookcase and began thumbing through one of the thick volumes. He seemed engrossed in it, but when Lea and I started discussing the kibbutz, he put the book down and came back to the sofa.

"I think it's going to be a bad summer," Lea was saying. She glanced up at Moshe, but he said nothing. "It's nothing you can put your finger on exactly," she continued, "but it's something we all feel. A feeling that this whole stinking business with the Russians is all leading to . . . to something horrible."

"Come on, mother," Neeli said sharply, "You're always exaggerating these things."

Lea shrugged, "You see? I tell you, all I can say is thank God for *their* confidence. Israel has always existed as far as they are concerned, and it always will."

"There is a lot to be said for this kind of confidence," said Moshe pedantically. "Because of their confidence we all can be hopeful."

"Hopeful? Of course we're hopeful," said Lea. "Who has any choice except to be hopeful. But I tell you sometimes I wish it hadn't worked out this way. You know sometimes I think it would have been a lot better if Moses received the Ten Commandments from some place like Mont Blanc. Seriously, you know, when our group from Germany first came to Palestine, the Jewish Agency asked where we wanted to settle. We said we weren't sure. 'How about the Beit Shean Valley?' they asked. 'No,' we answered, because at that time the Beit Shean Valley was all dust. 'Then how about the Jordan

Valley?' Again we said no, because the Jordan Valley was just desert. 'So what do you pioneers want?' 'Switzerland,' we said. 'We'll settle the Mont Blanc.' At the time it struck us as a funny answer, but now I think it was a pretty good idea."

"Look, on that fanciful note," Moshe interrupted, "why don't we go to dinner?"

"I second the motion," said Neeli, rising quickly out of her chair.

"Yes, of course," agreed Lea. "I'm sure Michael doesn't want to miss the Friday night dinner."

The dining hall was packed when we got there. The children, who usually ate their evening meal at the children's houses, were together with their parents now, and at each table there was a full family. In the corner of the dining hall, two candles were lit. ("Simply a tradition," explained Lea. "Nothing to do with religion.") And each table was covered with a white table cloth, and had a pitcher of flowers in the middle. It was hard to imagine that this was the same place where I had sat in the morning. We waited near the door a few minutes until a table opened up.

"*Nu*, like a restaurant in Tel Aviv, isn't it?" said Lea jokingly, as a girl in tight yellow slacks and low-cut blouse passed. Most of the younger women (under thirty) were dressed modishly like in Tel Aviv, whereas the older women still wore the fashions of the *shtetl*.

"Come on, mother," said Neeli. "You know you don't mind."

"Mind? Of course I don't mind. I'd like to be in a restaurant in Tel Aviv right now."

Neeli and I laughed, but Moshe sat there dead-pan, continuing to look around the dining hall, as if it were his first time.

Eventually, the food cart was wheeled our way, and instead of the eggs, herring and olives, there was chicken. A man in a starched, white apron and short pants served us each a piece, and we began eating hungrily. There was a long silence, and then Neeli turned to me (a chicken bone in her hand), and said she'd like to know how my family celebrated *Erev Shabat*. Did we go to Temple? Or did we stay home and just have a big dinner, like in the kibbutz?

"Well, frankly," I admitted, "we don't do anything. Some Jewish families do, but not mine. We are Reformed Jews. We have never celebrated *Erev Shabat*."

Moshe looked up from his plate. "They're like the Jews in Germany, they want so much to be assimilated that they have given up all tradition. Except even in Germany, Jews generally celebrated the Sabbath in one way or another."

Neeli seemed surprised. "Is that true, Michael? You celebrate nothing? Nothing at all?"

"We used to celebrate Passover when my grandfather was alive. But now we don't celebrate that anymore, either. About the only thing we celebrate is Christmas."

"*What?*" Lea asked unbelievingly.

"It's true. We've always had a tree and given presents. My parents consider it more an American than a religious holiday."

"I don't believe it!" said Lea. "I mean, I knew there were Jews like that in the United States, my sister has told me about it, but I had no idea that you were ... that you come from such a background."

"I do. I can't really say I'm ashamed of it either. Most of my relatives are not this way, and my grandmother has never quite forgiven my mother for it. But it's the way I was brought up. It's the way my friends are, my Jewish friends that is, and I got used to it. Up to a point I had gotten used to it, I should say."

"'*Up to a point!*'" Moshe interrupted, repeating my words, "Up to a point you can forget who you are, and then it hits you. Like it or not, you must admit you are a Jew. Either you admit it, or others will decide it for you."

Moshe's words irked me. It always irked me when one of these Israelis from the Old Country claimed he knew my fate, and like it or not, I would someday have to decide I was a Jew. The *sabras* said the same thing, but it didn't bother me so much when *they* said it, because it always sounded like something they had learned by rote. But the ones from Europe, these goddamned *alte cockers* from the Old Country, they always said it to you as soon as they met you, and always in the same words, and always like some goddamned thunder-bolt from heaven.

"It has nothing to do with my Jewishness," I said with obvious annoyance to Moshe. "It's something deeper, something more confusing...." I knew I was being vague, but then I was none too clear about it myself, and the last thing I felt like doing at that moment was laying out my background like a patient on an operating table for Moshe to slice open and poke at. Besides, I knew what his diagnosis would be, and I had no desire to hear it.

Fortunately, Lea caught my mood and said: "Look, this is Friday night. It's no time to be getting into these weighty philosophical discussions. Let's eat in peace." She licked her fingers. "Tell me, how's the work going? Orna told me you're in the *Lool*."

Silently, I blessed her for changing the subject. "The work is easy, and Bierman seems like a perfect boss."

"Maybe so." She sounded skeptical. "It's the beginning. In the beginning he goes easy with everyone. Later he gets harder."

Moshe wiped the corners of his mouth with one of the parchment-like napkins. "He's a stickler about his work. It's something special to him, he has no perspective about it. *Meshugat ovodah*, we call it. Work craziness. It's a thing that's dying out."

"And just as well! There's more to life than work, even if we didn't think so at one time." Lea smiled wisely, and reached across the table to take a small dish of fruit compote. She passed one to me too.

"Well, how about Zelda?" I said. "She doesn't seem any less enthusiastic about the work."

"Same thing," said Lea, swallowing quickly. "You're absolutely right. Zelda has worked so many extra hours that she has accumulated enough time to take a year off without working. And Bierman has about half that, about 150 days. And do you know he has a bad heart? Two heart attacks. The last was during the Six-Day War. The doctor told him he had to take it easy, but he pays no attention. He just goes right on working seven days a week, ten to twelve hours a day. I don't even think he takes a vacation."

"What is the normal work load?" I asked.

"Eight hours a day for men, seven for women," answered Moshe.

"Less if you're in school," said Neeli. "Only one day a week if you're a senior in high school."

"And vacations?" I asked.

"Ten days a year, besides Saturdays," said Moshe.

"Only eight days if you're under thirty," said Neeli.

"There are variations and exceptions to these rules," said Moshe, "but basically that's what it is."

"Who cares about numbers?" said Lea. "I want to hear more about the *Lool*."

"There's really not much more to say," I said. "In the egg section, hardly anybody talks . . . except for one person."

"Sadie!" Lea announced. "Never stops, I bet."

"She's nuts!" said Neeli. "Don't pay any attention to her."

"She has always been like that," said Lea. "Ever since the beginning. If anyone ever wrote down all that she said, there would be enough volumes to fill the Hebrew University."

Neeli burst out laughing and I laughed too. Moshe smiled and then added: "She's not as foolish as she seems. She's a lonely woman who talks all the time to fill the silence, but if you listen to what she says, you'll see that she is a pretty good barometer of how everyone else feels. They just have the sense to be quiet."

"One must be grateful for little things," said Lea.

Everyone laughed, this time even Moshe. Then, clearing his throat, Moshe mumbled something about "meeting Avram."

"Avram Schecter," coached Lea. "You mean, you don't know anything about him?"

"Yes, yes," I remembered. "The one who was cleaning eggs."

"You don't know that he used to be a *macher* in Ben-Gurion's government? Assistant Secretary of Agriculture, I think it was."

"Exactly so," confirmed Moshe. "Back in '48, the first government after the State was founded. Later, he became head of all economic enterprises for our kibbutz movement. He held that spot right up until a few months ago when he retired. He's over seventy, and couldn't work so hard any longer. But he still goes once a week to Tel Aviv as a consultant."

"And the rest of the week he works in the *Lool* cleaning eggs?"

"Right. We wanted to put him in the *Masceeroot*. We didn't want him to do physical labor. Apart from his age, it's been twenty-five years since he has done constant physical labor. Of course, now and then he did some physical work when he was here for the Sabbath or for his vacation, but nothing on a regular basis. So, about a year ago, when it became clear he was giving up his administrative work in Tel Aviv, we suggested he work here as an accountant. When he heard this, he refused. He wanted to do physical work."

"So he wound up cleaning eggs?" I repeated.

"He could hardly have worked in the bananas."

"Never mind, I think he likes it," Lea said.

By now, we had polished off the dessert, and everyone was anxious to leave. Especially Neeli. Just a few minutes before, a tall curly-haired soldier, had come over to the table (he barely said hello to Lea and Moshe), and told Neeli he was waiting for her. She told him she'd be right out.

"Well, get going already," Lea finally said to her. "You don't have to stay around with the old folks." She smiled apologetically at me.

"Yes, I know," said Neeli. "I don't need you to tell me." She got up from the table and excused herself.

"Shall we all go?" said Moshe. He looked down at his watch. "I believe there's a movie at 9:30 P.M."

"What is it?" Lea asked disinterestedly. Then to me: "I hardly ever go. It's almost always junk."

"I think it's something in French, *Les Temps des Loups,* something like that."

"It's probably not worth it anyhow," Lea said.

"I'm going to see it," Moshe said.

"Not me," Lea said.

"There are Hebrew subtitles," Moshe said to me.

"I don't read Hebrew so quickly," I said. "I think I'd better pass it up. Thanks anyway."

The cleaning crew had already stripped the tables. We said good night to each other, and I went back to my room, turned on the fan and went to sleep.

A Day of Rest

To wake up late on a Sabbath morning, about 9:00 A.M., say, and to hop into a clean pair of pants and a clean shirt, and then go have a leisurely breakfast which always had something extra like cottage cheese or chocolate spread, was for me the finest kibbutz luxury. Even veteran kibbutzniks felt the same way. More than the refrigerators, air-conditioners, radios, and week-long vacations by the sea, they valued this Sabbath morning rest, though they may not have said so — it generally wasn't acceptable to *love* rest — and besides, they had to work for all the other things, gathering them over the years, whereas the Sabbath morning rest came free and had always been there.

Of course, not everyone got to sleep late on *Shabat*. Someone still had to milk the cows, collect the eggs, irrigate the fields, and prepare the food, and each kibbutznik lost one *Shabat* morning a month doing these things. Then, too, there were the families with young children: the kids almost always spent *Shabat* with their parents, and often they would arrive early from the children's houses and wake them up. And finally, there were those unpredictable things that could louse up *Shabat* morning — bombings, for instance, or anti-aircraft fire — and these, of course, were the worst, not simply because they were dangerous, but moreover because they were a special head-tax that you alone paid, and almost everyone else in the world was exempt from.

But that Saturday morning — my first in Bilat — there was no mortar attack, no anti-aircraft fire, and as an outsider I was free from all the other obligations of kibbutz life. So I slept late — in fact, so late that when I arrived for breakfast I had to go into the kitchen to get some leftovers. I ate quickly and then took a short walk.

Actually, there wasn't very much to see. You couldn't walk more than a few hundred yards east (towards Jordan), because once you came to the middle of the banana groves, you were likely to meet some army patrol that would question you and send you back. Or, if you had no run-in with a patrol, you might come up behind a machine-gun position that overlooked the Yarmuk, or behind a tank position. Two British Centurion tanks sat like elephants in the heart of the banana groves. While none of this was terribly dangerous — the Israeli soldiers being used to foolish foreign volunteers who appeared out of nowhere — it still was no way to behave near the border.

So if you wanted to tour, you had to walk westward, where there were fields of date palms, eggplants and olive trees; or you could walk north and south on the main Jordan Valley road, where you could see other border kibbutzim. It wasn't really polite to drop into another kibbutz when you knew nobody, but there was nothing wrong in walking by them. You could do this heading northward, and after you passed three or four of these kibbutzim you would get to the Sea of Galilee. You could also hitch a ride to the Galilee — though you couldn't take a bus because they didn't run on *Shabat* — and you could get a ride rather quickly unless there was a girl or a soldier hitching near you.

Too lazy to try for the Galilee either by walking or hitching, I strolled over to the kibbutz swimming pool, and sat there until lunch, wishing that this gaping cement hole was filled with water. That would come later, Orna had told me, probably sometime after Passover; nobody had expected this kind of heat in April. However, Yehudah, the man in charge of the pool — he was one of five or six kibbutzniks who had given their German reparations payments to build the pool — promised that if the *chamseen* continued, he was going to check with the water allotment people in Tiberias, and see if he couldn't pump up a bit of the Yarmuk early this year. Maybe by next *Shabat*, if necessary.

After an uneventful, though tasty, beefstew lunch, I went back to my room and my fan, and went to sleep. I might have slept right through dinner if the high-school kids who lived nearby weren't playing their records at full blast, and Beatles' records at that. I woke, appropriately, to the strains of *Here Comes the Sun*, and somehow that reminded me that Bierman had invited me to his house before dinner.

Shaved and showered, I headed for Bierman's, only a couple of hundred feet away, across a large expanse of lawn (one of the few areas that, as yet, had not been marred by trenches). The sun was still out, though not so hot, and several families were sitting on blankets, taking their tea outside. Small children in short pants or swim suits were tossing around a beach ball, or else riding their tricycles along the path. And, off at the far end of the lawn, with the Gilead Heights in the background, a group of high-school boys were playing soccer. It seemed like some Jewish summer resort in the Catskills.

"So how's my American friend — the scholar?" Bierman grinned widely, and flung open the screen door of his apartment. "Or should

I call you a chicken man by now?"

He ushered me into the living room, where Hannah was seated. She had her feet propped up on a chair, and the fan was blowing gently on them. She held out her hand, "So how are you enjoying your first *Shabat* in Bilat?"

"Fine. Except, to tell you the truth, I slept through most of it."

Bierman led me to the brown sofa with the white doily on the back. "I'm glad to hear you're taking it easy, my friend. You don't want to overdo it, not in the beginning. It takes time to get used to working in this heat. Doesn't it, Hannah?" By now, Hannah was off in the pantry.

"Not many people get a chance to see what a kibbutz is. At least, they should spend a few months in one. Then if they don't like it, fine, they can leave. Nobody has to live in a kibbutz that doesn't want to, but at least they should see it first. . ."

Bierman paused as Hannah returned with some chocolate cake and her iced-coffee with the ice cream dripping over the edge. He began telling me how he had once been a recruiter for the kibbutz. Usually, the kibbutz would receive a letter of inquiry either directly from a family, or through the kibbutz movement office, and a representative would be sent to speak with the family. Bierman said he had enjoyed the job, that it had given him more insight into how outsiders saw the kibbutz, but he admitted that he never could understand why some people didn't want to join.

"Take for example this Bulgarian family I once visited. They lived in one of the worst run-down sections in Jaffa. The husband worked as a porter on the docks. The apartment was nearly empty except for a bare table, some crates for chairs, a few mattresses on the floor and four or five children who were running around in torn clothes and dirt all over their faces. In all this mess, his wife was preparing some soup which she invited me to eat, but I told her 'No thank you,' I had already eaten.

"The man was dressed in shabby clothes and looked like he hadn't shaved for a week. He wanted to come to Bilat, but first he wanted to know what it was like. So, I told him that each child lives with his own age group, not with the parents, and each child has his own closet of clothes, and the food is good and healthy. 'How will I pay for this? What work will I do?' he asked. I explained that there is no money in the kibbutz, except for a 150-pound allowance each year, and that the work he would do depended upon the work manager — bananas, cows, chickens, something like that. 'And how about my wife, what will she do? Will she take care of the house and cook?' I told him that his wife would work, too — in the children's houses, the laundry, the communal kitchen, it all depended. He was a little surprised by this, and he sat there thinking for a moment, and then asked: 'You mean my wife will not cook for me? Who will prepare my soup then?' I told him that we all eat our meals in the same place, kind of a restaurant, and that there is soup almost every day. 'What kind?' he wanted to know. That depended on who the cook was. If the soup cook is from Poland it's a Polish soup, if she's from Morocco it's a Moroccan soup. He began to shake his head. 'I don't think I'll go. If my wife won't be able to stay in the house and cook. . . .No, it won't be any good.' And that was that."

Bierman sat there, now shaking *his* head. "Who can understand it?" he said. "His children were dirty, his apartment was poor and empty, his clothes were shabby, and he doesn't want to come to the kibbutz because he likes his wife's soup!"

"Well," I said, laughing in spite of myself, "*I* like the kibbutz soup."

Bierman laughed, too. "You see, it is good."

"Very healthy, too," added Hannah.

"Hannah used to be the kibbutz dietician."

"I had to give it up. Too much time on the feet. So, now I make underwear. It's a sit-down job. Easier on the feet."

I nodded, and there was a short silence as everyone sipped iced-coffee.

"Tell me, Michael," Hannah finally asked, "how are *you* finding the work?"

"Not too difficult. I've had some experience with physical work before. I once lived a half-year in Kibbutz Hazorea."

"Of course, on the road to Haifa," Bierman said enthusiastically. "Not far from Kibbutz Yagur. That *is* interesting. Do you hear that, Hannah? He's been to a kibbutz before."

"Yes, I'm listening," Hannah said.

"Tell me more. Tell me about Hazorea. How did you like it there? What brought you there?"

Bierman was brimming with enthusiasm. I couldn't get out of it, I saw, not without some kind of excuse which he would recognize immediately as just that. Still, I couldn't be sure how he would react. I debated with myself how much I would say, and then decided I would let it flow.

"Some of these things, I perhaps shouldn't tell you," I began, "but I suppose I might as well let you know the whole story."

"Yes, of course," said Bierman, "the whole story. You are one of the family now, I want to know you better."

"I've told you that I once spent a half-year in Hazorea. That was in 1963, when I was twenty years old. I was not a very political person then: I knew nothing about political theory, nothing about Marxism, nothing about the Soviet Union, or Cuba, or Israel, or even America. I was not, to say the least, very well informed. I didn't even read the newspaper.

"So how did I wind up in the kibbutz? To this day I think it had very little to do with my Jewishness. My parents are Jewish, and so were all my grandparents, but I, personally, didn't feel very Jewish. You see, my connection with Judaism was superficial. My parents insisted I go to Temple and be *Bar Mitzvahed.* 'I don't care what you do afterwards,' my mother told me, 'but at least I want you to know some of the history.' Meanwhile my parents never went to Temple except on *Rosh Hashanah,* and we never celebrated the Jewish holidays, except for *Chanukah* sometimes, and Passover when my grandfather was alive. So, what was Jewishness to me? Nothing, to tell you the truth. Nothing except problems, because every now and then some gentile kid would make a rotten anti-Semitic remark, and you had to face him with it, or you felt lousy. Or someone would ask you what your religion was — a teacher or a kid, say — and you had to say 'I'm Jewish,' because if you didn't, then you were trying to hide it, and you felt ashamed.

"But actually, I'm making too much of these problems. Because, by the time I went to college, it was no longer an issue. I lived for two years with gentile roommates, though there were also Jews on the same floor, and I was in love with a gentile girl. Nobody made anti-Semitic remarks, except for the usual wise-guy college jokes and there was nothing very personal in this. I never went to Temple, I had nothing to do with *Hillel* — the college Jewish organization — I had no interest in learning Hebrew, and very little curiosity about

Israel. I still said I was Jewish if anyone asked, though as far as I remember, hardly anyone ever did.

"So why did I go to a kibbutz? Well I got bored with college after my sophomore year. I wanted real life experience, to learn by doing — not from reading. At the end of my freshman year, I had gone to France, not speaking very much French. I spent the summer on a farm there. It was the first time I ever did farm work, the first time I ever traveled by myself, and it seemed to me then that I learned more that summer than in my whole life. I wanted to do something like that again. So, after my sophomore year, I decided to travel and work for a year. I went back for a month to the French farm, and then spent two months on a Danish pig farm. Finally, I decided to try a commune. As far as I knew, there were two possibilities: a *kolkhoz* in Russia, or a kibbutz in Israel. The *kolkhoz* was out of the question for political reasons, so the kibbutz was my only real possibility. I came to Israel and wound up in Hazorea."

"The rest of the story is more complicated," I continued, "and perhaps less easy for you to understand. What makes it especially hard to understand, maybe, is that in all truthfulness I can tell you that I loved the kibbutz. I loved Hazorea. Of course, there were things that bothered me. In six months I never really became a part of kibbutz society, and only had two or three friends. But these seemed like small matters compared to what I liked. For example, I liked the fact that all people were treated as equals, that the kibbutz garbage man was on the same social level as the kibbutz chairman, and I liked the idea that these people seemed to believe in what they were doing. They had come here and made something out of nothing. But my feeling for the kibbutz never carried over to a love for Israel. Whenever I left the kibbutz and went to Haifa or Tel Aviv, I was put off by the rudeness and arrogance of Israelis. And then, when I spent a month in Jerusalem working on a construction crew, I felt convinced that Israel was a country like all others: the only thing special was the kibbutz.

"And I still feel this way, that Israel is just another country — like all the rest. And I guess this is why I've been so critical of Israel. You see, once I got back to college, events in America had begun to churn up. Martin Luther King had led a march on Washington the summer I was in Israel, and when I came back to college, most of my friends were involved with civil rights. Soon I was participating in demonstrations, school boycotts, and I even spent a short time in Mississippi as part of a voter registration project. I also began to distrust and dislike America.

"Then came the war in Vietnam. I began to do a lot of reading, gave up the idea of becoming a psychologist, and immersed myself in history and economics. After graduation, I traveled throughout South America, and what I saw there was worse than anything I imagined. This was the real face of American imperialism. I returned home distrusting my country, and ready to do anything I could to change it. I began to study political economics, Marxism and other things, first by myself and then in graduate school. I also got involved in radical politics. Marches, demonstrations, sit-ins, teach-ins, everything. I considered myself a revolutionary.

"I don't expect you to understand, but it was completely natural for me to be against Israel in the Six-Day War. We were all against Israel. We did not hate it the way we hated South Africa, or South Vietnam, or America. We did not oppose it that way. But still we felt that Israel had taken territory which didn't belong to it. It had thrown out the Palestinians, and Israel now stood in the way of Arab socialism. The most progressive Arab states — led by Nasser — were the ones trying to destroy Israel. And, since the Arabs comprised a hundred million, and the Jews 2.5 million, and since the Jews had no business being there in the first place — well, of course, we wanted to see Israel lose."

Bierman could not contain himself when I said this. "How can you say such things? Two thousand years they let it all go to waste, and you call *that* progressive! In fifty years we make it a garden, and you oppose *us*! I don't understand it, I just don't understand it!" He was angry, but there was no getting out of it. I tried to explain the New Left position.

I began by recalling some of the history of Palestine: the Zionist dream which called for the establishment of a Jewish State in spite of Arab wishes; the British sell-out of the Arabs after World War I; the exploits of Jewish terrorist gangs during the British Mandate; the conquest of Arab territory in '48. I mentioned them all, and at each point Bierman interrupted me. ("I don't know where you ever learned such garbage.") I made no effort to argue with him because

I no longer believed this was the whole story. Still, I had friends who believed it *was*, and since I had once been with them, I felt it necessary to at least state the case.

"Perhaps even more important than the question of Palestinian rights," I continued, "is the question of oil. You see, those on the New Left feel that the only way the Arabs are going to move out of their misery is if they can control their own oil. They cannot do so unless the foreign companies are booted out, and the only way to boot them out is for popular movements in the Arab countries to overthrow the pro-Western rulers — like Hussein, and Feisal, and all those little emirates in the Persian Gulf that are nothing more than the creation of imperialist powers. Israel's position in all this, the way the New Left sees it, is as a kind of outpost for the imperialist powers. As long as Israel exists, the progressive forces in the Arab world — Egypt, Syria, *Al Fatah* — are stymied. They must throw all their force into beating Israel, and they stand there humiliated. But, if they can succeed in beating Israel, Hussein will fall, so will Feisal, and so will the Persian Gulf emirates. It is a question of power politics and, the way American radicals see it, Israel is in the way and has to go."

Bierman exploded. "It's insane! How can you say such foolishness? How can you be so unprincipled? One-two, goodbye Israel, because the Arabs need oil! And how can you be so stupid to think the Arabs would get this oil? Don't you see what the Soviet Union would do? Can't you see what they've done in Eastern Europe? The Russians will take the oil just as the Americans and British have taken it. And what is more, they will squeeze the Arabs until there is nothing left of them. They have already begun to do it in Egypt, and just give them the chance, and they'll do it to all the Middle East. And, for this, your New Left wants to destroy Israel? Let them go to Egypt or Syria and see this Arab progressivism. Let them see how men are treated when they say something against the government, or how the women are kept almost like slaves. They want socialism do they, these New Lefters? Let them see Arab socialism, and let them compare it to Israel. We have more socialism here than the Arabs will ever have. Let them come and see that!"

He stared at me angrily, waiting. "All I'm trying to describe," I explained, "is how and why I *once* viewed the situation."

He shook his head slowly, appraisingly, and then in calmer tones said: "I don't mean to accuse you personally, my friend. I understand, I understand. It's the New Left of yours. Whenever I hear about them, it makes me angry. Especially the Jewish ones. When will they open their eyes?" I sat there silently, not knowing quite how to answer him, or whether to answer him at all. Then, he said: "Please, go on. I want to hear what changed you."

"I came to see that much of what you say is right. I don't mean to say I agree with you entirely. I don't really see the Russians as that evil, but I don't see them as saviors, either. They are in it for themselves, just as the Americans are. And I agree, a Soviet takeover of the Middle East would be no improvement. Czechoslovakia taught me that. I was there a few weeks before the Soviets came in with their tanks, and I saw how much the people hated and feared them. Since then, I have never been able to see the Soviets in the same way. I won't curse them like you do; I won't write against them, but I won't praise them either.

"But that was only part of my reason for pulling out of the New Left. You see, we were never so much pro-Soviet as we were pro-Cuba, pro-China or pro-Third World. We knew that in some of these countries violence had taken place, that people were still not able to speak openly; but all of this, we felt, was necessary for the removal of counter-revolutionary forces.

"Then I spent some time in Egypt in 1968. Actually, I had gone there for several weeks, but as things turned out I left early. I knew that Egypt was no revolutionary country, no Cuba, but it *was* the hope of the Arab world. When I got there and began to talk to people, I could see they were scared; most wouldn't say anything, and the rest just gave me the government line. Besides this, I saw that the social differences were enormous. The bureaucrats lived much better than the *felaheen,* and the women, at the very best, were second-class citizens. I had to admit that as rude and arrogant as Israelis were, you didn't have this. At least here, women were pretty much equals with men, and the class distinctions were small by comparison.

"What completely turned me sour on Egypt was the fact that after a few days of seeing these things, and asking questions, I began feeling uncomfortable, even scared. The cab driver asked my name, he wanted to know if I spoke Hebrew, and he followed me back to the hotel. And a student asked me in the middle of dinner if I had been talking to others as I had to him about Nasser, politics, and that sort of thing. I said yes, and he answered: 'You are asking the wrong questions at the wrong time and in the wrong place.' He told me that he would not leave the restaurant with me (I was probably already in trouble), and if he were in my shoes he would take the first plane out of Cairo. I took his advice. I caught the next plane to Cyprus, and then to Tel Aviv. Immediately I felt relieved. That very evening, I wound up in a political argument with the hotel clerk. I took an anti-Israel position and after an hour-long debate I went to bed, completely secure that I wasn't about to be informed on.

"I spent about three weeks in Israel that trip, including two weeks at Hazorea. I cannot say that I came to like Israelis any better this time. Hazorea was disappointing, because I began to feel that it was a closed society and the people in it were suffering a kind of village isolation.

"In any case, I returned to the States and gradually started moving away from the New Left. I finished graduate school and started free-lancing as a journalist. I no longer demonstrated much — by now the demonstrations had become more violent, and you didn't just get arrested. You were beaten up in the process. I began to feel that the violence we had once talked about so glibly, was a heavy price to pay for anything. I also saw that we had talked too easily about giving up — in the name of Revolution and Socialism — the right to openly say one's mind. I kept thinking back to Czechoslovakia and Egypt.

"Then, in this somewhat changed frame of mind, I started to read seriously about the Middle East, and I saw that not only did the Arabs have rights to Palestine, but so did the Israelis. I also came to realize that important as the oil was to the Arabs, Israel's defeat wasn't necessarily going to be followed by nationalization of the oil companies: Israel could lose, and the oil companies go on. Or even if the oil companies *were* expropriated by Arab nationalists, would the people get the benefit of the oil? I wasn't sure. In any case, it no longer seemed like a good enough reason to wish for Israel's destruction. The whole situation, in fact, began to look to me like a tragedy; the Palestinian refugees having their claims and the Israelis having theirs, and I really didn't know where I stood, though I felt Israel had the right to exist.

"This was pretty much my viewpoint when I wound up here last summer. I cannot really say whether I have changed much since then; I still see the situation as a tragedy. What is not very clear to me is why I somehow feel bound up in the thing. I do not love America by any means, but I am surely far more American than Israeli. And even though I know a few words of Yiddish, and can speak Hebrew, and like gefilte fish, I do not see where this makes me much of a Jew. I would like to figure these things out. Perhaps then, I'll also have a better idea where I fit into America. Anyway that's why I have come back, and that's why I am writing the book."

It was a long story and I was exhausted from telling it. I was not sure Bierman had followed me. There were, after all, so many turns, so many twists which I, myself, could not explain, that I could hardly expect Bierman to weed through it all and come up with any sort of understanding. I just hoped that in my desire to level with him I had not made an enemy.

Bierman sat there, his eyes focused not on me but somewhere else, somewhere far-off. Hannah said nothing, she just looked at him. Then, Bierman looked at me and said: "A book is a very great thing, Michael. I am a lover of books, and I tell you that if a man writes a book, a good book, he is making a gift to the world.

"But there are some important things you do not understand yet. You do not understand what is a kibbutz, you do not understand what is Israel, and you do not understand what is a Jew. And because you do not understand these things you do not understand yourself. You will be here three months. I hope that will be enough time for you. Perhaps you will need more time. I can only tell you that it is important for you to learn about these things, more important, maybe, than anything else you will learn in your life — more important even than your book." He paused a moment, gauging my reaction.

"To me your story is not a puzzle," he continued. "I have heard many stories like it. It is the story of a Jew. A Jew, not just because his mother and father are Jewish, but because he is a man without a place, without a country. You can turn against America, fall in love with Russia, join the New Left, become a revolutionary, because you are a Jew. Who was Marx, Trotsky? Who were half the men who made the Russian Revolution? So when you tell me you are a revolutionary — excuse me, *were* a revolutionary — and in the name of Revolution you turned against Israel, the one country that is really your own, you do not surprise me. It hurts me, yes. It makes me angry, yes. But it does not surprise me.

"We too were revolutionaries once. Not the same kind of revolutionaries as you, because while we turned against our native countries — like Poland or Russia — we felt we would create a revolutionary new country here in Palestine. And in many ways we did. But look also what has happened to us. For more than twenty years the Arabs have been trying to destroy us. They sit at our door and wait for the first chance to come in and murder us. And then they bring along the Russians, once our friends, once our heroes even, and they sit there together and prepare to annihilate us. What could we do? What *can* we do? We must survive. And to survive you need friends. Is it our fault that we have wound up with Germany, South Africa and America as our friends? Do you think we wanted it that way? Do you think we wanted the socialist countries to turn against us? We didn't. But this is the price we have had to pay to survive as a Jewish nation.

"So you say, if that is the price, you don't want it. If you must be against Russia, and Cuba, and all them, you don't want it. But do you think that Russia and Cuba and the rest are any different? Cuba hates us because she needs Russia, and Russia says hate Israel. And Russia hates us because she wants the oil and control of the Middle East. Every country, every people is in it for themselves. Sooner, or later we all have to discover that. The only people who are not in it for themselves are the Jews around the world. They love everybody, all the poor, all the miserable. And do you know why? Do you know why they are such great internationalists? Because they have forgotten themselves. They are *luftmenschen*, men of air, men without a country. You can only place everybody else first, when you place yourself last. That is what you have not learned, Michael. You have not learned that about Jews. I think you will. If you stay here awhile, you will. I am sure of it."

Bierman was smiling now, and Hannah, who had sat stonily through all of Bierman's talk, was smiling too. And so was I. I felt none of the anger that I had felt towards Moshe the night before when he told me that like it or not, I would have to decide I was a Jew. Bierman's message was the same, but there was no talk of anti-Semitism in it. I wasn't really sure what was in it. Most of the things I had heard before, but I had never put them all together in the same way. I would have to think about it. In fact, I wanted to leave Bierman's house right then and start thinking, but there was no chance. A young couple and two children had just come in.

"Don't tell me," the woman said, "This is Michael." She flashed me a smile, her white teeth lighting up her tanned, bony face. She reminded me of a fox. "Glad to meet you, Michael. I'm Yael. This is Eton, my husband; and Kinneret and Tamar, our daughters."

Eton, a large man, smiled stiffly, and the two girls, who couldn't have been more than two and four, hid behind Yael.

"Yael's our daughter," Hannah said. "We have two daughters. Ruthy is in another kibbutz." Hannah asked Yael and Eton to sit down, to "have something to *nosh* on," but Yael shook her head no.

"We'll miss dinner, mother. It's almost eight."

Bierman stood up abruptly. "She's right Hannah. We'd better get a move on it."

Although it was late the dining hall was still half-filled, probably because it is *Shabat*, I thought. The flowers were still on the tables, and the kibbutzniks had a scrubbed look about them. The children played outside. We sat down, all of us except Kinneret who took a piece of bread with jelly, and went off to join the children.

Then it happened. I had been dicing a cucumber into my salad when I heard it. Fssooooosh.....Boom! First like a whistle, and then breaking like some enormous firecracker in your ear. I jumped to my feet. Fssooooosh.....Boom!.....Fssooooosh.....Boom! The windows shook, and everyone in the dining hall was up. I expected to see a sudden, mad dash for the doors, but no, they seemed to stop short, almost frozen. Drora, the kibbutz chairman, stood in the middle of the room, her hands raised, signaling everyone to move slowly. And over by the door, another kibbutznik, a young man I didn't recognize, was yelling, "Take it easy! Walk! To the rear shelter! Slowly!" And everyone obeyed. Like a crowd exiting from a theatre during intermission, they headed calmly to the rear door.

Bierman, who had run to the front lawn where Kinneret was playing, now had the girl in his arms. He was cautioning us to watch our step. There were planks with nails in them lying alongside the unfinished shelter, and the staircase was still shaky.

There must have been one hundred of us down in the shelter. It was not at all crowded because it was an enormous room, but it had the dank smell of wet cement, and was badly lit by a string of light bulbs that dangled from the ceiling. There was no place to sit, so everyone milled around in small clusters, talking excitedly, speculating about what was going on outside.

"Revolutionaries," Bierman said angrily to me. "*Al Fatah's* revolutionaries! Nothing but a bunch of rotten cowards. And that's what your New Left calls heroes!"

I didn't answer, though I wondered how he was so sure it was *Al Fatah*, and not the Jordanian Army, or the two divisions of the Iraqi Army which were said to be stationed just over the Gilead Heights.

"All they can do is fire *Katyushas* at civilians," he went on.

"Take it easy, Bierman," Hannah said. "Getting excited won't stop the rockets."

The children were no longer together in a group, but had joined their parents. One mother was playing "clap-hands" with her two daughters, another was feeding her son a sandwich which she must have brought with her from the dining room. A man was holding on tightly to a six-year-old boy who was crying.

"I want my parents!" the boy yelled, trying to escape from the man.

"Not till the rockets stop," the man said.

"I want them! I want them!"

"Your parents are in a shelter, too. You can't go there now. Not until it stops."

A woman brought over something for the boy to eat, but he pushed it away and kept shouting. The man said nothing now, but continued to hold the boy tight. Everyone ignored them, as if this were a common occurrence. Calmly, they went on talking to each other, a few even joking, and the only thing that temporarily interrupted them was the noise from the bombs.

"Tell me, Michael, this is the first time for you?" Bierman asked, "The first time you've heard rocket fire?"

"No," I said. "There were some shellings the last time I was here, but nothing as close as these."

"You're right," he answered. "These were close. Probably landed inside the kibbutz. Wouldn't you say so, Eton?" He turned to his son-in-law, who had thus far been silent.

"Yes," Eton answered, in a somewhat detached voice. "It's the first time in weeks they've come so near. *Al Fatah* no more knows how to fight a war, than a donkey knows how to walk on two feet.

"Take these *Katyusha* rockets tonight," he continued. "It was pure chance that they had landed this close. Usually, they landed far away — in the fields or out by the road. A good army uses spotters, but not *Al Fatah*. They simply planted the rocket launchers in the hills — as far away as twenty-two kilometers — and pre-set them to fire at a given hour. Then they scamper away to hide."

How did he know that these were *Katyushas*, and that *Al Fatah* was firing them?

"Oh, you develop an ear for such things," he answered. "Besides, the Jordanian Army hardly ever bothers us. They know damn well that if they do, we'll go after their cities, like Irbid. So, about the only time we have any trouble with them is when we go in with our planes and strafe *Al Fatah's* hideouts; then the Jordanians throw a little anti-aircraft fire our way. That's about all."

"So *Al Fatah* are the only ones shooting in this area?"

"Sure! Why should they care?" Bierman answered sarcastically. "The heroes of the people, the heroes of the Palestinian cause, why should they care if we have to retaliate on innocent villages? They can't be responsible for *that*, can they?"

"The Iraqis are the same." Eton added. "They've got a couple divisions just over the Heights, and they fire on our settlements the same as *Al Fatah*. Why should they care if we retaliate on the refugee villages or Jordanian towns. It's not *their* towns. . . ." He stopped momentarily, looking at Yael and Hannah who had just moved over to join us. ". . .But what you hear now is not the Iraqis. They fire with cannons. And cannon-fire, in case you don't know, is very different. None of that whistling sound you hear with *Katyushas*. No, with cannon-fire, you have no time to duck. You hear them when they land, and that's it."

"Aaaach!" muttered Hannah, flapping her hands disgustedly

towards nobody in particular. "I tell you, the whole thing's enough to drive anyone *crazy*." She took hold of Yael's wrist lightly. "Go ahead, tell Michael what happened to you a few weeks ago."

Yael shook her head no. "He just got here, and already you want to scare him off?"

"Yes, I suppose you're right," said Hannah, not quite convinced. "Some other time, Michael."

"You've already started," said Eton. "You might as well finish."

But nobody said anything, except for Bierman who began telling me how Bilat was really a very lucky kibbutz. The only things ever hit were buildings: apartment houses, the machine shop, the cowshed, and twice almost the *Lool*. In fact, with the exception of Reuben Ben-Zvi, who once caught a small mortar fragment in the leg, nobody had actually been hit.

"No?" said Hannah, incredulously. "What about Yael?"

"I wasn't hit, mother!"

"No! You were only knocked to the ground and had half the dining hall on top of you."

"A little debris," said Yael to me. "Nothing serious."

"She was almost killed," said Hannah, "and she calls *that* nothing serious!"

"Take it easy," said Bierman. "No need getting excited."

Hannah ignored Bierman. "That's the trouble here," she continued, addressing everyone. "Too many heroes. Nothing serious, nothing serious, they go on saying. You'll see, we'll go back upstairs and there'll be people still up there. Didn't even go to the shelter. Why? Because it's nothing serious, is it?"

And Hannah was right. When we returned to the dining hall — about a half-hour after the initial shelling — there were three or four tables of young people, some high-school couples and some soldiers, who from the looks of things had gone on eating through the entire attack.

"See what I mean," said Hannah, as we headed back to our table. "They never left. They'll stay there until someday something happens."

"Come on, let's not get excited," repeated Bierman.

"You're making too much of it, mother," Yael said. "It's their business, they can do what they want."

"It's understandable," Eton said to me, but so that everyone else could hear. "None of this is new to us. You spend a month and a half each year in reserve duty, and there's usually a lot more than a few shells, believe me. Especially if you're on the Canal, where most of us have been at one time or another. It's understandable that when you're at home you don't want to be bothered by this kind of thing."

We finished our dinner in peace. There were no more surprises except for the appearance of a short, middle-aged man named Shimon, who told us that two of the rockets had landed in the stacks of hay next to the cowsheds. The hay had been damp where they landed, so nothing burned.

"Well, what about the *Lool*?" Bierman asked him.

"You know they don't dare hit the *Lool*."

Everyone chuckled, including Bierman.

"If they ever hit the *Lool*," Yael said to me, "my father will go after them himself."

"With his bare hands," added Eton.

"What about everything else?" Bierman asked.

"The rest of them must have hit in the vineyards," Shimon said. "Nothing else came into the kibbutz."

"Good. But, are we going to have to go back to the shelters later?"

"I don't think so. We've had no word yet, in any case."

"They're talking about a possible counter-attack," Eton said to me. "Sometimes after an attack, we go right after them with our planes. The army lets us know so we can be in the shelters in case there is anti-aircraft fire or a return volley of any sort."

"You better put the children to bed, just the same," Bierman said to Yael.

"I was planning to," Yael snapped back.

Bierman kissed Kinneret and Tamar goodnight. As they went off with their parents, Bierman took hold of my arm and told me not to go.

"I want you to stay around and see the *asifa*, the weekly kibbutz meeting. Here in the dining hall, in another twenty minutes or so. . .Did you ever go to an *asifa* in Hazorea?"

"We weren't allowed."

"Well, here you're allowed. I invite you. I want you to see what is real democracy."

The *asifa* was just getting underway when I returned. The kibbutzniks, about a hundred of them, were facing the side of the dining hall, where one of the *Masceeroot* functionaries — a man in short pants and a short-sleeve shirt, with white Ben-Gurion-like hair flowing over his ears — was just then testing out the microphone. I took out my notebook, and scribbled some notes: one hundred kibbutzniks equals roughly thirty per cent of the membership; almost everyone present seems tired, old (Where are the young?); oh yes, two tables of young — twenties, early thirties — on the opposite side of the dining hall, near the door (Ready to leave?); some high-school kids peering in the rear windows, giggling, making jokes (They can't attend, Bierman had said, until after high school when they become members); on the formica tables, there's some food — oranges and cake — and everyone is eating; flowers are still on the tables, lasted through the shellings; how long is this going to last?

"The topics to be discussed tonight are two," intoned the speaker over the microphone. He ran his hands through his long white hair, and looked out at the audience. "They are: (1) The Shatz Library, and (2) Nimrod Tevlin and the Gardens. We will begin with the library, I think we can dispense with that quickly enough. Uriel will discuss the blue-prints and if there are any questions, raise them afterwards." The speaker waved in the direction of a tall, dark-haired man with glasses who approached the microphone. The lights went off, and a floor plan of the library was projected on the screen behind the speaker's stand. It was all too technical for anyone to follow. Five, ten, fifteen minutes, the voice droned on. When he finished and the lights flashed back on, several older men in the middle of the dining hall appeared to be drowsing. There were two questions from the floor: one about the size of the building, the other about the location of the bathroom. With a voice vote, the members approved the plan.

"Now let's move on to the question of Nimrod Tevlin," the speaker said. Three young people rose and left, one of them carrying an armful of oranges. "All of us, I think, are familiar with the general background of this problem. But, just to make sure, I would ask Nimrod to come forward and state the situation. Is that agreeable to you, Nimrod, or would you just as soon we go ahead without it?"

"No, I'll be glad to come up."

When he approached the speaker's table, I recognized him as Orna's father. She spoke of him, I remembered, in a peculiar way — the way one speaks of a friend or a business associate. She was warm and sympathetic in her words, but somehow detached, and I remembered wondering whether this was typical of kibbutz relationships.

Orna had told me that Nimrod — she called him Nimrod — had gone through some difficult years. Her mother had been an invalid ever since Nimrod was forty years old; she died three years ago. Orna and Nimrod had nursed her mother right up to the painful end, and Nimrod had suffered a great deal. His only distraction was his work — he had been the kibbutz gardener from the beginning — and this is what kept him going. However, in the last two or three years, just when he was finally free from looking after her mother, his work became a terrible frustration. Security measures required trenches and underground shelters, and all this had to be done quickly with little consideration for beauty. And Nimrod, who had carefully planned the landscape — "It was one of the best in all Israel" — watched the trees knocked down and lawns dug under, watched the security people override his suggestions, and eventually, when he couldn't stand it any longer, he quit. Orna understood how hard it had been for him, and agreed that Nimrod's suggestions should have been listened to. But still, the most important thing was getting the shelters and trenches made, and Nimrod should have understood this.

"I cannot understand, I don't care how many times I hear it, I will not accept that we do not have the manpower or equipment." Nimrod, a thin, bald man with a soft voice was speaking — really lecturing — to the members. "If you want me to come back, if you say that Talik cannot take my place, that he has not done the job well because he is not a professional gardener, then why do you refuse to take the advice of a man who *is* a professional? I need a tractor, I need five more men, two steady and the rest volunteers. Otherwise I cannot come back. Let's not talk about what has been done to the landscape. That's water over the dam. But if we are to repair the damage, we must go about it wholeheartedly, with the right equipment and the right number of workers. Otherwise, I must say no, I cannot go back." And Nimrod sat down.

The discussion that followed was heated. One by one, members came up to the microphone and stated their opinions. First Talik apologized for the condition of the landscape, but repeated that gardening was not his profession; he was a shepherd. Then Drora, the kibbutz chairman, commended Talik for his fine job, especially since he had filled in for Nimrod with so little notice. In her opinion, everyone ought to be grateful for his work. Next came Bierman who said he was perfectly aware of Talik's difficulties, but the members ought to remember that Bilat once had "the finest gardens in the country" thanks to Nimrod, and that if Nimrod said he needed more men and a tractor, then the kibbutz must provide them; he didn't care how. Two more spoke, one echoing Drora, and the other seconding Bierman. Then Yankel, the kibbutz accountant and one of its most respected members, slowly came to the microphone and argued at great length that Nimrod had no right to just pick up and leave his post, and that quite apart from any decision on men and equipment, he ought to be told to return immediately. Nimrod winced visibly at this, but said nothing. Finally, a young man named Elie, the only one of the younger generation to come up to the microphone all evening, said there was no sense getting all heated up over such things. There were far more important matters in the country and in the kibbutz than the appearance of the gardens, and while he, too, wanted the kibbutz to look well-kept, there was no sense quibbling about it. Give Nimrod as much as possible, tell him to go back, and enough said.

It was almost 11:00 when the speaker called for a vote. Almost everyone supported Nimrod's immediate return to the post of gardener. All was well. Someone, of course, would later have to figure out where to get the money, but in the meantime the gardens would be looked after and Nimrod would be happy.

I looked over at him, and he did look satisfied. He continued to stand by his chair, near the front door, and as everyone filed out, he accepted their congratulations, grinning like a schoolboy. I decided to go over and introduce myself, and hopefully arrange for a meeting with him sometime in the near future: I wanted to know more about him. To my surprise, he agreed on the spot. ("I'd be delighted. Orna has already told me about your mission with us.") He smiled warmly, and said that anytime during the week, after dinner, would be just fine.

I went out the front door of the dining hall into the warm, mosquito-filled night. The stars were out and the datepalms were silhouetted against a half-moon. As I began crossing the lawn to head back to my room, I noticed on the bench near the far entrance of the dining hall, a slight young man who — perhaps because he was sitting alone — seemed like a spectator, observing both the night and the kibbutzniks who were filing by. I walked a bit closer and saw that it was Rafael.

"So how's it going, my fellow *kolkhoznik*," he greeted me with a laugh, motioning for me to sit down.

"Fellow what?" I asked.

"*Kolkhoznik*. You've never heard of a *kolkhoz*?"

"That's what I thought you said. Sure I've heard of them, but I never heard a kibbutznik refer to his kibbutz as a *kolkhoz*."

"So how's it going?" he repeated, this time slapping me on the shoulder.

"Fine. How come I didn't see you in the *asifa*?"

"Me go to an *asifa*? Hell, no. Never. I just sit out here and listen — for entertainment. Come to think of it, it's not that bad — as entertainment, I mean. In fact, considering that everything else is closed during the *asifa*, it's the best thing going."

We both laughed, and Rafael started to give me a humorous lecture on why he didn't like going to kibbutz meetings. "None of the young people like to go," he said. "There's too much talking. For hours on end these *vateekim* [oldtimers] can go on about nothing. They never get tired of talking. It's a Jewish sickness. The *vateekim* brought it over with them from Europe, and after forty years, they still haven't been cured. About the only thing you can do is laugh at it.

"You take this business about the library. Did you ever see anything so stupid? I bet you didn't follow one word of it, did you? Of course not. You need technical training to follow that stuff. I assure you, there weren't more than two people in there besides Uriel who knew what the hell he was talking about. But everyone's got to hear it, right? Otherwise it isn't a democracy. And the crazy thing is that all it would have taken is that one old buzzard who said he didn't like the location of the bathroom. And if he said it convincingly enough, they would have voted down the whole plan, just to please him. Believe me, I've seen it happen!"

"So what's the alternative?"

"Who knows? To sit out here and enjoy it, I suppose. . ." A tall, blonde girl in skin-tight shorts, passed. She looked about nineteen, and had a terrific smile beamed at us. "That's the alternative," he whispered to me.

"*Lyla tov*, Rafael," sang the girl, fluttering her hand in our direction.

"Hey, that's no way to say good night," Rafael answered. "Come over here, I've got something to tell you. . ." He looked her up and down. "Something about. . .about your shoes."

The girl smiled. "Never mind. You can tell me tomorrow. Good night."

"A *quiet* night, she means," Rafael whispered to me. "If she came with me, then it would really be a *good* night." Then loudly to the girl: "Good night, lovely one. And remember what you just said about tomorrow!"

"I think I better be going off to bed, too," I said. "I've got to get up early tomorrow."

"Where are you working?"

"The *Lool*."

"Ah, the *Lool*. Our old-age home. I hope you're going easy on your boss. You don't want to break him in too quick."

"Thanks for the advice. Good night, now."

"Quiet night, you mean."

A Gardener's Story

The first few days of that week before Passover, the *Lool* work remained as dull as it had been the first day. I swept, made box tops, cleaned eggs, sorted and packed them for market. The only departure from this routine was on the fourth day, when I spent several hours with three other men, vaccinating the ten thousand chicks which had hatched and were being prepared for export. Bierman and Zelda fluttered back and forth that day, carrying the chicks from the vaccination table to the packaging table. And as they worked, they flapped at each other, usually in Yiddish, and usually with Bierman coming out on top. All of this was somewhat amusing to me, but the three men I was working with, all oldtimers except Dodik, completely ignored it. In fact, they almost completely ignored each other, with only Dodik now and then making a bad joke, which he alone laughed at.

I tried to somehow break into this silence. Perhaps, I thought, a new face, a young face, would arouse their curiosity. Nothing doing. About two or three sentences worth of curiosity was all I could stimulate, and even that was more politeness than anything else. I began to feel that maybe Rafael was right: maybe this section of the kibbutz *was* something of an old-age home. I decided to go that evening to visit Nimrod.

Through the screen door I could see him sitting on a rocking chair, swaying back and forth in front of the fan. He was talking to a woman. I knocked lightly and Nimrod came to the door. He was wearing a pair of clean work boots (several of the oldtimers preferred work boots to shoes), gray cotton pants, and a tee shirt. His face was sunburned and so was his nearly bald head.

At first, he didn't recognize me, and I had to remind him of our conversation of a few nights before. Embarrassed ("I was a bit overwhelmed that evening."), he ushered me into his home — the usual three-room flat, but crowded with pots of flowers that jutted from the corners or vined up the walls, and family photographs over the mahogany desk, and padded chairs, an ornate coffee table, and glass-doored bookcases. It was unlike any other kibbutz flat I had visited.

Nimrod introduced me to his friend — a woman of about the same age, who worked in the kibbutz kitchen. She promptly went off to make "our guest" some coffee. Then, Nimrod asked what I wanted to know. He had heard about me from his daughter, Orna, and he would be glad to assist me in any way.

"But first," he raised his finger, "we must wait until Becky comes back from the pantry. If I am one of the so-called founding fathers, then she is one of the founding mothers." Nimrod moved the fan that had been blowing hard on one of the potted plants. While he was walking back and forth, looking for just the right angle to put the fan, I told him I would like to know something about the *asifa*. There was something that still puzzled me.

"What would have happened if the kibbutz said no, it couldn't provide the extra help and equipment. Could they compel you to go back, anyhow?"

He looked at me, astonished. "No . . . no, we don't do things like that here."

"I see. Then what that fellow Yankel said about the kibbutz telling you to go back . . ."

"Michael, look, let's not discuss the *asifa*," he interrupted, in a voice that was part pleading, part angry. "That's water over the dam. If you want to know about other things in the kibbutz I will be happy to oblige you. But nothing about the gardens, let's leave that alone."

Nimrod continued to look for the right angle for the fan. When he finally found it, he sat down, waited for Becky to bring in the coffee and a blintze-type cheese roll she had baked. Then — of all damned things — he took out an electric razor and began shaving his white stubble beard. At the same time, he started to tell me about himself, his background, and the founding of Bilat. It was, he said, "a story as long as the Bible," but he would give me an abridged version.

"It begins, in Kazatin, Russia, where I was born in 1899. Kazatin was — I don't know if it still exists — but then it was a small Ukrainian town of some five thousand people, in the Kiev region. It was also an important junction on the railroad line that runs from Moscow to Odessa, and many of the Ukrainian families worked on the railroad. The rest were farmers. Jews made up about half the population, and were merchants — grocers, tailors, carpenters, barbers. And while we lived right with the Ukrainians, integrated you could say, socially we were completely separate.

"My family descended from a long line of rabbis on both my mother's and father's sides. We were five children. I was second to the oldest. For a long while we lived in one huge house — the seven of us, and uncles, aunts, nephews and nieces. In addition, there were constantly people, young people, coming in and out because our house was the center of Zionist meetings. My father was the leading Zionist in the area, so they would gather in our house to discuss Zionism and to sing songs of *Eretz Yisrael*. My father taught Hebrew in our local school and, of course, I learned how to read, write and speak it.

"Before the war and revolution, when I was still a young boy, my father promised me that I could go to the high school in Jaffa, Palestine. This hope never left me, not even when it became impossible due to the upheavals. Instead, in 1916, I had to go to the Polyteknikon in Kiev. I spent a year studying engineering. The Ukraine was already in a huge depression. I went to the school barefoot, and there was almost nothing to eat. Just to get bread was not easy, and what we did get was of poor quality. This, and a thin soup made of cereal and water, and once a week a small bit of beef, was all we ate.

"Things were even worse in Kazatin. Since our town was a railroad junction, thousands of Jews passed through it, homeless, and with nothing to eat. We did what we could, gave them bread and water, and put them up for a short while, but it was not enough. And these were only a few of the hundreds of thousands of people who were displaced during that period.

"Kazatin, itself, was passed back and forth between the Bolsheviki and the White Russians. The Bolsheviki mostly left us alone, but the White Russians were brutal. They beat us, killed us, raped our women. And the Ukrainians who had lived with us all those years, were no better. Boys I had grown up with rode through the streets on horseback and grabbed old men by their beards until half their faces ripped off. I saw them take little girls off, God knows where. Some never came back, and those that did were ruined for life . . ."

Nimrod's whole body heaved a great sigh. He looked out the window and then back at me. "These are things I have tried to forget," he said. He smiled faintly, rose from his rocking chair, and turned off the fan. He opened the window to let in a thin breeze that had begun to stir outside, and then sat down again to resume his story.

"Let me tell you about something a little less depressing," he said.

"Something about the *Chalutzi* or Zionist Pioneering Movement that I joined. Remember, in my father's house I had been raised on the milk of Zionism. Well, the revolution only intensified this feeling. All nationalities in Russia experienced a great surge of national feeling, and we, as Jews, were no different. True, some were members of the Jewish Bund — a Jewish socialist party — and they opposed Zionism. But most of us in Kazatin were Zionists, and the desire for a national homeland was so strong you could almost taste it in the air.

"I joined the *Chalutzi* movement when I first went into the Polyteknikon, and stayed in it for the next six years. A group of Polyteknikon boys and girls, about twenty of us in all, joined the movement together. After the first year of school, we decided to quit and spend full time preparing to emigrate to Palestine. Hardly any of us, however, had backgrounds as workers — heavy physical work like farming was considered work for *goyim* — and there was no possibility for us to get this training in Palestine. We couldn't get there. Russia's borders were shut. True, there were rumors that you could make it through the Caucasus, but we didn't want to try because the mountains were covered year-round by snow, and we knew that some of us would never survive it. So, we decided, at least in the beginning, we would train ourselves in Russia until an opportunity came to leave.

"The first two years we spent in the Smolensk region. There was a large railroad construction project going on there, and people from all over Russia were brought in to work on it. We worked with Tartars, Kirghiz, Byelorussians, the lot. The boys and a few of the tougher girls did heavy construction work, and the rest of the girls worked in the kitchen. Our group lived as a commune. We slept at night in empty railroad wagons, twelve to a wagon, and we pooled our earnings to buy the food. Actually, the food sold by the government wasn't bad; the bread was good and the soup had cabbage in it. As long as you could work from dawn to dusk you could be sure there was food, and in those days that was a blessing. There was no chance to save any money, but we didn't care because we looked upon the work as an apprenticeship.

"In the winter of our second year, we saw a possibility of getting to Palestine. The government announced that all those who were nationals of another country or empire, and had been detained in Russia due to the war, could now be repatriated. From Batum, on the Black Sea, several shiploads of refugees were leaving for places like Greece, Turkey and Palestine. Our group, in hopes of getting on one of these ships, moved to Tiflis. There was all sorts of finagling going on to get the right papers, and this took time and contacts and money. While we tried to make these arrangements, we worked — the women in town, and the men on a hydroelectric project. For two years we carried on like this, and in the end we never got the right papers. The frustration and disappointment split us up, and we dispersed — some staying in Tiflis, some returning to Smolensk, and others to the Crimea.

"I was one of those who went to the Crimea. There, in Yalta, was a Zionist collective farm that was training future farmers for Palestine. There were several throughout Russia. Our farm was called Tel Hai, and about sixty of us worked there. It was here that I met my wife, Miriam. She died a few years ago . . ." Nimrod pointed to the largest picture in the room. It hung on the wall behind his rocking chair, and showed a young, heavily muscled woman in short pants — smiling, as she dumped out the contents of a wheelbarrow. It was taken in Tel Hai.

"It was really a marvelous place, though for many years it had gone untended. It used to belong to a nobleman, but when he fled the Bolsheviki in 1917, the city government confiscated it. We rented it from them. You know, I can still see it all — it was so beautiful. There were cypress trees and almond trees and eucalyptus trees. It was the first time I saw such trees, and there was a natural lawn, one that didn't have to be planted. In the center was an immense, beautiful park with rolling hills and flower beds, and beyond the park were the fields where we grew tobacco and vegetables. We were helped in our work by an agricultural specialist — a Greek — but after a year or so the city government decided it didn't want a Zionist group there, and we were forced to leave.

"Fortunately, just about this time, we got news that the *Chalutzi* people had reserved a place for us on a boat sailing for Jaffa. It was the last of these repatriation ships, and by some stroke of luck we got a place on it. We traveled, actually, as four or five families. The authorities would hardly have been willing to repatriate sixty 25-

year-olds, so some of us, the older-looking ones, grew beards and pretended we were the fathers. And some of the girls put on three and four dresses and pretended they were mothers. Somehow it worked, probably because the authorities were drunk most of the time on vodka, and in 1924 we finally arrived, without a kopek or a place to go, in Jaffa. Jaffa, Palestine. We had finally made it."

Nimrod smiled widely, and glanced over at Becky. She smiled back. The two of them began chatting about Jaffa (evidently, Becky had arrived there too; but from Lithuania, some years before). They joked about how easy it was for an *oleh hadash*, a new immigrant, to come to Israel nowadays, compared to the long journeys they had to go through, and the long waiting periods before they could even get permission to go. "Seven years it took me to get to Palestine," said Nimrod. "Though, I guess it's not really so bad when you consider that Jacob waited twice that before he received Rachel." They both laughed joyously at this.

Nimrod rose from his rocking chair, went over to the bookshelf, and meticulously set the electric razor back into its case. He kept the razor case with his books. He came back with a large album of photographs and began showing me some early pictures of Bilat: the rock-dirt desert, the stone buildings and tents, the first trees that he had planted, and the founding fathers in their short pants, sandals, tee-shirts, and a few even with Arab headdresses to protect them from the sun.

"I want you to have a feel of it," he said, closing the photo album abruptly. "I'll show you a little more what it was like in a moment. But first, let me give you a brief history of the kibbutz. It'll give you an idea how things have changed.

"Kibbutz Bilat was started in 1924, on a small plot of barren land (fifty acres), some four miles to the south of its present location. He did not come there until 1927. The real founding fathers were from Becky's group — some twenty Lithuanians, who were sent by PICA, the privately financed Palestinian Colonization Agency, and they were the first Jewish settlers in this part of the Jordan Valley. At the time they were sent, the place was inhabited by about ten Bedouin families who made their living by raising sheep and smuggling. PICA moved the Bedouins across the Jordan River onto another patch of land they also owned, a patch that is now in Jordan. When

Nimrod's group from Russia joined the Lithuanians in 1927, PICA gave them an additional piece of land to work, about a thousand acres that was located four miles up the road. It was these thousand acres that they were living on today. They didn't move here until 1934."

"Why was that?"

"The arrangements at the time for forming a new kibbutz were rather makeshift. There was no solid organization like the Jewish Agency today. In fact, the principal organization, PICA, was not at all in favor of forming kibbutzim. As far as they were concerned, communal living was only good for young, unmarried people. Once you began to have families, they thought, the kibbutz would break up. So what PICA wanted was for us to break up into families from the start, each family getting a small plot of land. If we agreed to do that, then we could live on the thousand acres here. If not, we could only farm that land, and we would have to go on living on the small plot. It was their way of putting pressure on us to break up our communal life.

"We stayed together and went on working the fifty acres there and the thousand acres up the road. Eventually, however, we became frustrated and secretly began making plans to move here. This was in late '34. There was an old Turkish law which the British left on the books, and this law stated that if a man or group of men put up buildings on a piece of vacant property, and they managed to get the roof up before they were stopped, then the property became theirs. It makes sense when you think of it: he who works and lives on the land, deserves it. Well, this is what we did. We laid the foundations for some living quarters and kept the side walling and roofs down the road. While working on the foundations, we kept a man on lookout in case an automobile came up the Valley. We knew, you see, that the only one likely to be driving an automobile in the Jordan Valley was the PICA representative. Once, in fact, he did come, just as we were finishing the last of the foundations. We went down the road to meet him, and asked him to join the post-harvest party. Leading him off to the far side of the fields, we took out a harmonica, some bread, olives and wine, and we threw a party. By the time it was over, he was tired, maybe even a little drunk, and he had no desire to tour the land. Shortly after this incident, we brought up the side walling and roofs, and in a couple of hard days we were established. We had formed our own new kibbutz. Part of our group, particularly some newcomers from Germany, stayed on the original plot; but the bulk of us, the Lithuanians and Russians, moved up here.

"The PICA people, of course, were angry, and for two years they cut off all loans, and wouldn't speak to us. However, once they saw how well things were going for us, how even with families we continued our communal life, they resumed their support and even began to bring around guests to show them 'an example of PICA's work in the Jordan Valley.' That's right, we became *their* famous example of Jewish communal life in the Jordan Valley."

Nimrod and Becky chuckled over "those good old days," and then Nimrod showed some more pictures. These were mostly shots from the late 40's and early 50's, and as he showed them, he kept flipping back to the earlier pictures ("The exact same spot, if you can believe it."), and pointing out how Bilat had become a "Garden of Eden."

However, in those first years they had lived in tents, in huts with corrugated iron roofs, and a few ruins that were still standing from Roman times. In summer, there was no escape from the heat, and in winter, the rains came washing through the living quarters. The only thing that was at all "civilized," was the food — though sometimes, of course, it was a little burned because of their primitive kitchen facilities. But, at least, there had always been enough to go around: bread, vegetables, and a little meat and fruit.

The dining hall, a stone-walled building, was then — much more than now — the center of their lives. They ate there and in the evening, they would stay on for hours, talking and singing. There was no other place to go except back to the tent or hut, with its kerosene light. And besides, there was much more of a feeling of togetherness in those days, much more a feeling of building something. They, of course, had no idea that what they were building would become part of a Jewish state — not in their lifetimes. "What we did feel, was that we were resuscitating the earth, giving our lives to the Land. The earth — as you can see from the photographs — was almost completely barren here. Except for a little bit of summer grass that grew up along the banks of the Yarmuk and Jordan Rivers, there was no vegetation. We saw our lives as dedications, the fertilizer you can say, for the rebirth of this Land.

"So, hard as these first years were, they were in a way the best years. We had nothing and yet we had everything. No electricity, no television, no pool, and yet we had a harmonica and we had the rivers where, under the moonlight, we could go bathing at night. Naked even. In many ways we lived like — I hate to say it — hippies. Didn't we, Becky?"

Becky nodded, and began to say something about the changing social mores of the kibbutz, but Nimrod cut her short. "It's getting late, and I want to get on to this Arab thing, that Michael asked me about earlier." I had asked him about the Arabs, when he told me how the ten Bedouin families were removed by PICA.

"Everyone always wants to know: What was life like with the Arabs in those days? But what does it really matter?" He was speaking now as he had spoken at the *asifa* the other night, his soft voice reaching for those higher notes of prophecy. "If I tell you that things were good, then you want to know how it went bad. The only thing that matters now is that they are fighting us, and that all we built here, all we created out of this desert barrenness, they say belongs to them. And that cannot be. Never."

He stopped and shook his head slowly. He was going to continue, but he had to get this anger off his chest. I didn't say anything, and neither did Becky. Nimrod continued to sit there, very silent, picking at the dirt under his thumbnail. Then, slowly, he began talking about the Arabs.

He knew them well, he said. Probably more than most Bilatniks, because, purely by chance, his contact with the Arabs was greater than that of most. He had worked with them. "You see, before I became the kibbutz gardener in 1935, I used to plow and harvest in some of the Arab fields. For pay, of course. They had no machinery, only horses. But we had a tractor (We got the first one in '27.) and a combine. They had never seen a combine before. They used to ride along with us as we cut the sheaves of wheat and turned out the final sacks of grain. Eventually, word got around and some of the wealthier Arabs — those in the government ministries — employed us to work in their fields. We even plowed and harvested some of Emir Abdullah's fields. We were paid by the hour, or by the acre, depending upon the arrangement. In fact, from the early 30's until about 1944, some of us worked this way in Arab fields.

"Aside from this contract work we also helped them build a pump so that they could irrigate fields, and we taught them how to grow tomatoes, cucumbers and other vegetables. In return they helped us out — with weapons. They, the Bedouins, sold us arms — British and French rifles — and ammunition. At night these dealings would take place. We'd meet at the Yarmuk and receive the weapons, fire them to see if they were all right, and then pay for them — always in cash, Palestine sterling.

"They came to visit us now and then on our holidays. Just the men, of course. Their women stayed home, except when they came to our doctor, and then they were accompanied by men. They couldn't understand how we let our women go around alone in slacks, or riding horses. They thought we were some kind of free-lovers, with no family system. It was all very strange to them.

"We also visited them on their holidays. I speak some Arabic, but not very much, so when I went, I brought along Zakkai, who the Arabs considered our *sheikh* because he spoke fluently. Zakkai's parents had come from Yemen; he was born in Tel Aviv.

"When we visited their tents they prepared a feast for us which lasted about five hours. They entertained us with horse racing and mock fighting with swords on horseback, and they fed us to the brim, until we convinced them we had enough. You've heard how the Arabs do it, right? Belching. It was hard at first, but we caught on soon enough.

"Usually, the meal was mutton with yogurt and *pita*, a thin bread which they make on a grill. It was paper thin and delicious, not like the stuff you get now in Tiberias. I used to get sick sometimes from all the food. They, of course, were used to all that grease and curdled milk. They had stomachs like camels. They could eat that stuff for three days in a row, and then go another three without eating.

"After the meal came the coffee; that was a ceremony in itself, and took about two hours. They took the green beans and with a pestle they ground them and then toasted the flakes on the fire. The grinding was done with a rhythmical tak-tak-tak, and when the elders of the village heard it being pounded out they knew it was time to come and join us. Usually ten or so would come in for the coffee.

"The conversation during the meal and coffee time was always the same. They'd ask us about our families and then about our cattle and our crops. When we finished telling them, they would begin again asking about the family and the cattle and the crops. They could ask the same thing ten times. In between they would drop questions about the business between us — plowing, buying or selling. It was all very strange to us. We were practical-minded and used to getting down to business immediately. But even with this strangeness, there was a good feeling amongst us, a feeling that we could live well and even work together."

Was there ever any quarreling or fighting?

"Only in the bad periods — like the late 20's and late 30's, when the situation was bad all over the country. Otherwise, we got along fairly well, as I have just indicated to you. Now and then, of course, there were small squabbles over stealing or grazing in our fields. It was the old story of Cain and Abel — Abel being the shepherd and Cain the farmer. The Arabs were shepherds and the best grazing places were in our fields. There's nothing new in this. In fact, the Bedouins had done this amongst themselves for years and still do it today. We were not selected for special treatment. When it did affect us, we usually settled the matter by sitting down with the *sheikh*. When this failed, we settled it ourselves. We could not rely on the police because they were, themselves, Arabs on the British payroll. So we made use of dogs.

"I remember one day a dog bit one of the Arab shepherds. That night about a hundred of them came after us — with a few guns, knives and sticks. The sticks had a heavy wooden ball on the end; one hit on the head and you were finished. Our weapons were also primitive. We had a few rifles, and our work tools — spades, pitchforks, that kind of thing. Anyway, that night when they came up after us, shouting 'Death to the Jews,' there was a little fighting. One or two of us got hit badly and had to be taken to the hospital, and we cut up a few of them, too. But, before the thing got totally out of hand, some British officers came in and settled it. To tell you the truth, the worst part was all the noise."

Nimrod stopped and shrugged. "So that's how it was with the Arabs," he said. "Make of it what you want. I can tell you from my own life that none of us ever thought it would turn out as it has. But that is life — surprises. Right? We have had to learn to accept these surprises and go on. It is not easy, it is never easy" — his head was shaking back and forth, and he was smiling sadly — "but it is something we have learned to do. Call it a special talent of the Jewish people: learning to adjust to surprises."

Accident

"A 40-year-old volunteer was shot dead in error on Friday night while doing guard duty at Bilat, and his companion was seriously wounded.

The two men, both members of the Rotary Club in their home town, were on their appointed round, when they approached an Army position from which fire was opened on them, apparently without warning.

The country's Rotary clubs every weekend send volunteers to the Jordan Valley settlements to relieve the settlers of guard duty. The Army has ordered an inquiry into the incident."

That is what Israelis heard on the radio late Saturday afternoon. It was on the T.V., too. And in Bilat, it was all over the people's faces.

I first heard about the accident early Saturday morning. About thirty of us had assembled at 5.30 A.M. with cheese sandwiches, hard-boiled eggs, tomatoes, and halvah. We were waiting for Misha, the Culture Chairman, to bring around the truck, so we could get going on our excursion to the archaeological excavations on the Golan Heights. Everyone was lively and expectant, like a class of school children going on a field trip. Then Misha appeared, without the truck, and nervously cancelled the trip. "Last night the two Rotary guards were shot. One is dead and the other is in critical condition . . ."

As if a mortar had just fallen in their midst, the kibbutzniks scattered. No words were spoken, no questions asked; they simply bolted away, each one heading in his own direction.

I stood there stunned, not only by the news, but also by this terrible, sudden, silent dispersion. Americans would have hung around, would have wanted a few of the details. I tried to get a little more information from Misha, but he wasn't talking. "There's nothing more to know," he insisted. "The trip's off. Sorry." And then he walked away, too.

Late that afternoon, I found out that Shimon had been on guard that night, and I asked if he would tell me what happened. He didn't want to; not then. The police and Army had spent a couple of hours with him that morning, and he didn't want to talk anymore. Tomorrow, he said, if I came over to his house in the afternoon, perhaps he could tell me what I wanted to know.

"There's nothing much to tell you," he said the next afternoon, as I sat there with him, his wife, and three children. We were all drinking cola. "You've heard the radio, read the newspaper, listened to the speculations. What more can I tell you? I came off guard duty at 2:30 A.M. The accident happened a half-hour later. I was here sleeping."

Hadn't the police and Army told him something about it?

"If they knew what happened, they wouldn't have come asking me. Look, this I can tell you: the Rotary boys were shot while inside the kibbutz. All guards stay inside the kibbutz fence. Nobody goes outside. They were coming back from the cowshed. The guard at the gate thought they were terrorists, and he shot them."

"Did he shoot them without warning?"

Shimon stared at me, annoyed. There was a long silence.

"Daddy, it had to be without warning!" Shimon's seven-year-old daughter blurted out.

Shimon ignored her. "Nobody knows," he said unemotionally. "Look, all we know is that he emptied his magazine — all 50 shells — on them and then went running to the commanding officer. Said he got two *Al Fatah*. The officer came, saw who they were, rushed the wounded one to the hospital, and called the police."

The police?

"Of course. You don't just shoot a man, and then walk away scot-free. This isn't America, you know."

I ignored the barb, and instead asked who the fellow was who did the shooting.

"A reservist. From Tiberias. Most of the guards here are reservists."

What will happen to him?

"He'll be tried and sentenced. Dereliction of duty."

But did he, Shimon, think the guard had been sleeping?

"Not my business. I have no idea. Now, if you'll excuse me . . ."

Passover

Ma nishtana halyla hazeh m'col halylot? When I was nine years
old, I recited this slice of Hebrew for my grandfather, during the
traditional Passover *seder,* and he beamed. It was always something
of a magical incantation for me; I never understood why saying
these strange-sounding syllables should bring such happiness to him,
especially when the translation was nothing more than, "Why is
tonight different from all other nights?"

"It's different this year," Edo said flatly. It was the morning
before the *seder.* "It's worse. You don't get over what happened the
other night so quickly."

I nodded, but said nothing.

"You see," he continued, "this is not the first time something like
this has happened to us on *Pesach.* Do you know Ayelah?"

"No."

"She was sitting right across from us at breakfast. Her son was
killed two years ago on *Erev Pesach,* just a couple of kilometers from
here. He had requested that the Army restation him near the kibbutz
for a month. Ayelah was sick, and he wanted to be nearby. He had
just been restationed when he got hit. A piece of shrapnel in the
head."

Edo stopped. We had come to his tractor, one of those armored
tractors used in the banana groves. He climbed on. "Since then," he
continued, "nobody really wants to celebrate *Pesach* here. We even
thought of changing the day of celebration. But we decided that we

couldn't. It wouldn't have been right." He started up the tractor and rode off.

"Come in, my friend, come in," Bierman called, "but quickly! There is something terrific on the radio. Come here, listen to this," Bierman shouted. "It's almost over!"

"In the early morning, it must have been about 5:00 A. M.," a man's voice was saying over the radio, "we disembarked in Haifa. We were exhausted. The journey must have taken thirty hours and we had mostly old people with us. One of these old couples, it turned out, was the parents of a dock-worker, and the dock-worker came running up to them, shouting in Arabic that they had arrived in *Eretz Yisrael*, The Land of Israel. They all kneeled and kissed the ground . . ."

Bierman clicked off the radio. "Can you imagine it!" he said excitedly. "In this day we can pull off things like that. Who would believe it? Only us; a *yiddishe kopf*, a Jewish head. That's what it is!"

"Why don't you explain to Michael what went on before he came in," Hannah suggested.

"Right. The name of this story is 'A Modern Exodus from Egypt.' It took place in '56, during the Sinai Campaign, and it is all true. The fellow you just heard was one of the two sailors who took part. They landed in Egypt wearing civilian clothes, the modern kind from Paris. Both spoke French, and, pretending to be tourists, they went into a camera store. They bought some film and began to make light conversation with the store owner. Nothing important. They asked how people in Port Said enjoyed it there. Fine, they were told. And what kind of people lived in Port Said besides Egyptians? Were there many French, many Armenians? Greeks? A few that lived down near the water, they were told. And how about Jews, do you still have any of *them* around? Not so many anymore, just a few ragged families who lived in a run-down part of town. Hmm, and where's that? Near the center, you couldn't miss it. They talked a little more about film and cameras, and they walked off.

"When they got to the Jewish quarter, they met a little boy. They asked him in French whether any Jews lived there. He was scared and hesitated. They asked him again, this time in Arabic, saying

they were French tourists. The boy told them of a building where
they could find a few families. When they entered the building and
knocked on the door, an old, very poor man greeted them. They
asked if he knew about Jewish families, and the man said yes, he was
a Jew. They asked to come inside. Then they explained to him that
they, themselves, were Jews, and had come to take some Egyptian
Jews *out of the land of Egypt.* They put it in those words. The man
was startled. They couldn't tell him any more about it, they said, but
they promised that they had come to *deliver* them. The man
hesitated, and said he would have to speak with his neighbors. They
went along with him. Almost all the neighbors were old people, very
poor and very religious, and they told the two sailors that they had
been waiting all their lives to be 'delivered.' Were they going to
Palestine? The sailors said they couldn't tell them any more, they
only promised again they would 'deliver' them.

"Well, the men talked it over and they decided that about fifteen
or twenty families would go. They were ready to leave immediately.
And what do you think they took with them? No furniture, no
suitcases, no clothes. Just the *Torah.* That's right, only the Bible,
that's all they took with them. Three thousand years later and
nothing has changed. Can you imagine it?. . . ." Bierman slapped my
knee solidly, and took a long drink of the iced-coffee. "And then,
when they reached Haifa, miracle of miracles happened . . ."

"Bierman, he has heard that part," Hannah interrupted. "He
came in at the end."

"The part about the dock-worker meeting his parents? You caught
that?"

I nodded.

"Well, what do you think? Isn't it wonderful? And it's all true.
Three thousand years later and we are still escaping from Egyptian
bondage!"

There was a sudden, loud rapping at the door, and a voice
announced: "And here we are at last, bondage or no bondage!" It
was Yael. Behind her were Eton, the two girls, and a young man I
didn't know.

"Well, it's about time," said Hannah, as they came in.

Yael ignored her. "And how are you Michael?" she asked.

"Michael, I don't think you ever met Uzi," Hannah interrupted.

The young man and I shook hands. He was about twenty years old and seemed rather distant.

"Uzi is our nephew," said Hannah. "His father is my brother. Aaron lives in Haifa, but Uzi is a member of Bilat."

"He's also a top-notch soldier," added Bierman.

"All right, father, no sense getting carried away," said Yael.

Everyone took a seat around the coffee table, and Hannah went off to the pantry. She came back with a tray of silver shot-glasses, and a bottle of cherry brandy that was made in Haifa. It was the first liquor I had seen in a kibbutz home.

"Well, shall we have a toast?" asked Bierman.

"Why not?" answered Yael, promptly raising her shot-glass, and then adding: "I propose a toast to the Egyptians . . ."

Only Uzi raised his glass with her.

". . . to the rotten Egyptians, whose bondage — thank God — we are no longer in."

"Come on, Bierman," said Hannah, "you make the toast."

Bierman raised his glass and we all followed him. "I propose a toast to the holiday," he said slowly, "To *Pesach* and to our special guest from America, our Jew from America. May we all celebrate together and enjoy ourselves. *Le Chaim!*"

We drank up.

"Mommy, aren't we ever going to eat dinner?" asked Kinneret, tugging on Yael's arm.

"Yes, right now," answered Bierman, stroking his granddaughter's cheek. "Come on, everybody, let's go eat hearty. Tonight's a night to celebrate. Let's not be late."

The dining hall was filling up when we got there, and the kibbutzniks, dressed in their holiday best, warmed the room with their conversation. There were many faces I had never seen before, and I assumed these to be the guests from the city. The kibbutz was expecting 250 guests. It was wonderful for the kibbutz to have them, Hannah had told me on the way to the dining hall; especially this year. The past two years hardly anyone from the outside had come on the holidays; they were afraid of the bombings. But this year, with the situation worse than ever, they came. "We are a strange people," she had said. "When the times are golden, we act badly to each other. But when the times are bad like now, we are as good as gold."

"Well, what do you think of it?" Bierman said. "Where have you ever seen so many Jews come together and celebrate in their home?"

Bierman fumbled in his pocket and took out some pink, numbered slips of paper, and began whispering to himself in Yiddish (he always counted in Yiddish). Then, taking Hannah by the elbow, he led us slowly across the dining hall, stopping several times along the way to shake hands with the other kibbutzniks and their guests. He seemed to know them all, guests included, and to have a private word for each of them, much like a rabbi strolling down the aisle of his synagogue after the Sabbath morning prayer.

Eventually we made it to the far end of the hall to the last table, where we found our assigned seats. There were six long tables running down the entire length of the room, with enough space for about 750 people. The tables were covered with white cloths and had pitchers of roses every few feet. The food was already on them —gefilte fish, *knaydlach*, pickles, cold chicken, fruit compote, matzoh and wine.

"You sit next to me, my friend," Bierman said.

I sat down between him and Yael. Eton, Uzi, and Hannah sat across from us. The girls were next to Yael.

"Is it this way every year?" I asked.

"Every year."

"Always the same decorations, the same food?"

"Yes, always. Tell me, does your family celebrate *Pesach* in America?"

"Not any more. We only celebrated when my grandfather was alive."

"So you have forgotten everything? You don't know the meaning of these words on the wall?" Bierman pointed around the walls of the dining room to four or five long, paper signs which had some very literary Hebrew written on them.

I shook my head no.

"They're quotations from the Bible," he said. He picked a small, gaily decorated booklet off the table. "Here, they're repeated in the *Hagadah*. Our own *Hagadah*. We made it ourselves. Two of the quotations are from *Exodus*, celebrating our deliverance from

Egyptian bondage, and three are from *Song of Songs*, celebrating spring. You don't know them at all?"

"No."

"My friend, my dear Jewish friend, you *do* have some things to learn."

"Bierman, lower your voice," Hannah interrupted. "The children are coming out."

A hush fell over the hall as the lights dimmed, and a piano at the far end of the room sent up a slow, swaying rhythm. Twenty or so children, boys and girls about five years old, came tip-toeing out of the door near us, each child waving a sheaf of wheat. The children were smiling and giggling, and slowly they tiptoed up to the lighted stage next to the piano. One of the children recited the traditional four questions, and they sang several songs. Then the lights went back on, and the children jumped down off the stage and went running excitedly back to their parents.

"Beautiful, no?" Yael said to me. "Next year, Kinneret's class carries the wheat, don't you, Kinneret?"

The little girl blushed and hid behind her mother. Yael began play-wrestling with her.

"Sssh!" said Hannah, "show a little respect!"

Now there was a deeper silence throughout the dining hall; nobody seemed to move, except for a solitary figure in black who walked quickly up the center aisle to the stage. It was Drora, the secretary of the kibbutz. She looked remarkably like Golda Meir, with her thick body and statuesque head with the gray hair pulled straight back, the wrinkled forehead, and that long, sure nose pointing right out at you. She tapped the microphone. It was working. "Comrades of Bilat," she began, her voice heavy. "A member of the Rotary Club fell while guarding our home. For two years now they have come to us, the members of the Rotary, sharing our burden, sharing our danger, day and night in our time of need..." Drora continued for ten more minutes, stopping several times in the middle as her voice cracked, and then going on again, breathing heavy and pushing each word out to us, until the last words came blurting forth, "Happy holiday to all!" Her body drooped and she walked slowly from the stage.

Havaynu Shaaaaalom, Aleichem, Havaynu Shaaaaalom Alei-

chem . . .," the kibbutzniks sang out, and before Drora reached the floor, the dining hall was reverberating. *"Shaaalom, Shaalom, Aleichem"* — on and on they went, singing loud and hard, until there was no room left in the dining hall for anything but the song. Bierman was singing loudest, and when almost everyone else had stopped, he was still booming away.

"All right, all right, Bierman," Hannah said loudly, almost shouting.

Bierman stopped slowly. "Come on, let's have a toast," he said. He reached over and grabbed the bottle of sweet red wine, and poured us all a glass.

"Le chaim!" we said together, and drank deep.

There was a long silence, as we passed the food around and began eating. I was gobbling a slice of gefilte fish, when I noticed that Eton was watching me. "You're really enjoying it?" he said, surprised.

"Sure. It's my favorite."

"Not mine!" said Yael, defiantly, "Gefilte fish, *knaydlach* — you can have it, not me."

"It's delicious," said Bierman.

"Just right," said Hannah.

"They like it," Yael said to me. "But not us. Not the *sabras.*"

"What's there to not like about gefilte fish?" Bierman said. "Sometimes you make no sense, Yael."

"Who said anything about sense? I said it doesn't taste good, that's all."

"Come on, let's not argue!" said Hannah, decisively. She repeated a Hebrew maxim that goes, "About taste and smell there is nothing to argue" — and with that, nobody said another word.

We ate the rest of the meal in silence. For awhile, Eton, Uzi and Bierman got into a brief discussion about tractors, but this broke off when one of Uzi's army buddies came over and began talking to him. Yael and Hannah were busy feeding the two girls, both of whom were more interested in the matzoh than anything else. And I ate and drank quickly until there was nothing left around me.

Then, as dinner ended, there began a half-hour or so of entertainment. Zakkai, the man with the Yemenese accent who everyone claimed spoke the most beautiful Hebrew in the kibbutz, rose, went to the stage and read a long section from *Exodus*. He read this same section every year, Hannah said. After this, some children danced, while a muscle-bound man who worked in the cowshed accompanied them on the flute. Then Bierman rose, and read a selection from *Song of Songs* — the same section that he read every year. And finally, there was some more singing, capped off with a poem about spring, read by Nimrod, the gardener.

All of this had the air of a talent show, one act following the next, and those around me, except for the guests, seemed bored by it. The young children, the ones who weren't performing, walked up and down the aisles, many of them still eating matzoh or fruit. When Nimrod finally finished his poem, there was a quick shuffling of benches, and most people moved off to the doors. Then, from out of nowhere, appeared the clean-up crew in their white aprons, and suddenly the white table clothes were coming off and the food remains were thumping into the garbage pails.

I was still sitting there, watching the sudden disintegration of the party, when somebody tapped me hard on the shoulder. I turned around, expecting to see Rafael or Edo, but it was Lea.

"A fine fellow you are," she said in mock anger. "*Erev Pesach*, and you don't even drop by to say hello."

"I was meaning to."

"When? At three in the morning?"

"Tonight, after the dinner. Really."

"Well, if that's really true ... Then I forgive you. But not completely. You've been making a hermit of yourself. Do I have to send a formal invitation for you to stop over and say hello?"

"I was hoping to run into you in the dining hall."

"And now you have. And let me tell you, you do not need an invitation. You may come by anytime. But tonight is a bad idea ... You should stay around for the party."

"You're not staying?"

"No, not me. I'm too tired, and besides I'm not really in the mood for it. But don't let me keep you. They've already started." A small group was gathered around the piano, singing traditional Passover songs. "But *do* drop by sometime. Sometime before you go back to America, all right?"

At the piano they were singing *Dayaynu*, and I found that I remembered most of the lyrics. It was like suddenly recalling a poem you had memorized way back in sixth grade, and even though you had changed completely since those days, or so you thought, suddenly the old lyrics came tumbling out, and it was you singing them.

Those sitting and singing next to me seemed to be experiencing another kind of nostalgia. The lyrics were there all right, they hadn't forgotten *them*, but while they sang they kept turning their heads toward the other side of the dining hall, where most of the kibbutzniks were drifting away. This made them sing louder, but to no avail. Our group never got much larger than forty people, almost all of them middle-aged or old people, who were running out of tune.

The entire evening seemed to be droning to an end, when a group of young people, the army-age set, came rushing in with a tape-recorder, and began playing hora music. The woman at the piano, a severe type, was annoyed by the interruption, but everyone else seemed happy for an excuse to quit and go home. A few of us helped clear the center of the room, and then the dancing began. There was now almost nobody in the dining hall over twenty-five years old. First they danced horas, and then some rock, a cha-cha and a samba, all of which they performed in group style. It was the first time that entire evening I felt that people were really enjoying themselves, not just going through the motions.

"Hey, fellow, how come you're not dancing?" It was Shmulik, Orna's husband.

"I overate."

"That's no excuse."

"Well, what's your excuse?"

Shmulik's face dropped. "Have some?" He pulled a pint of *Canadian Club* whiskey from his pocket, and poured two shot-glasses full. "Well, *hag sameach!*"

We touched glasses and drank up. There was silence for a few moments as the whiskey made its way past our vocal chords. Then I asked where Orna was.

"She went back to the apartment."

"I haven't seen her the past few days."

"She's been having a rough time. The Rotary guards. She takes

care of them when they're here. Brings them sheets, fruit, things like
that. They come over every *Shabat* and have coffee with us."

"Did you know the two who were shot?"

"Not well. We know some of the others better. They're different
each week."

"How is the wounded one, he made it didn't he?"

"He made it, all right, paralyzed from the waist down." Shmulik
shook his head slowly. "Look, this isn't the time to be talking of such
things. Why don't you have a good time? Get in there and dance!"

He walked off with his *Canadian Club*, calling a couple of soldiers
to come join him for a toast. I noticed for the first time that he
limped.

"He's a good guy, Shmulik," said an eighteen-year-old boy who
had been standing near us. He was a big kid, with wide eyes, and I
had seen him around, though I had never met him.

"Yes, he is," I said noncommittally, somewhat surprised to be
suddenly talking about someone I knew with someone I didn't.

"I work with him sometimes in the machine shop," the boy said.
"That is, when I work. I'm still in high school."

"I see."

"Every now and then it bothers him and he gets lousy, but the rest
of the time, there isn't a better guy around."

"*What* bothers him?"

"His leg. You don't see how he walks?"

"Yes, I see that he limps."

"He lost it in World War II. From the knee down. He was with
the Jewish Brigade. He once told me how it happened, but I forget.
On a mine, I think it was."

I looked over at Shmulik. He was standing about fifteen yards
away, talking to the soldiers as he poured them a drink. I couldn't
hear what they were saying until they lifted their glasses, and
Shmulik lifted the pint-bottle, and they all clanked together, and
Shmulik boomed out, "*Hag sameach!* Happy holiday to all of us!"

A Movie

On Tuesdays, Thursdays, and sometimes on Fridays or Saturdays, there was a movie. It was usually not a good movie, but the kibbutzniks went devotedly, and all the mosquitoes in the Jordan Valley weren't enough to keep them away. The mosquitoes knew this. And thus, every movie night squadrons of mosquitoes gathered inside the theatre (which was actually a former airplane hangar), and flew regular missions. None of this, however, seemed to faze the kibbutzniks, for they came protected with socks, long pants, mosquito repellent, and thick skins.

I probably would've skipped the movies altogether, if it weren't for the fact that — even considering the mosquitoes — there was nothing better to do. The reading room and exhibition room were closed; television, which ran from 6:00 P. M. to 10:00 P.M., was dull, and besides, eight of the nine sets were located in the muggy shelters; and finally, there was hardly anyone to talk to because almost everyone went to the movies. So I went, too. In fact, during the first three weeks, I had seen four movies, including two American westerns, one American war movie, and a French film I didn't understand at all. The kibbutzniks didn't understand the French film, either; but the American films were plain enough, and the kibbutzniks liked them — especially, the most recent American film, *Glory of Heroes*, which featured a unit of American Marines beating the hell out of an unusually seedy and vicious battalion of Japanese. This film, which we had seen a day or so before Passover, made me swear off all future American films. Better to spend those evenings alone in my room. So, a week later, when I saw an announcement on the bulletin board stating that the evening's film was called *Besieged*, I prepared to spend the evening at home, until someone informed me that it was not another American film at all, but an Israeli film on *their* war.

I went back to my room to put on socks, long-sleeve shirt and mosquito repellent. On the way back, I bumped into Rafael.

"So there you are, my fellow *kolkhoznik*," Rafael greeted me with his standard salutation. "You're going to the cinema, I presume?"

"Yes. You're heading there, too?"

"After I stop at the 'services,' I am. I have to take a leak." He entered a communal toilet along the way, a leftover from the early days of Bilat.

"Mission accomplished," he said when he came out, still working on the buttons of his fly. We resumed walking towards the theatre. I asked if he knew anything about the film, and he said yes, he had heard it was something about the war, and the current situation in Israel. Then grinning widely, he added: "I doubt if you'll appreciate it, though. Not enough sex in it."

We both laughed, and Rafael grabbed me quickly by the arm, nodding towards a long-legged girl in short pants who was walking just ahead of us, and about to turn into the theatre. "Have you met *her* yet?"

"No."

"Well . . ." He slapped me on the shoulder. "Perhaps it's just as well. You'd only waste your time. You see, she uses SAM 3's."

"She uses *what*?"

"SAM 3's. Surface-to-air-missiles, like in Egypt. You can't get near her."

We laughed again.

"Of course, there's not very much up here," he tapped his head lightly, "but, have you ever seen anything better to go on than those legs? Believe me, I know all about her. Or rather, I ought to. God knows, I spent enough time trying. For three months I tried. Even took her on *Shabat* to the beach, whenever I could get one of the kibbutz cars. But every time I thought I was going to get into gear, I wound up back in neutral. Or worse, in reverse: she'd push me away. I couldn't figure out what I was doing wrong until it was all over. And, you know what it was?" Rafael shook his head slowly. "She wants to get married. She knows the only thing she's got going for her is her legs, and she's not about to let any guy get his hands on them until she's sure he'll marry her. Not bad reasoning, eh? You know, now that I think of it, I don't really blame her."

The movie was, as Rafael had said, about the current situation in Israel. The drama focused on a woman in her mid-twenties, who lost her husband in the Six-Day War, and is left with a small child, a large empty house, and her husband's army buddies to console her. She never cries. She goes about her life — work, the beauty parlor,

the supermarket. Never breaks, and never laughs much, either —
until she meets a new man. In between these scenes, are flashbacks
of her husband, the war, and even Arab women going to the graves
of their men. The viewer is never sure what happens with the
woman and her new man. He goes off to reserve duty on the Jordan
border (there are flashes of the Bilat sign), and a week or so later, she
gets a telephone call that he has been seriously wounded. She is
rushing off to the hospital to see him, when suddenly the action
freezes, the movie ends, and the viewer is left to fill in his own
conclusion.

When the lights flashed back on, the kibbutzniks were still sitting
in their seats reluctant to move. Then slowly, they rose and filed out
of the theatre. It was not like the American war films, which they
had left in high spirits. Now they were silent. All you could hear
were their footsteps and the sounds of the night — crickets, and
sprinklers watering the daisies next to the theatre. I looked for Rafael
— he seemed to have disappeared — and then I noticed he was just
in front of me, walking quickly away, his hands thrust deep in his
pockets, and his head bent, eyes fixed on the pavement in front of
him.

I was a bit unsettled too; not so much by the movie, as by the
reaction of everyone around me. Rafael, who had entered the theatre
laughing, was now fleeing without a word, and the rest of the
kibbutzniks were jostling by, as silently as if they were going to a
funeral. Just like the time when the guard was killed, I thought.
Nobody hangs around for details or catharsis, they just go home and
sleep it off.

But, what had there been in the movie, really? The events were
believable enough, but the film, as a whole, seemed overdone and
melodramatic; even the acting seemed unreal. The woman had been
too much of a superwoman, a woman who never shed a tear, not
even when she was alone, and not even when her new man got
wounded. I couldn't believe it. And yet, the audience had obviously
been affected by it.

Lea's apartment was in the row of flats next to the theatre, and
from the path, I could see that her lights were still on. It was about
9:30 P.M.

"So it's you!" she said with mock surprise.

"I hope I'm not disturbing you."

"Don't be silly, come in!"

We went through the living room, and into the new room which was no longer littered with wood shavings and plaster chips, but still had the fresh smell of paint. There was a cot and a wooden table on the far side, and the walls were already hung with paintings — a Van Gogh flower print, and two reproductions of Chagall's stained-glass windows. The table had a pitcher of roses on it. "Neeli's room," Lea said, almost whispering.

I looked at her, surprised. I had thought Neeli lived with her high-school group. Wasn't that the rule?

"But sometimes she likes to stay here. Not often, but sometimes. And now, you see, it's more convenient, more comfortable."

I smiled.

"It comes a little late. She has to go off to the Army in another few months, but it will be waiting for her when she comes home on leave."

"Doesn't the kibbutz give her a room of her own, then?"

"Not until the end of their army duty. It's so stupid!" She shook her head disgustedly, and motioned me back into the living room while she went to the pantry for some grapefruit juice and homemade oatmeal cookies.

"Neeli made them this afternoon," she announced. She picked one up, tasted it, and smiled approvingly. "Not bad, are they? I'm finally getting her to bake. Teaching her myself, while there's still time." She sighed, and massaged her forehead with her thin, white hands. "But let's not talk about *that*. Tell me, what's doing with you. You're enjoying yourself, I hope."

I nodded.

"And the work? It hasn't become too hard, yet?"

"Not yet."

"That's good to hear. I was hoping Bierman would go easy with you. I know he doesn't want to give you a bad impression of us."

Lea turned on the fan. (You weren't allowed to use the air-conditioning after 6:00 P.M.; it ate up too much electricity.) Then, smiling coyly, she asked who else — besides the *Lool* "birds" — I had managed to meet. Any girls? There were a lot of beautiful girls in Bilat, and she was expecting that by now I would have met at least one. I told her that, sorry as I was to disappoint her, I had met only guys — Rafael, Edo, and a couple of others.

"Really?" she asked, her expression suddenly collapsing into seriousness. Then, almost to herself: "That's very curious."

"Curious?"

"Yes — that you should have met *them*."

I shrugged my shoulders, and said something to the effect that they seemed like good guys to me.

"Oh yes, of course. It's just that both of them have problems. Neither of them is — How should I put it? — well, very settled."

She began to tell me about Edo, and how his parents had divorced and left the kibbutz when he was a teen-ager. He had stayed on, but in her opinion, he had never gotten over it. Oh, he was a bright boy, all right — Moshe had him in his history class, and said that he was the most politically astute student he had ever taught. But emotionally, Edo was still "all plugged up."

"What hurts," she continued, "is that he might have grown out of it in some other circumstance. But, with the current situation as bad as it is, he'll never snap out of it."

"I don't follow."

"The war. The pressure on all of us to be tough, and have a stiff upper lip. And then with Edo there is something special."

"What's that."

"He killed a man. Not an Arab. One of our soldiers. He shot him by accident during training exercises. He's never talked about it, but in a kibbutz, it's one of those things everybody knows.

"It's a terrible situation. You want to help. But sometimes there is nothing you can do. Take Rafael: he's another one. He hasn't suffered so much from *this* war — no more than anyone else I should say, but he's still suffering from the last one, World War II. His parents were in a concentration camp in Italy. He was brought to Israel when he was a child. Six or seven years old, I think."

"I had no idea. . ."

"No, you couldn't. He doesn't talk about it either, I'm sure. Nobody talks much about these things. It's the way we are about it." She sighed again, and looked at me closely.

I looked away, not knowing what to say. Even with their reticence on personal matters, I did not think Edo, or especially Rafael, had been through anything like this. I felt young, and very naive.

"I begin to understand why the movie seemed so unreal to me." I said softly.

"I don't exactly follow."

"The actress in the movie. She seemed kind of catatonic to me. She never cried, not at all. Up to a point I could understand her hardness, but never to cry at all seemed a little unreal to me. Like they were overstating the case."

"They're not overstating anything. That's the way they were. That's the way they *are*. You read the newspapers, don't you? Every day now, someone is getting killed. It happens so often, there is not enough time or strength for tears. I can tell you right from our experience here, that's the way it is. Do you know Mimi, or Esther, or Ayelah?"

"Ayelah. I sat next to her at breakfast once."

"She lost her son. So did Esther. Mimi lost her husband. All of them have suffered more than you can imagine. But tears? Never. Michael, you may have been born in America, but God knows, you ought to be Jewish enough to understand that we do not measure our suffering in water. That, you at least ought to have learned by now!"

Another Accident

"I suppose you heard what happened this morning," a fellow said as Edo and I were finishing lunch. He seemed to be talking to me.

"You *are* the visiting journalist from America, aren't you?"

"Yes."

"Didn't you tell him about it, Edo?"

"No," Edo answered.

The fellow looked away momentarily, as if he was thinking what to say next. Then he turned back to Edo. "Well, don't you think he should hear about these things?"

"He'll hear about it on the radio when they announce it," Edo said. "There's no rush."

"Yacob, if you're so anxious to tell him, go ahead already," the woman at his side said to him.

"I'm sure Edo knows more than I do about it. He works out there."

"Someone got killed this morning, Michael," Edo said, without looking up from his plate. "Down in the banana groves, on a mine."

There was a long, uncomfortable silence, as Edo sat there polishing off the rest of his meal. "You can find out about it on the news tonight. There's nothing more I can tell you."

And with that, he got up and left.

After Edo was gone, Yacob finished telling me what had happened. Bilat's banana groves, he said, grew right up to the banks of the Yarmuk River (the border with Jordan), and were irrigated by water from the river. In most of the groves the irrigation system went on and off automatically. This system had been installed in late '67, when they first found mines in the groves. However, there were still some groves that were not irrigated by this system. These bordered on the groves of the neighboring kibbutz, and both of them were watered from the Yarmuk by the same set of pipes. Consequently, members of the two kibbutzim took turns going down to the river and turning on the water.

What happened this morning, Yacob continued, was that *Al Fatah* terrorists sneaked across the Yarmuk, cut the double-row of barbed wire, and attached a mine to the water spigot. The man who turned it on happened to be from the other kibbutz: a young fellow just out of the army. He was blown to smithereer.s.

May Day

It was another hot, muggy morning, and there on top of the water tower, the highest point in the kibbutz, two flags flapped listlessly: the blue and white of Israel, and the solid red of socialism. It was May 1st.

Seven years before, I had also spent May 1st in Israel, in Kibbutz Hazorea. I had never been in a country that celebrated May Day, so it was a bit strange that we took the day off from work and went to an enormous parade in Haifa. I knew nothing about politics at the time, but I had been properly educated in America, and thus I knew that the red flag was the banner of communism. I remember asking one of my friends from Hazorea why it was that he, and so many around him were carrying small red flags. since this was, I thought, the flag of communism. "But we *are* communists!" he answered, with a laugh. "The kibbutz is our commune."

Along the path leading to the dining hall, someone was putting up more flags, and though he hadn't quite finished, the ratio was now about three Israeli flags for every red one. I was curious to know more about this — especially, since in Bilat we were celebrating May 1st by working — so when I neared the fellow who was setting up the flags, I was happy to find that I knew him. It was my new acquaintance: Yacob.

"Good morning, *tovarish*," I greeted him.

"Good morning," he answered, without a smile.

"You don't know any Russian, I see."

"I know 'tovarish,'" he answered, dead-pan.

He stood up abruptly, flashed me a bored look, and then went on to the next flag. I followed him making some crack about the three to one flag ratio, which he answered curtly: "Don't take the symbolism too seriously, we just happen to own more Israeli flags." I asked him whether Bilatniks had always worked on May Day, or whether this was something new.

He jammed a red flag into the ground, and began wiring it to the iron bar alongside. "Bilatniks used to celebrate May 1st by going to the big parade in Haifa," he said. "But after the Six-Day War — without any official kibbutz decision being made — we decided not to go to the parade anymore, but to work a full-day. What better way to celebrate May Day, than with work?"

Moreover, he continued, in the cities almost everyone now worked a half-day, and their earnings, matched by an equal sum from the employers, were donated to the Border Kibbutz Fund. That was the Fund which paid for shelters, trenches, new roads, and all the other "adjustments" that border kibbutzim had to make. "You don't think we'd stay here and fight alone," Yacob said, "if we didn't know the country was totally behind us?"

"No," I answered, flatly, "but that still doesn't answer why you don't celebrate May Day anymore."

"We *do*, dammit! That's what I'm telling you. Not the same way as before, but we *do* celebrate it!"

Back at the *Lool*, the flurry of activity had already begun. Bierman and Zelda were rushing back and forth, as they always did on the days we vaccinated the new-born chicks and packed them for market. But today they seemed to be rushing more than ever. "You're late, my friend," Bierman said sharply. "The others have started without you." I promptly went to the rear room and took the empty seat next to Dodik. Pinchas was there, too, absorbed in his work, as usual. Across from him was Sadie, replacing Zvi, one of our vaccination crew regulars. Sadie was the only one who looked up when I came in, though she didn't say anything because she was already into one of her monologues. When she finished whatever it was she was saying (something about her native town in Poland), she pointed to a pail of rags on the floor. I thought she asked me to fetch her one, but when I went over and handed it to her, she seemed shocked.

"No!" she said sharply. "I meant for you to take it."

"I don't understand."

"That little mess near you." She pointed irritably at a small puddle of water on my section of the table.

"Oh, I didn't see it."

"I would never ask you to stoop down and hand me a rag from the floor." She was completely serious. "Only in the city do women behave like that!"

"I'm sorry, I didn't mean to offend you. It just didn't seem like such an unusual request."

"Never!" she said, now pointing her finger at me accusingly. "Never in a kibbutz will anyone ask you to stoop down and hand him something from the floor. Never!"

"I'm sorry to offend you," I repeated, "but even in a kibbutz it doesn't seem like an unusual request."

"Never!" she repeated, her finger still pointing at me.

"All right, never," I said sarcastically. "It never happens in a kibbutz, all right?"

She lowered her accusing finger and became silent, satisfied at last that I understood her.

The rest of the morning and afternoon continued without incident or excitement. Pinchas and Dodik didn't say much except for a short conversation about the Russians, none of it very enlightening. And Sadie joined in to curse the Russians and the way they acted in Vilna, Poland, in World War I. When we finally finished at 4:00 P.M., we rose and went our separate ways.

I was about halfway home when Bierman caught up with me, complaining that I had left too quickly. He wanted me to know that we had all worked brilliantly today — another ten thousand chicks to export, and another nine thousand Israeli pounds for the kibbutz. He was sorry that we had to work so long on May Day; but, of course, I shouldn't forget that there was a big dinner and party tonight, and of course, he and his family were expecting me to go with them.

As usual, the festivities were being held in the dining hall. The Biermans and I arrived at about 8:00 P.M., but only half the kibbutzniks had come so far. Those that were there, had taken their seats at the long tables — arranged as they were on Passover — or else they were milling about, particularly in one corner where there seemed to be something going on.

"What's happening over there?"

"The Remembrance Day exhibition," Bierman answered tersely. "Photographs from the Holocaust."

"Go have a look, Michael, if you want to," Hannah said.

"He must have seen them already," Yael said. Then to me: "The photographs of the Nazi atrocities. Your American soldiers took most of them when they conquered Germany. You must have seen them."

"Yes, in books."

"You mean, you've never been up to the Holocaust museum in Kibbutz Lochameem Haghettaot (Ghetto Fighters), just past Acre?"

"No."

"Then go have a look at the photographs," Hannah said. "Tomorrow is Remembrance Day, perhaps you ought to go over and see them."

I joined the crowd, composed mainly of young people, gazing at the photographs on the wall. Most of them were familiar. The stacks of bones, the piles of shoes, trousers and gold teeth, the skeletons in a ditch, the rows of skulls, and the lines of frightened people being marched off through a German street, to a train, a camp or a grave. Yet, as often as I had seen these, they always seemed unreal. They were not scenes you could identify with, anymore than you could identify with scenes of slaughtered Indians in cowboy movies, or slaughtered Vietnamese in Song My, and in the end, they were so far removed, so unimaginable, that you looked at them as a spectator, not so much horrified as curious.

"Terrible, isn't it, Michael?" said a woman behind me. I turned around and was a little annoyed to find it was Sadie. She looked different now without the red bandana and the work smock, and without the scowl she had worn on her face during our interchange that morning. She had tears in her eyes. "Just terrible, isn't it?" she repeated. "It's always terrible. Always. It never changes." She took a deep breath and coughed into her handkerchief. "Every year, the same. We have to do it. For the children. They don't know what it was like. Every year we must put up the photographs again. We must remember it. Otherwise they would forget." She pointed up to one of five signs that stretched along the walls.

"I have vowed to remember it all, to remember so that I will never forget," she read quickly to me. "That is why we must do it. So the children will never forget."

"I understand."

"Good. It's important for you to understand, too." She smiled sadly, and went away. I went back to Bierman and his family.

They were sitting now in almost the same spot they had sat in during Passover, at the last long table near the windows. There were only four of these dining-hall length tables this time, instead of six; evidently, not too many guests were expected. But again there was a stage at the far end of the dining hall, and again it was decorated with kibbutz-grown flowers. The long paper signs on the wall were only partially familiar to me. The two about workers and socialism were taken from Marx — the *Manifesto* and the *Gotha Program;* but the other three, including the one Sadie had read, were laments or maxims I had never heard before.

When I sat down, I asked Bierman why there were these different signs on the wall, and he explained that we were celebrating both May Day and Remembrance Day together. May Day was in honor of workers, and Remembrance Day, tomorrow, was in honor of those who died in the Holocaust. I asked him if the signs on the wall were always the same.

"Yes, always the same."

"Not exactly," said Yael.

"What's different?"

"There's one missing, the one about 'All the workers of the world are one.' Very pretty, no?" She was being flip.

"We always used to put it up," said Eton to me. "In fact, this is the first time I can remember not seeing it."

"Why should we put it up?" asked Yael. "It's a joke."

"It's no joke," said Bierman.

"No joke?" asked Yael, suddenly aroused. "All workers of the world are one! One *what*?"

"One — together," said Hannah.

"It's nothing to joke about," said Bierman to Yael.

"It makes no sense," said Yael. "You mean to tell me the Russian worker and I are one? The Chinese worker and I are one? And how about the Egyptian worker and the Syrian worker? Are we one, too?"

Bierman looked at Yael angrily, but whatever he was thinking, he kept to himself.

"There's no need pressing the point," Eton said to her gently.

"I'm not pressing anything," Yael answered. "Three days ago they tell us the Russians are flying in Egypt. And I'm supposed to go on saying 'All workers of the world are one?'"

"You see the sign is down."

"And that's where it belongs."

After dinner there was an hour or so of entertainment, much of it resembling the Passover show. There were songs, dances, and poems, although this time the poems were not about spring, but about Warsaw ghetto fighters and the Jewish struggle for survival. Many of the same people who performed on Passover were up there again: Nimrod reading a poem, the muscle-bound fellow from the cowshed playing the flute, Zakkai reading a section of the Bible, and the austere piano teacher leading the songs.

To conclude the program, a group of eight-year-olds read original compositions which their young teacher, Ruthy, introduced as "Prayers for Our Soldiers." I knew these kids. They were housed about a hundred feet away from my room, and consequently, the five or six times we had been bombed during the night, I had run down to share their shelter with them. Evidently, I was not supposed to do this, but nobody ever said anything to me; not even the first night when I came running down the stairs, my trousers still in my hand.

Having watched these kids sleep right through the attacks, undisturbed and seemingly unaffected, I was now curious to hear their compositions. Perhaps they would reveal something. So, as each of them came up to the microphone and slowly recited his composition, I quickly copied down the words. What I didn't catch right then, I filled in a few days later from Ruthy.

To the pilots: I pray that you and your families have a nice holiday. We always see your planes in the sky and we pray that you will keep the borders safe. I pray that you will be the bravest heroes in the world, and that you will come back safely from all your flights. I hope that peace will come soon, and that you will not have to use the Phantoms.

To the sailors: I pray that for the simple sailors and high officers, in the reserves and regular Navy, peace will come rapidly and you will be able to come back soon.

To the border guard: I hope you will keep the border safe, and that there will not be many infiltrators. I hope you will be able to go home, and that you will also be able to have a nice holiday, and while you are gone there won't be troubles here.

To the tank soldiers: We send you our prayers that you will succeed in all your actions and that your tanks will be improved. We pray that their anti-tank guns will not hurt you.

To the parachutists: I hope that you are good parachutists. Just don't jump in places that are bad to jump in. Happy holiday to all of you.

To the soldiers on the Canal: Keep the Canal safe so that the Egyptians will not get through. I pray that you will be brave and strong. I pray that you will beat the Egyptians and not let them kill us.

To the soldiers in the Jordan Valley: Thanks to you, the terrorists don't get through. You keep watching out for them and ambush them and catch them when they try to get through. In spite of heat and tiredness you stay at your positions. After a hard night you go back and begin again. I pray that you will keep the Jordan Valley borders safe. I hope peace will come rapidly, and that you will be able to go back to your homes and take it easy.

The Children and the Shelters

"The real point is that the children here in Bilat aren't any more afraid than the children in Haifa or Tel Aviv. They take more interest in the war perhaps, but that doesn't mean they are particularly scared about it; nor does it mean that they find sleeping in shelters abnormal. You've been down there enough times to know. Tell me, have they looked particularly frightened to you?" Ruthy shrugged her shoulders and took a deep draw of her cigarette. She hadn't really answered my question, which was whether she thought the compositions she just read me gave any indications that the children were afraid or insecure. She didn't see any point in analyzing the compositions. The real point was that the kids were not frightened, and anybody who went down in the shelters during the attacks could see it clearly for himself.

And really, she continued, there was every reason for the children to feel secure, at least now that the new shelters were built. Two years before the shelters had been inadequate, and separated from the children's houses. Then she could understand that the children were frightened. But now with thse new shelters, there was no reason for insecurity. The new shelters connected directly to the children's houses, and they could go right through the reinforced concrete corridor, and downstairs to safety. And, of course, at night they slept in these shelters which, about six months ago, had been reinforced with boulders, so that now even a direct air attack could not harm them. The children knew this. So really, why was there any reason for them to be frightened?

The most immediate problem, she continued, was that the shelters were ugly and sometimes uncomfortable. But this, too, was being taken care of. All ten of the children's shelters were now equipped with air-conditioners, and in most of them, something was being done to brighten up the walls. In the younger children's houses, there were plans to paint the walls with pictures of animals, clowns, and toys. The kibbutz was looking for someone, maybe a volunteer, to do the job. In the older children's houses, they were using drawings made by the children themselves, and everyone seemed to like them. But even with these improvements, the shelters looked like wine-cellars, and with the double-decker beds (used to conserve space), it was impossible to make them look *very* beautiful. She thought the solution was to do what they had done with the two newest shelters: to use a large square room with single beds along the floor. This way it wouldn't look like a shelter.

"But what does it matter if it *looks* like a shelter, if the children don't mind sleeping in shelters?" I asked, feeling there was some contradiction in what she was saying.

"It looks better as an ordinary room. That's the point. Would you rather sleep in a wine cellar or a bedroom?" She seemed annoyed that I was pressing her.

"You mean to say, then, that nobody is insecure now? It bombs and nobody is frightened?"

"I didn't say *nobody* is frightened. I said the children are secure. Not all of them, most of them — just like anyplace else."

"In every children's shelter someone goes down when bombs fall?"

"Yes. That is the practice. Except in the youngest grades — kindergarten and first grade — someone sleeps in their shelters every night. One of the men."

"What grade are your children?"

"Second."

"So they are alone at night?"

"Completely alone. You seem more worried about it than they are."

"Well, to be honest, if I had an eight-year-old child, I'm not so sure I would like him sleeping down there by himself at night."

"He wouldn't be by himself. There would be eight other children."

"I mean without an adult, without a grown-up to look after him in case something went wrong. Suppose he were sick, or uncomfortable or had a nightmare, I would like him to know that an adult was right there to take care of him."

"There are two women who make the rounds of all the shelters at night, you realize. And there's the intercom that goes into all the children's shelters — the 'electrical baby-sitter.' You must have heard of that, too."

"Yes, I have." The 'electrical baby-sitter' was the kibbutz's name for the expensive communications equipment which hooked up every children's shelter with a central location, where the night-watch women sat. They could hear any loud sound — such as crying — that went on in the shelters, and could talk to anybody in the shelters. "I know about all this," I said, "but let's just say it would be difficult for me, as a parent, to get used to it."

"I suppose," she granted.

"And because I feel this way, it's also difficult for me not to imagine that some of the parents are concerned about it too. Particularly with the bombings."

"Some of them are. Not many, a few. The point is that we're not all running around like a bunch of chickens with our heads chopped off. We're rather calm about it, as a matter of fact. Maybe to *you* this doesn't seem possible, but that's the way it is."

Ruthy snuffed out her cigarette and got up from her chair. "Why don't you speak to the doctors, the nurses. They'll all tell you the same thing. You can even go speak to the psychiatrist if you want to. Ask Mical, the nurse, to get you an appointment."

The psychiatrist was a large man in his early thirties, with a fleshy face, a red mustache, and dark rings under his eyes. He lived in Jerusalem and worked at the Talbieh Hospital, but once a week he came to the Jordan Valley to visit border kibbutzim. It wasn't volunteer work, he said, because the hospital paid his salary, yet it was true that he didn't have to come if he didn't want to. For the past two and a half years he had been making these visits, and while there was no fixed schedule to the appointments, he usually came to Bilat once every three weeks. Mostly he would talk to individuals — about five every visit, and mostly children — but occasionally he spoke to groups — teachers and parents — and sometimes to the entire kibbutz. As might be expected, he said, the border war had created "a new set of socio-psychological problems," and there was a need to discuss them openly. However, this was not always so easy to do in a kibbutz, as he knew only too well (He had been born in a kibbutz.); but as he thought back on the past two years or so, he felt there had been some real changes in the kibbutzniks' attitudes.

"You see, in the beginning — late '67 or early '68 — when the bombing first started here, the general attitude was that it would go away. This kibbutz had been at peace for about twenty years, and everyone looked on the shellings as only a temporary inconvenience. And really, in the first half-year or so, the shellings *were* irregular. For a couple of nights they would land close, even within the kibbutz, and then for a couple of weeks, or a month, there would be nothing. In the intervals, some people were able to forget about it, but many — perhaps most — began to worry. Particularly the mothers. They didn't sleep well, they had insomnia. Their work deteriorated and they began to get into more frequent arguments with other kibbutzniks. They wouldn't take sleeping pills because then, they said, they wouldn't be able to hear the bombs. And they *had* to hear the bombs. The children were sleeping upstairs.

"All this was very bad for the children, too. There were these terrible scenes when the bombing attacks did occur. The parents would come running, often from far off. They would arrive breathless, and snatch the child, sleeping or not, from his bed, and carry him to the shelter. Often the parents didn't know where to run first. If they had several children, they had to choose: the mother went one way, the father the other. The night-watch women took care of some, but then, they had a limited number of hands, too. All of this was terrible for the children. Even those who were too young to understand why they were being taken to the shelters knew that something was drastically wrong. The parents couldn't help but give them this feeling. They were scared themselves.

"Now, given such a bad situation, you would have thought that the parents would be eager to have the children sleep in the shelters. But that was not the case at all. They fought it all the way. They argued and resisted, and no matter how much I or anybody else warned them of the possible ill-effects of their refusal, they wouldn't hear of the children sleeping in shelters. Some of the reasons they gave were medical: the children wouldn't be able to breathe well, they said. The shelters were too stuffy, too hot in the summer, too damp in the winter. There was some point to this because, at that time, the shelters were not well equipped and they were badly ventilated. But some of the other reasons they gave made less sense: for instance, one woman said she didn't want her children sleeping like mice, underground. That it wasn't natural. Or another man had spent his boyhood in World War II Rumania, sleeping in shelters, and he would be damned if his kids were going to have to do the same thing here in Israel. Not many people argued so illogically, but it is safe to say that most felt this way; and for a long time, they wouldn't change. But eventually, more than all our arguments, it was the bombs that changed them. And in mid-'68 they decided to move the children, all those between one week and eleven years, into the shelters at night."

Had the shelters alleviated the anxiety of the children and their parents?

"No question about it. The shelters have been a blessing. For the children, the parents, for everyone in the kibbutz. You need to have been here for the past two years to fully appreciate how much they have helped. Most kibbutzniks are much calmer, and sleep much better. The change has been remarkable.

"But, as you can imagine, none of this took place overnight. It was gradual, and in the beginning, even slow and difficult. For some of the children it took months to get used to sleeping in shelters. They insisted that their parents stay with them. One boy, a four-year-old, wouldn't let his parents leave him day or night. The same with some of the older children. One eleven-year-old boy was a terrible problem: he kept getting sick all the time, so that he could sleep upstairs. In a way, all of this was predictable. The shift to sleeping in shelters had been made suddenly and traumatically, and as I've told you, the shelters weren't adequately equipped in the beginning. There was no intercom, so that if a child woke up frightened, he wasn't able to speak to any adult. Instead, he would wake up his whole group, and they would all come to the night-watch women.

"Incidents like this still happen, but they are fewer and less serious. With only a few exceptions, the children have adjusted to sleeping in the shelters; which is not so surprising when you think of it, because for many of them — those five years or younger — it is really all they can remember. In fact, the paradox we now face is that if we ever get to a point where it will be safe for them to sleep upstairs, we are going to have some problems. Already we see signs of it. For example, when families go visiting in Haifa or Tel Aviv, some of the children do not want to sleep in bedrooms. Even when they are told that there is no bombing in the cities, they complain that they want to go back to the kibbutz and sleep in the shelters.

"This is where they feel secure. It is their imaginary return to the womb, so safe and secure that not even bombs can harm them there. I remember, in this connection, an incident which one of the women told me this past winter. During the winter there are sometimes heavy rainstorms, and on one night it was raining and thundering particularly loud. When she went down to a shelter where one of the youngest groups was sleeping, she found one little boy who had awakened and was very frightened. She thought for a moment what she could tell him to calm him down, and then she finally said: 'Don't worry, it's only some bombing.' The boy relaxed and went back to sleep.

"The point, of course, is that children learn to adjust to anything — no matter how strange to adults. I don't mean to say that all of the children have, or someday will, come out of this situation psychologically undamaged. Some won't. But often what is now interpreted as psychological damage, is really not that at all. Some of the parents, for instance, complain that their children are always playing with guns and tanks. They don't like to give them these toys, they say, but that's what the children want to play with. So what can they do? I try to explain that none of this is abnormal. Children all over the world enjoy playing with toy weapons, and that play of this sort is really healthy for them. Playing is for children what words are for adults. It's their way of getting out their anger and fears.

"And you know, children are really quite ingenious in the way they manage to work out their anxieties through play. One woman who takes care of the three and four-year-olds was telling me how sometimes the children in her group would play a game called 'Bombing,' and they wanted her to get under the bed for shelter. She didn't know what to do. Should she go along with them, or should she tell them that it wasn't really bombing, so there was no need to go for shelter? I explained to her that the children constantly feel on the defensive. Someone is always bombing them and they must go to the shelters. They have no real way of getting back. In fact, until they are about four years old they're not even sure who it is they want to get back at. But they *do* want their chance to make someone else pay for their discomfort. And she is the natural target. I'm not sure how she eventually handled it, but to me, the wisest path was to go along with them."

The doctor paused, and I told him a little about my conversation with Ruthy, and how she seemed to be annoyed whenever I suggested that some of the children might be afraid. He smiled knowingly, and then his expression became serious, even sad.

"This is one of the cruelest problems we face. Everyone is expected to be a hero, to show no fear, no matter what his age. It's as if the society, feeling itself under attack, must counter with a collective defense. If any single individual revealed his fear, it might become contagious, and then the society would be in danger of dissolution. The cruel thing about this is that nobody is allowed the comfort of openly expressing his fears. And you can be sure that everyone is afraid at one time or another. He wouldn't be normal otherwise.

"This atmosphere of stoicism or bravado, whatever you want to call it, is particularly hard on the children. Just today I had a six-year-old girl here who is up against this problem. Her mother told me that the girl's troubles began about a year ago. It was tea-time and there was a mortar attack. The mother ran off to look after her baby, who was in the baby house, and a neighbor looked after the young girl. The two of them went running to the shelter and on the way the girl fell and cut herself badly. She had difficulty getting up and continuing to the shelter. Since then, she always wanted to go to the shelter even if there is only a slight bombing in the distance.

When she is playing she always seems to be listening for the bombs. She is never fully involved in what she is doing. I asked the girl if her friends were as afraid as she was, and she said they weren't paying attention to the noises. Her biggest fear, it turns out, was not that the bombs were going to hurt her, but that the rest of her friends would find out that she is afraid, and then they would make fun of her and not want her to be in their group anymore.

"Where do the children learn to react this way? Is it natural for them to ostracize one of their group because he or she is afraid? Or is it something that the parents and teachers have instilled in them unwittingly? Unfortunately the answer seems to be the latter. The adults, for reasons I have just told you, have felt it necessary to show a stiff upper lip. Some of this may be necessary and unavoidable, but the degree to which they carried it in the beginning was unbearable, even psychologically damaging I would have to say. There was intense criticism of anybody who showed the slightest outward sign of fear. That was a good part of the reason why it took a half-year or so to convince them to put the children in the shelters at night. And it was also a major cause for the various other anxiety reactions people were developing — insomnia, irritability, and sickness. People were unable to say openly that they wanted a vacation, a chance to get out of the kibbutz and be away from the strain; instead they felt obliged to spend their free days here, even if they didn't enjoy them. Or take another example: mothers could not say openly that they were afraid to have more children, that they preferred to wait; instead they went right on getting pregnant, and of course what happened is that many had miscarriages.

"The only group that was at all immune from this intense atmosphere of bravado was the old people — those sixty years and older. Like any place else, the old people here were able to get away with behavior that was seen as a bit queer or abnormal by everyone else. They were able to show their fears — not completely, but more than others. And this is fortunate because it is probably also true that they were more frightened than anyone else. Here in Bilat, about five of them still sleep in the shelters regularly, and they are joined by others when there is a particularly bad week of bombings. In another kibbutz, Kfar Ruppin, there is a group of about ten old people who go to the shelter each night at sundown, and nothing can bring them out. In fact, on one occasion a woman in this group was brought the news that her youngest son had just broken his arm in a basketball game, and even though it was absolutely quiet outside, she couldn't be persuaded to come up. This is an extreme case, of course, but it gives you an idea of the fear involved, and the permissive attitude toward the old. No young person could have gotten away with such an open expression of fear.

"Fortunately, however, there is no longer such a stringent taboo on admitting one's fears. No longer do you get the argument that one must not go to the shelters unless the bombs are falling very close, because *that* is just what Al Fatah wants — to keep them on the run constantly. People have become more reasonable. They go to the shelters when they should — in a walk, not a run, of course — and if someone wants to take his vacation outside the kibbutz, he does so. He may not say 'I want to get away from the strain,' but rather something like 'I work hard, I deserve it.' The point is, he goes. Now too, you begin to hear some parents — quite a few in fact — openly express their worries about the effect of the bombs on the children. They don't pretend that nothing is wrong. They talk to one another about these fears, and while they may not speak so freely with you as an outsider, you can be sure they are more candid with each other. However, all this does not mean that the kind of thing you heard from that one teacher isn't still a problem. It is. And, no doubt, what she told you is what she really believes. It's just that there is a limit to which any group can hide its fears, and it's a good sign that many people are beginning to recognize this, and loosen up." The doctor stopped.

"But let me ask you this," I said. "Now that the parents are beginning to speak more openly about their worries, what kind of things do they say? What do they think will be the long-term effects of the shelters and bombings on their children?"

"Not what you might expect," he answered. "I mean, the kind of worries that you might have for your children if they were in the same situation, are not the ones the kibbutzniks have. If you were raising children here, what would *you* worry about ?"

"What you told me about some of the children becoming dependent on the shelters: the ones who wanted to sleep in shelters even though they were in Haifa or Tel Aviv. A generalized insecurity, I suppose you would call it."

"That's what I thought you would say. But it's not what the kibbutzniks are worried about. Not the main thing, anyway. You see, many of them have gone through very tough and dangerous times, and they aren't terribly insecure because of it. What worries them most is not that their kids will be timid or dependent, but the opposite. That they will become too toughened, too enameled by the situation. Golda Meir said recently that she might someday be able to forgive the Arabs for the damage they have done to Israel and the killing of Israelis, but she would never be able to forgive them if they turned Israelis into destroyers and killers. You are Jewish, no doubt; so you will recognize this as a particularly Jewish outlook, and it is indeed the deepest worry of the most serious and thoughtful kibbutzniks. Especially those who came here as pioneers. They are very worried that the children are becoming thick-skinned, not just in their outlook on Arabs — many of the adults, themselves, to some extent share this — but in their general outlook, their world-view, so to speak. They know that their children are not as broadminded and tolerant as they were, nor do they have the same big dreams and ideals. And they are afraid that if the war continues, the children will become less and less inclined to broaden themselves."

"Well, how *do* the parents explain the current situation to their children?" I asked. "What *do* they tell them about the Arabs?"

"It varies. Mostly they try to explain that not all Arabs are bad. They try to raise the children without hatred. But this is extremely difficult, because over the years some of them have come to, let's say, strongly dislike the Arabs. Just the same they try not to convey this feeling to the children. The problem is that time works against them. The longer the war continues, the less likely they are to succeed in raising their children without hatred. Everyone knows this, but there is not much that can be done about it."

"Let me ask you one more thing, then," I said. "Suppose the war does not continue. Suppose, somehow, peace is achieved. What do you see as the effect on the kibbutz?"

"As you can understand, this is not a question that really worries them. After the Independence War in '48, there was a fairly large exodus from kibbutzim. All those who had been holding on due to ideological reasons, or because they would have been ashamed to leave when the situation was difficult, well, they left the kibbutz immediately after the war. I imagine the same thing would happen if there were peace. Here, for example, the number of young people leaving the kibbutz has diminished greatly since the bombing began. I don't know what the exact numbers are, but something like a third or a half were leaving before; now hardly anybody goes. It's one of those ironic, but fortunate, effects of the bombings, and in a way it sums up everything else I told you: the worse the situation gets, the more everyone is convinced he must sit tight and hold on."

"No, we would never leave. We wouldn't want to. Both of us were born here, you know. It's our home." Ofra smiled that wonderful smile of hers. She was, I thought, the most beautiful woman in the kibbutz, with her short blonde hair, blue eyes, and that terrific, natural smile. In fact, everything about her was spontaneous — her expressions, her gestures, her opinions. And having spent all of her thirty-odd years in this kibbutz, she was surely one of the most convincing endorsements for kibbutz living. The same was true of her husband, Baruch. Baruch had been away for a while, since the beginning of Passover. He was a lieutenant in the infantry, and now he was somewhere on the Golan Heights serving a chunk of his annual seventy days' reserve duty; he was due back in a couple of weeks, the end of May. Like Ofra, he was a spontaneous sort, big and joyful. Largely because of him I had enjoyed my short stay here the year before, and even my work stint in the olive groves, where he was one of the bosses. He had invited me a couple of times to visit them in their flat, and we had chatted — not about anything very substantial — and tried out some spiced tea that Ofra had bought in Jerusalem. We all got along well together, and even now that Baruch was away, I would have liked to visit Ofra alone, but this was not a polite thing to do, not for an outsider anyway, and I was afraid Ofra might have felt uncomfortable. However, sitting there on the bench outside the dining hall, while her three children played in front of us, was perfectly all right. And since I had just that afternoon had the talk with the psychiatrist, I was eager to hear what she would say.

"I agree with him that some would probably leave if there were peace," Ofra continued. "But not those of us who were born here.

Certainly not Baruch and I. It may not look like an ideal life with all this bombing, but even with that, I love it here. So does Baruch. The bombing is just something you learn to ignore."

"And the children?"

"It depends. Some ignore it, and some don't."

When the bombing first began a few months after the war, she said, it had been "a bit difficult" for everyone. At that time, there were only about ten shelters, and some of them were quite a distance from the children's houses. In the daytime, she knew that if there were an attack, the *metaplot* (kibbutz women who take care of the children during the day) would bring them to the shelters. But at night, it was up to the parents.

"I would go to one shelter — the one nearest our apartment, and Baruch would go to another. It wasn't just the parents who rushed to bring the children downstairs. Everyone did, children or no children. Sometimes I'd get to the shelter and the children would already be downstairs. They'd be frightened. They didn't talk, they just cried. Some were even a little hysterical. Ilan was five at the time and he was always hysterical when the bombs fell. I used to have to hold him tightly to quiet him down.

"But now, thank goodness, he's all right. If it bombs during the day he goes quickly to the shelter. He doesn't panic. And at night, he sleeps calmly, even if there is an attack. I don't have to go to the shelters anymore. You see, it's a big difference now that they sleep downstairs — for them, and for us. Everyone is calmer. Of course, Baruch and I don't feel free to go away from the kibbutz for more than a day. But still, the situation is much better than it was in the beginning."

What did she think the effect of sleeping in the shelters would be on the children?

"I really don't think much about it."

"You don't think it will affect them badly?"

"No, not really. Take what happened to us — we who grew up here. We lived through the British period and the War of Independence, and in a way that was worse. My mother almost lost us altogether; because of the British, not the Arabs. I remember how the British came one night and wanted to take me and my sister away. I was six and she was ten. I don't know what they wanted to do with us, but they wanted us to go with them. They said we were not Jews, we looked too Aryan. They said my parents had stolen us, and they wanted to take us back. I can still remember my parents arguing, and then my mother actually fighting with one of the British." Ofra smiled, "And as you can see, my parents won!"

"So you don't think it will affect your children adversely?"

"Look at me," she was now almost laughing. "I am married, a mother of three children, happy. Why shouldn't my children be the same?" Noticing that Hagar and her three friends were leaving the area, she asked where they were going. To the children's house, the girls answered; they wanted to take showers before going to bed. Ofra nodded her approval, and shouted to Hagar that she would come by shortly to say good-night.

Then, turning back to me, she asked if there was anything else I would like to know. Yes, I said. How did she explain the war to her children; why they were being bombed, why the Arabs were against them?

Ofra nodded her head slowly. "A tough question for all of us. It's not so difficult when they are Hedi's age . . ." Ofra pointed to her daughter who was somersaulting near the bench. "At three, they don't know what is happening. They hear the bombing, they hear the other children talk about it, but how can they understand it? Hedi, for example, is always talking about dead animals. She says that soldiers are shooting the foxes because the foxes are eating the chickens. And she says that she must go to the shelters because she can get hurt. But that's all she says, and for the time being, there is nothing to explain."

"What *do* you say when they realize somebody is shooting at them?"

"That's the tough part. We don't want to poison their feelings. We tell them that there are good Arabs and bad Arabs. We cannot say that all Arabs are bad, we have Arabs living here in Israel. So we say there are good ones and bad ones. The good ones live in places like Nazareth and are farmers like we are. The bad ones shoot at us from across the border. It's really the same thing *our* parents used to tell us. Before '48, there used to be Arabs in the villages across the Yarmuk, and they would come up to buy grain or vegetables from us, and we would go visit them and drink lemonade or eat pomegranates. They were the good Arabs, we were told. But the other ones, the ones who would fight us with sticks and knives, they were the bad Arabs.

"We tell them that we have come here because we need a country of our own and Israel is our special place; that we bought the land, and that during the Independence War some Arabs fled — most of them, and some of them were conquered."

"You use the word 'conquered'?"

"Of course. Until recently, it was always used freely. Now we are a little sensitive about it, perhaps, but we still use it. Haven't you seen the plaque over our exhibition house, the Uri and Rami exhibition house? Uri and Rami were two sons of the kibbutz. Malcolm's sons. Rami died of a snake bite, and Uri died in Lod during the Independence War. That's what it says: Uri fell during the 'conquest' of Lod."

"What do the children say when you tell them you 'conquered' some of the Arabs' territory?"

"Some of them ask why. So we explain that for reasons of security we needed certain places, certain territory. With Jerusalem we tell them it is our most important place. We didn't succeed in getting it in 1948, but we did in 1967."

"And what do they say?"

"Nothing special. For them the present territories and Jerusalem were always ours. Look, you can ask them about these things yourself if you want. I'll call them." Ofra called Ilan over. At this point he was playing tag with several smaller children, and answered that he was busy, but when Ofra shouted that "the American journalist" wanted to talk to him, he and two girls came running over.

"Ask them anything you like," she said, as the children stood there fidgeting.

"Well, why don't you sit down first," I said to them.

The children sat down quickly, Ilan in the middle, with a small chubby girl on one side, and a thin red-haired girl on the other.

"Tell Michael about the Arabs," Ofra said. "He wants to know what you think of the Arabs, Ilan."

Ilan shrugged his shoulders.

"I would like to know who it is that does the shooting at us," I said.

Ilan giggled, as if he were astonished that an adult could ask such a stupid question. "*Al Fatah*," he said. "Everyone knows that."

"Are they the only ones shooting at us?" I asked.

"Yes," all the children said together.

"Do you know why they are shooting?"

"They're idiots!" said Ilan.

"Stupids!" added the chubby girl.

"Are all the Arabs shooting at us, Ilan?" Ofra coached.

"No."

"Some of them work here," said the other girl, the red-haired one.

"*They* don't shoot at us," said the chubby girl.

"Where do they come from?" I asked.

"Tiberias," said the chubby girl.

"No, silly, they come from Nazareth," said the red-haired girl.

"Do you know any of them?"

"No," they all answered.

"Do any Arabs do good things in Israel?"

"They build the shelters," said the red-haired girl.

"So they do some good," I said.

Nobody answered except the red-haired girl. "Yes, they build the shelters." There was a pause.

"And they build the children's houses, don't they?" Ofra said.

"They put a new roof on our house," added Ilan.

"Reinforced concrete," Ofra said to me. "They're new this past winter."

"Some are farmers," said the red-haired girl.

"What do they grow?" I asked.

"I don't know," she answered.

"They don't grow anything," answered Ilan. "They raise animals."

"What kinds?"

"Sheep."

"Did you ever eat any?"

"I don't like sheep."

"I ate some once," said the chubby girl. "In Haifa, at my aunt's house."

"How did it taste?"

"Good."

"We don't eat much mutton or lamb in the kibbutz," Ofra said to me. "The children don't know very well what it tastes like."

"I know what it tastes like," said Ilan. "I don't like it."

"You've tasted it once, how can you say you don't like it?" Ofra asked him angrily.

"I don't like it," he repeated.

"All right, wait a second," I interrupted, trying to get back on the track. "Let me ask you this: if some of the Arabs are farmers and some of them make shelters and houses, then they do some good in Israel, don't they?"

"There are good ones and bad ones," said Ilan.

"The bad ones shoot at us," said the chubby girl.

"*Al Fatah* are the bad ones," said Ilan.

"How often do they shoot?" I asked.

"All the time."

"Does anyone get hurt?"

"No. They shoot lousy."

"What do you do when it bombs?"

"I go to the shelters and eat tea, cookies and chocolate," said the chubby girl.

"We all walk to the shelters," said Ilan.

"Are you at all scared?"

"I'm not if my parents are here," said the red-haired girl.

"I am," said the chubby girl.

"What are you scared of?" Ilan asked the chubby girl, accusingly.

"I just am. So are you."

"I am not!"

"You just don't remember, Ilan," Ofra said calmly. "You used to be scared a few years ago, too."

"Now I'm not," Ilan announced, with a tough-guy expression.

"You mean you don't run to the shelters when it's bombing, Ilan," Ofra said to him teasingly. "Come on now!"

"Only when it's near. When it's not near, I walk calmly."

"I go to my parents' apartment if I'm close by," said the red-haired girl. "I lie under the bed or go into the bathroom."

"So do I," said the chubby girl.

"Who taught you that?" I asked them.

"The security people talk to them," explained Ofra. "Their

teachers tell them, too."

"My father told *me*," said the chubby girl.

"Her father is Jason," said Ofra. "You probably don't know him. He just got back from the reserves. He was away a month and a half."

"Two days ago he came back," the chubby girl said.

"Did you think about him when he was away?" I asked.

"Yes."

"What did you think?"

"Oh, nothing." Then to Ofra, the girl said excitedly: "He almost got wounded this time! A bomb came flying right into the bunker, right where my father was standing. But it didn't explode!"

"I didn't know that," Ofra said calmly.

"My father was wounded in the Six-Day War," said the red-haired girl. "He almost lost his hand."

"My father was on the Golan," said Ilan. "They captured a Syrian fortress. He's up there now, too."

"All right, Ilan, that's nothing to brag about," said Ofra.

"Are you scared at all, Ilan?" I asked.

"No."

"Yes you are," said the chubby girl.

"I am not."

"We all get scared," said the red-haired girl.

"Not me," said Ilan. "Just when there is bad news."

"Do you listen to the news?" I asked.

"Yes."

"So do I," said the chubby girl.

"We all listen to the news when our fathers are away," said the red-haired girl.

"They know where their fathers are stationed," said Ofra, "so they follow the news when they're away."

"My mother doesn't listen," said the chubby girl.

"What do you mean?" asked Ofra.

"Not when my father is away," said the girl. "She doesn't listen."

Ofra looked over at me, her eyebrows raised. "You caught that?"

"Yes."

"Look, kids," she said, "I think it's time to be going. It's getting late."

"Are we going to be on television?" the chubby girl asked.

"He's a newspaperman," said the red-haired girl.

"We're going to be in the newspapers, stupid," Ilan said to the chubby girl.

"That's no way to talk," Ofra said.

"She should know he's not a television man."

"Perhaps nobody has told her."

"I want to be on television," said the chubby girl.

"Maybe someday you will be," I said.

"Good!"

"You're too ugly," Ilan said.

"That's enough of that!" Ofra said. Then to me: "You can see, we'd better be going." She and the children began to walk off.

"Thanks very much, Ofra."

"Sure. Good-night."

"Good-night," the children said.

A Lecture

It had taken the kibbutzniks a few weeks to get used to it. At first, (in late April) when the government initially announced that Soviet pilots were flying operational missions in Egypt, everybody was angry. They cursed the Americans, and as resident American, I suddenly became responsible for my government's actions. It was not at all unusual for someone I had never met to sit next to me at lunch and begin a harangue on how my government had lost its guts, how the Russians were able to do whatever they wanted, and how Americans wouldn't give a damn. Maybe a tear or two over Israel's grave, yes, in Brooklyn and the Bronx, yes, but what about doing something beforehand, so nobody would have to cry about it.

I remained silent because I secretly felt that the Israelis themselves, in their decision to bomb around major Egyptian population centers, including Cairo, had in a sense brought on the Soviet-Egyptian counter-escalation. This was not an opinion held by any kibbutzniks, or if it was, it was never mentioned. And I was not ready to debate these points. It was one thing to hold a dovish opinion if you lived in New York or Tel Aviv, but it was quite another to flaunt it on the border.

Just the same, I was curious to know how they would react, and for this reason, I was happy to see that the invited lecturer that night was Jacob Talmon, the well-known historian from the Hebrew University. He was the third lecturer who had visited from the Hebrew University since I had been in Bilat, and he was by far the most famous. I had never heard him speak before, but I knew from some of his writings — including a published exchange of letters with historian Arnold Toynbee, shortly after the Six-Day War — that Talmon was, in the spectrum of Israeli politics, a dove. Therefore, I was a bit surprised that the kibbutz had wanted him to speak; but, then, the kibbutzniks were no longer as riled up as they had been after the first announcement about the Soviet pilots. The fear beneath the anger was now almost gone, as the Israeli jets continued to pound Egyptian artillery emplacements along the Canal; and the American government was hinting that it would send the Phantoms and Skyhawks after all.

"That's what we need — the planes. All the talk in the world isn't going to do us any good without the planes. Everyone knows that. So what's the sense talking about it?" Rafael waved disgustedly in the direction of the dining hall, where the crowd was beginning to gather for the Talmon lecture.

"Do you know of Talmon?"

"What's there to know?"

"They say he's a dove."

"Nice bird. We ought to send one to Nasser."

"They say he's got an interesting point of view."

"Who's they? The Americans?" I didn't answer. "Look, I'm sorry. I mean no offense. Besides, I don't really look upon *you* as one of them, anyway."

"Why don't you go in with *him*." Rafael pointed towards Edo who was walking in the door alone. "He's our Russian expert."

Edo had taken a seat in the rear of the dining hall, among a small group of soldiers and high-school students. No sooner did I join him, when Orna came rushing up to us. She was out of breath.

"Come quickly," she said to me. "I want you to meet Talmon."

We went up to the front of the dining hall where a rather rumpled looking man was sitting alone at a table. He was sweating, as if he had run all the way from Jerusalem.

"So you are here from America?" He was shuffling through some papers and didn't bother looking up.

"Yes, about a month and a half now."

"And how do you find it?"

"I haven't decided."

"No? Well, I can tell you it's different than it used to be. Much different." He stopped as if he had just summed it up. He poured himself a glass of grapefruit juice which had been set out on the table for him.

"They're older now. Much older. I used to make these lectures several years ago. The faces have changed. They used to be young, lively. Now take a look."

I didn't have to. It was mostly the older kibbutzniks who came to these cultural affairs; the young, like Rafael, usually weren't interested.

"The young people don't go to lectures much," I said.

"They're the ones who need to hear it. Not the old people."

"I suppose."

"It's not like America, is it?" He was still going through the papers. "There, the old aren't interested, and the young are the fire-eaters."

"True."

"A real mess. I was there in '69. And it's worse now from what I hear. I get letters from friends and they say it's coming apart at the seams. A real mess. That's what we're worried about here. If America comes apart, what will happen to us? It's a real question. That's what I want to discuss tonight."

He stacked his papers neatly, and placed his pencil down on top of them. "Well, we'd better get going. Before everyone out there, and I, too, fall asleep."

I returned to my seat next to Edo, and the professor began talking. He spoke informally, much as he had chatted with me — sometimes seeming tired and disinterested, and at other moments, when he was making some intellectual point, appearing suddenly alive and roused. The audience, however, was mute, barely reacting to anything he said, except for a few Yiddish jokes which Talmon used to illustrate his case.

Talmon argued that the Israeli government had been remiss in not stating forthrightly, prior to any negotiations, what its ultimate territorial demands were. They were the victors; the Arabs had been humiliated, and as everyone knew, the Arab mentality was too prideful to allow them to come quietly and request a settlement. The Jews had to go to them. They couldn't pass up any opportunities.

What's more they had to be realistic in understanding that in a significant way, the match was no longer just between the Israelis and the Arabs, if indeed it ever was. It might be good rhetoric to say that the Big Powers should stay out of it, but the fact was they were in it. The Russians, as everybody knew, were in it up to the gills, but so were the Americans; and really, it was now up to the two of them to lead the Arabs and Israelis into a settlement. As far as he could see, the Russians were not about to try to cross the Canal. They were satisfied, at least for the time being, to establish a foothold in Egypt. Of course, it was possible that they could be dragged into something they didn't want. They might suddenly find themselves eyeball to eyeball with the Americans as they had been in Cuba, and from there anything could happen. But he prayed that the situation would not be allowed to deteriorate this far, and he expected that the two Big Powers would take a more sensible course.

The professor sat down. He looked even more tired than when he had started, and sad that he had to be the bearer of such news. He said he was willing to answer any questions, to make any clarifications. From the audience, there was a long silence, then a few kibbutzniks stood up by their chairs and made short speeches about the United States and Russia. While none of it was very substantial, it was obvious they had been irritated by the professor's reasoning. Finally, a short, old man from the back of the room yelled out that he had something more to say. It was Avram, Avram from the *Lool*, the man who, according to Lea and Moshe, was once Assistant Secretary of Agriculture in the first Ben-Gurion government. I was surprised to see him stand up now, and even more surprised when he went to the front of the dining hall, to the table where Talmon was sitting. He seemed too shy for this. No matter how much I had tried,

I had never been able to get more than a peep out of him. He always went right on cleaning eggs, as if he didn't hear or wasn't interested. But now he was standing there, in front of the whole group, lashing out at all the demons that had just come into the room.

What did the professor mean that Israel had been remiss in not stating its territorial demands? What did he mean that the Israelis had passed up opportunities for peace? Who was it, the Israelis or the Arabs, that had refused to come to the peace table; that talked about "throwing the vermin into the sea"; that had made three wars to wipe out the other side? What had the Israelis done wrong? He knew. For fifty years, they had committed the one unpardonable sin of wanting to live like everyone else, in their own land. And now they were supposed to go begging their enemies to sit at the same table with them, nay, to grant them the privilege of existing as an independent state, a privilege they had already won with blood. This was absurd. Everyone should know that the reason they had lasted so far, was because they did not bow to these demands. Moreover, as soon as they showed the slightest sign of bending, everyone should know what would happen. The Arabs would take it for weakness and try to annihilate them. No, they had to stand upright, independent, strong, and only then would the Arabs someday come around. Meanwhile, nobody needed the Americans to do their bargaining or fighting for them. Let them stay out of it. Give the planes and stay out of it. Israelis could handle the rest.

And Avram sat down. There was a long silence and nobody sought to break it, not even Talmon, who seemed a bit taken aback by this onslaught. Perhaps he hadn't expected it. Or perhaps he had, but not so rough. The kibbutzniks, at any rate, seemed relieved, not just because the lecture was over, but because Avram had spoken so well for them, and the professor hadn't answered him back.

"He's right," said Edo, as we were walking out of the dining hall. "Completely right."

"Avram, you mean?" I asked.

"Of course. He's old, but he still has a head on his shoulders."

"And Talmon?"

Edo's eyes narrowed like a machine-gunner's. "He's just like one of the Jews in Germany who marched off quietly to the gas chambers. Everything would be all right, they thought, if only some outside force intervened. They couldn't believe they were going to be wiped out. Nobody would let it happen to them — not God, not the outside forces, not even the Germans. And look what happened!"

"So, what are you saying?"

"That we must rely on ourselves. Nobody but ourselves."

"Does everybody here see it that way?"

"Everybody. We have no professors on the kibbutz."

A Day in Class

The school year was coming to an end, and Moshe advised me not to wait until the final week, in late June, to visit: it would be too chaotic. It was better to come a few weeks before final exams, he said, when the students would be eager to receive me, and also eager to discuss their ideas.

It was exactly 7:30 A.M. when the school-bell rang, loud and tinny. The fifteen or so high school students who had been sitting on the lawn, and a few others who were coming up the path, headed for the second of three classrooms in the long, dormitory-like building that served as part of the high school. Most of them were dressed no differently for class than they would have been for work: they wore short pants, short sleeve shirts that floppd over the pants, sandals or no shoes at all, and several — the boys — had not bothered to comb their hair. Their teacher, on the other hand, a young woman named Ilana, was wearing red bell-bottom slacks, a white blouse, eye make-up, and that short, almost crew-haircut which I usually associated with Parisian women.

Ilana's literature class turned out to be somewhat disappointing. The subject matter — analysis of a sixteenth-century Spanish poem, translated into Hebrew — was not stimulating enough to wake most of the students from their early morning lethargy. So they sat there, heads in their hands, looking out the window, or even talking to each other. At one point, Ilana stopped in the middle of writing something on the blackboard, turned around, and reprimanded one talkative boy ("David, the least you can do is to be quiet if you're not interested."); and the boy shook it off ("It's all right, Ilana, I'm not disturbing anybody"). Nobody seemed to find this at all disrespectful, not even Ilana. She turned back to the blackboard, finished what she was writing, and then carried on her discussion with the few students who were interested in it. This continued for about a half-hour, and then just before the bell rang, Ilana made a homework assignment — analysis of another Spanish poem. Those who had been listening to the discussion copied it down. David, and several of the others, paid no attention.

This general pattern continued in the chemistry class. But Rebecca, an older and heftier woman, was far more stern than Ilana, and when a couple of girls began chatting loudly during her lecture, she stopped, stared at them, and waited until they were silent. Again, less than half the students were actively involved in the lecture, but at least this time, David was tuned in. He kept looking up and down from the blackboard to his book, and twice he called out to Rebecca that she had made a mistake. The first time, she agreed with him, but the next time she said she would have to check on it later. David had grinned knowingly at this, and a plump, pretty face across the room shouted over to him not to be such a big shot; to which David yelled back, that if there was anything big in the room, it was certainly not on his side. The students laughed at this crack, but the girl gave him a dirty look, and Rebecca went back to talking about hydrogen atoms.

When the chemistry class ended, Rebecca came over to me and explained that there was a half-hour break before the next class — Moshe's — and if I wanted to, I could come to the teachers' room and have coffee with them. I accepted gladly and we went to a small room at the end of the building, where Ilana and Moshe were already drinking coffee and talking.

They looked up suddenly as I came in, and then became silent. They seemed uneasy. Moshe poured Rebecca and me a cup of coffee, and began making small talk about the weather, joking how this was probably my easiest day so far in the kibbutz, sitting as I was in an air-conditioned classroom and taking notes. Rebecca seemed to stiffen with this remark, as if Moshe were somehow demeaning their work by calling it easy, but she said nothing. She simply took out a crumpled blue handkerchief and mopped her forehead, her expression now as stern and uncompromising as a set of chemistry equations. We all became silent again, and Moshe went over to the small refrigerator in the corner of the room, and brought back a dish of grapes. Then, as if the thought had just occurred to him, he said: "I'm curious, Michael, how are you finding it so far?"

I knew what he meant, but I answered: "My first day of class, you mean?"

"Yes."

Everyone was staring at me, especially Rebecca, whose small, dark eyes had narrowed almost accusingly.

"Well . . . to be frank," I began slowly, "there have been a few surprises for me."

"Like what?"

"The informality. I'm not quite used to it."

"You mean the short pants and the sandals?" Moshe asked, casually.

"Yes, I'm not used to it. And calling the teacher by the first name, and talking out without raising a hand . . ."

"This is a kibbutz, you remember, not a public school," said Ilana gently.

"We're comrades here," said Rebecca, predictably. "We see the students every day. Not just in school, but in the dining hall, and at work. It's not the usual student-teacher relationship we're involved in."

"I understand."

"No, I know what he means," said Moshe. He was trying to be diplomatic. "It takes time to get adjusted to it. For the students, though, it's completely natural."

"It's the healthiest type of relationship," said Rebecca. "We know them as whole people."

"You find you can do the best teaching under these circumstances," said Moshe.

"Besides, it's more enjoyable this way," said Ilana.

I then asked several questions about the students and the curriculum. Moshe did most of the answering, since he was principal

of the secondary school, as well as the history teacher. It was not a
large high school program, he said; only forty students in all three
grades. The ones I was seeing this morning were the oldest —
seventeen and eighteen — and next year they would be going to the
army. The students were a bit lax these last few weeks, but normally
they studied seriously. Each student selected his own program —
five or six classes a day — but there were certain required courses
such as literature, science, and in the last two years, Arabic. There
were also four hours of homework each day ("They do it if they are
interested," admitted Ilana), and, of course, there were tests every
few weeks. "I don't want to boast," concluded Moshe, "but
everyone here gets an excellent education."

"You mean nobody ever fails?" I asked.

"Never," answered Rebecca, promptly. "Every kibbutz child goes
through high school."

"How about college?"

"They go if they want to."

"If you have the desire *and* the ability, well, then of course you
can go," said Moshe.

"How many go as far as a B.A.? More than ten per cent?"

"Not yet," said Rebecca. "But, eventually, at least that number
will go. We are not standing still, you know. The trend in the city is
towards higher education, and it's the same in the kibbutz."

"And how about you, the teachers. Did you all go to college?"

"Teachers' college. It takes two years. But some have their B.A.'s.
Take Moshe, he has a law degree."

"How many hours do you all work per week?"

"The same as everyone else in the kibbutz, 48 hours per week —
24 in class, 24 in preparation. When there are vacations in school, we
work in the dining hall or in the fields." Rebecca looked at her
watch. "As a matter of fact, I must get ready for my afternoon math
classes. You'll excuse me, please." She got up and left the room, and
Ilana went with her.

When Moshe finished his introduction and left the classroom,
there was a short silence. The students sat there at their wooden
desks, two to a desk, waiting for me to break the ice. A few of them I
knew, of course: Moshe's daughter, Neeli, and David (he was the

boy who had told me about Shmulik on *Erev Pesach*), and the plump pretty-face girl whose name was Ruthy. But most of the others I had seen only occasionally in the dining hall, and I hardly knew them at all.

I decided to open with some easy, factual questions: Who reads the newspaper every day? (Almost all raised their hands or shouted out something, indicating that they did.) Who reads books and magazines in addition to what is assigned in school? (A few said they did, but most admitted it was rare for them.) How many hours of homework do you have each night? (Ruthy and a few girls said four hours, but David and most of the class said this was an exaggeration; two hours was more like it.) Who plans to go to college? (Nobody answered at first, and then a short muscular boy at the rear of the room yelled out: "Three years from now, who knows what will be? First there is the army!" Everyone seemed to go along with this.)

"Let me ask you one more short question," I said. "Is there anyone here who is not a *sabra*?"

Two boys raised their hands. One was from Argentina and the other, a dark-skinned boy with hair down to his shoulders, was from Morocco.

"I see, but everyone else is a *sabra*?"

The students nodded. I then asked how many of their parents were also *sabras*. Only one hand went up. Their parents were almost all immigrants, mostly from Europe.

"Then let me ask you this," I said. "What differences do you see between your generation and your parents? Are the two generations close together in their ideas and attitudes? Or do you have a generation gap?"

Everyone was silent for a moment and then David said: "There is always a generation gap. Wherever you are."

"How do *you* know?" Ruthy glared at him. "Where have *you* been?"

"You just have to pick up a magazine or a book and read it," David answered.

"I don't know about that," said Ruthy. "It seems to me you've got to live in a place before you know what's going on there."

"Let's not argue about that," I interrupted. "The question is about Bilat. Is there, or is there not, a generation gap here?"

"Of course there is," said David, matter-of-factly.

"How do you experience this gap?"

"Our parents are more conservative," said Neeli, speaking up for the first time.

"In what way?"

"They pay more attention to manners and things like that. We are more informal."

"If I want to walk around looking sloppy," said David, "my mother gives me a hard time. To me it doesn't matter. Shirt tucked in or not tucked in, hair combed or not combed, it's all the same to me."

"And try to wear your hair like Hassan's," said the slim boy from Argentina, pointing over to the Moroccan boy. "See what they say about that!"

"What do they say?" I asked. I had never heard any specific comments, but the previous week I *had* seen some older kibbutzniks eyeing one rather shaggy volunteer from England, as if they were Iowans getting their first close-up look at a hippie.

"*What* do they say!" repeated the Argentinian boy, dramatically. "You mean you've never heard them? Tell him, Hassan, what they've said to you."

"It's not worth it," said Hassan curtly.

"They call him pretty boy, if you want to know," said David. "'How are you today, sweetheart?' Things like that."

"Everybody?"

"No, no, not everybody. Just a few of the older ones that have no manners. Those that don't say it, are thinking it anyway."

"Has anybody ever said you have to cut it off?" I asked Hassan. "No."

"How about you, Ruthy," I said, "what do you think of all this?"

Ruthy had her head cupped in her hands, looking disgusted. "I think they're exaggerating. You heard what Hassan said, nobody has ever told him he has to cut his hair."

David and Hassan stared at her but said nothing.

"And how about you, Neeli. What have you got to say or add?"

"I think what David says is true. The older people, most of them anyhow, are conservative. On many things."

"I want to know more what you mean by that."

"Well, take things like walking arm in arm with your boyfriend, or kissing in public. They act as if it's immoral."

"How can that be?" I asked. "Some of your parents have told me how they used to swim naked at night down in the Yarmuk."

Everyone laughed.

"Yeah, isn't that the damndest thing!" said David. "It was fine for them, but for us, it's immoral."

"You can do it," Neeli said, "but you can see they don't like it. Not all of them are this way, you understand — like my mother, she says she sees nothing wrong with it — but many of the others are prudes."

"It's not so bad," said Ruthy, looking over at Neeli. "It's not like the city, where you're living in the same house with your parents, and they watch over you. Here we live by ourselves and you can do what you want. Everyone knows that."

There was a silence and it seemed that everyone did know it, but nonetheless objected to the way in which Ruthy had said it.

"You're missing the point," David finally said to her. "The point is that we have our differences with them. There are things they want us to do, and that we don't want to do. It's as simple as that." David stopped as if he had just summed it up.

"Are there any other examples?" I asked him.

He contemplated for a moment and then said: "Take what happens when we get out of the Army. You finish your three years, and immediately the kibbutz wants you to come back and start working."

"What's so strange about that?" asked Ruthy, belligerently.

"He asked me, not you," David said to her. Then to me: "They also want you to give all your army severance pay — it's about nine hundred pounds — to the kibbutz, except for a hundred pounds of it, which they let you keep. I say, why not let us take the Army money, and any other money we can get our hands on, and take a vacation. Maybe a year off. Go to Europe. In the city, that's what everyone does. Why can't *we* do it?"

Opinions exploded around the room. David had evidently touched a soft spot, and everyone was suddenly involved.

"David's an egotist!" announced Ruthy. "You heard what he just said. The kibbutz can make one decision, and he'll make another."

"That's not what I said at all," yelled David.

"Who is the kibbutz?" Ruthy asked rhetorically. "All of us, right? What is the meaning of collective life, if *we* can say one thing, and you do another? The kibbutz doesn't say you must come back and work immediately after the Army, just to cause you problems. It says you must come back because you are needed here. If everyone were to take a year off, we'd be short-handed."

"She's right," said a girl sitting in front of her. "Ruthy's right!"

"She doesn't know what she's talking about," Hassan said.

"Look here," shouted the short, muscular boy in the rear of the room. "David's not saying he should be able to take off time, when the kibbutz says he should be here. He means the kibbutz ought to change the rules."

"That's right!" said David. His face was now tight with anger. "The rule is lousy. It ought to be changed. I'm not the only one who thinks this way!"

By now, Ruthy was on her feet yelling at David, and he, pretending to be unmoved, began whistling to himself. To bring things under control, I decided to put it to a vote. At least two-thirds of the class favored the year off, and the other third — mostly girls — were rather hesitant about raising their hands.

"You're all egotists," shouted Ruthy, when the vote was over.

"And you're crazy!" answered David.

Again they were at it. Two girls got up from their seats and left the classroom ("We're sorry, but we're expected in the kitchen shortly"), and everyone else seemed ready to follow. I decided to make one more bid for their attention.

"Look! We're running a little late," I announced. "Unfortunately, I've left the best questions for last. But, if anyone has to leave, please go now." Another girl and boy got up and walked out. There were only about twelve students left, but they — thanks to some yelling from Neeli — were at last quiet.

"Now to some extent these remaining questions are hypothetical," I began slowly, "so you're going to have to think a little about them . . ."

"I'm thinking, I'm thinking," shouted the muscular boy. "Go ahead already!"

"All right. Next year all of you are going into the Army, correct?"

Everyone nodded. "And all of you must go, like it or not."

"We want to go," yelled the muscular boy. "This isn't America!"

"Wait a minute! Wait until you have heard the entire question. Now, suppose it were not compulsory to serve; suppose only fifty per cent of Israeli youth were needed in the Army, and the rest could remain in Tel Aviv, or wherever they lived. Would you enlist, anyway?"

"Of course!" shouted the muscular boy.

Two or three others shouted in agreement.

"Hold on!" said David. "Do you mean voluntary enlistment *and* the same situation as exists today with the Arabs?"

"Yes."

"Then of course we'd enlist."

"Is everyone in agreement?"

"Yes," they all answered.

"All right," I said, "one more question. I want you to imagine that you were born not here in Bilat, but a little distance from here — across the Yarmuk, in one of the Arab refugee villages — and that your parents once lived in, say, Tiberias. How would you look upon Israel?"

The class was silent, except for Uriel who let out a grunt. It was, of course a loaded question, deliberately vague; but the facts were not at all unimaginable. Two of the Arab villages that sat right across the Yarmuk, clearly visible from Bilat, were inhabited — until the Six-Day War — by Arab refugees from Tiberias, Nazareth, or Haifa. This was common knowledge among the older kibbutzniks, and I assumed the students knew it too.

"I'm supposed to imagine I'm an Arab refugee!" said Uriel, sarcastically. "Next thing I know, I'll be Arafat, himself."

The class laughed loudly.

"Almost," I said. "Kosygin is next." The class laughed again, except for Uriel. "No, seriously, I want you to put yourselves in the place of an Arab refugee, and tell me how you think you'd look on Israel."

There was another silence, and then Neeli said: "Well, if I look at it with my own head, I'd say they have every reason to be part of Israel. Everyone knows that the Arabs living here have a higher standard of living than those in Arab countries. Why fight us? If there were peace, the living standard throughout the whole Middle East could be elevated easily. Everyone knows that. But, that's with *my* head. If I grew up among Arab refugees, who knows how I'd think? Probably I'd think like they do."

"Look what's happened," said David. "Twenty years they've been used as a political football. You talk about being a refugee in one of the villages across the Yarmuk. Why couldn't Hussein have let them settle further inside Jordan. Or why couldn't they have gone to Syria or Iraq where there is plenty of arable land. I'll tell you why. They wanted them to sit across the border from us and hate us, so that someday there could be another *jihad*." He said the word *jihad* (an Arabic word meaning "holy war") mockingly.

"All their lives they're taught to hate us," said Uriel. "All they hear is that we threw them out, that we took their land. They never stop and think who started it, that it was they who wouldn't live in peace with us, from the first days we came here until they rejected the partition scheme in '48. All they can say is that we threw them out."

"Wait a minute," I said, "we seem to be going off the track some. The question, remember, is how do you think you'd look at Israel if *you* were an Arab refugee?"

"And that's the answer," said Uriel. "You'd be taught to hate it."

"Do any of you think you would want to join *Al Fatah*?"

"Here it comes," said Uriel, throwing up his hands. "Here comes the Arafat stuff."

The class laughed again.

"No, I know what he means," said Neeli. "Like I said before, if I grew up among Arab refugees, of course I would think like they do. If I were a Palestinian refugee I'd want my own country. Not all of those in *Al Fatah* are barbarians. We know that. Most of them join *Al Fatah* for the money, of course. But some are idealists who think they are fighting for a Palestinian country."

"Come on!" shouted Uriel.

"You don't know a damned thing about Arabs!" yelled Hassan.

"Let her speak!" said Ruthy.

Neeli continued rather calmly: "I'm not saying the Arab refugees ought to come back and live with us. They must have their own country, that's what I mean."

"We all go along with that," said Ruthy.

"More or less that's true," said David.

"A separate Palestinian state?" I asked.

"Yes," said Neeli. "On the West Bank. Not part of Jordan, not part of Israel, but still under the jurisdiction of our army."

"Is there anyone who doesn't agree?"

"I don't," Hassan said.

"What do you propose?"

"There's nothing to propose. Let the Arabs come sit and talk with us and then we'll see what they can have back. In the meantime, why should *we* propose any give-away schemes?"

"You're not with Menachem Begin, are you?" I asked.

Hassan clicked his tongue — an Israeli way of saying "no" — but added nothing more.

"Nobody here supports Begin's Greater Israel scheme," announced Ruthy.

"No?" I looked at Hassan but he was peering out the window.

"Of course not. What do we need the West Bank or Sinai for? We'd only fill the Arabs with greater hatred. But look, not even Begin believes in all this."

"Ruthy, he's been saying it for years," said Neeli.

"He's part of the government now. He says that to distinguish himself from Eban and the doves. It's all politics. He'll support the government in the end. He'll learn to live without a Greater Israel."

"I doubt it," said Neeli, almost to herself.

"Anyway," continued Ruthy, "the Jewish people have too much experience with being pushed around, to do it to others. We didn't come here to push anybody around."

"Just a second," I said, "wasn't it impossible to establish a Jewish State without at least a little pushing?"

There was a sudden hush, as if I had finally asked the forbidden question.

"Oh boy, here we go!" said Uriel.

"Don't you know the history of Israel?" said Ruthy, angrily. "The land used to belong to effendis — wealthy Arabs who lived in Damascus and Beirut. At the time of the Balfour Declaration, there were only fifty thousand Arabs living in Israel."

"I don't know how accurate that is, Ruthy. The figures I'm

familiar with refer to all of Palestine, and in 1917, some 600,000 Arabs lived here."

"I'm talking about Israel, though. And anyway, the point is that we didn't throw anyone off the land, we bought it."

"You mean no Arabs were living on the land that was bought from the effendis?"

"Almost none."

"That's not exactly so," said Neeli to Ruthy. Then to me: "There were Arabs living on some of the land — not most of it — and they were made to leave. Some *were* provided for, like the Arabs who once lived on Bilat's land, but some were not."

"Come on, Neeli!" said Ruthy. "You're exaggerating. There were only a handful who had to leave. Look at Nazareth or the Upper Galilee or Haifa. The Arab refugee problem has nothing to do with this. It has to do with the wars they fought against us, that they *chose* to fight against us. We begged them to stay. They ran. How can anyone call that forcing them off their land?"

"Why did they run, Ruthy?" I asked.

"Because they're cowards!" shouted Uriel. "All they know how to do is talk, and make propaganda. When it comes to fighting, they aren't worth a damn!"

"No, they ran because they were told to run," said Ruthy. "They were told that if they just left for a few days the Arab armies would clean the Jews out, and they could come back and claim their properties and ours."

"You're talking about the '48 War?"

"Yes."

"Look what happened in Haifa," said David, "We actually begged them not to leave, and still they fled. Those that stayed, like in Nazareth, are still there today."

"How about in Ramla and Lod?" I asked.

Nobody answered except for Neeli who said: "They were conquered there and forced to leave, that's true."

"Nobody would have conquered them if they didn't choose to fight us," said Ruthy.

"Do you think the people in Ramla and Lod chose to fight Israel?"

"Their leaders chose," said David. "They paid the price for

having rotten leaders."

"That's my point," I said. "The Arabs themselves didn't choose to fight in all cases. Many were innocent victims who were caught up in something they never wanted. People run in time of war out of fear, because they are being shelled."

"We don't!" yelled Uriel.

"That's right!" shouted several others.

"*That* is the real point," said Ruthy. "We can't afford to run. We've got no place to go. They do. They can go to their brothers in Jordan, Syria or Lebanon. But where can we go? Back to Europe? Back to the Arab countries? We've got no place and that's why we belong here."

"I agree Israel belongs," I said. "That's not what I'm arguing about. I'm only saying that in some instances, in fact quite a few instances, Arabs fled out of fear. And if you want to be completely accurate, in some cases the fear was deliberately instilled by the Jews."

"What!" cried out Uriel.

"Come on!" said Ruthy.

"Deir Yassin," I said, naming the famous Arab village where some 250 men, women and children were killed by Menachem Begin's *Irgun,* prior to the Independence War. "Surely you've heard of it."

"Yes, we've heard of it," said Ruthy in disgust. "We've heard of it until it's coming out of our ears."

"True, the *Irgun* operated against the wishes of the Jewish Agency at that time, or so I remember, but do you think the Arabs could make this distinction? This, too, explains the phenomenon of Arab refugees, and if you want to be completely accurate, you can't leave it out."

"You talk about atrocities," said Hassan angrily. "I know the Arabs, and when it comes to atrocities they are the masters!"

"That's right!" said Uriel. "You want to talk about what the Irgun did in the 1940's. How about what the Arabs do to Israelis today? Or, how about what happens to Israeli prisoners of war? I don't hear you saying anything about that. Or don't you know about these things?"

"I have some idea."

"Allow me to fill you in. Do you know what happened to our pilots who were captured by the Syrians in the Six-Day War; those that came back, I'm talking about? They didn't go to the hospital for their wounds, they went to psychiatric wards. You tell me, what kind of people is it that takes a man, ties him up, puts him out in the desert in the sun, covers his body with honey, and lets the flies go all over him. What kind of people is that?"

"Barbarians!" shouted Hassan. "That's what kind of people. Barbarians!"

"Come on," I said. "I'm not trying to make a case for Arab atrocities. You should know that."

"But you're sure willing to talk about Jewish atrocities," said Uriel.

"Look, all I've been trying to say since we got into this, is that there were some wrongs, some injustices done to the Arabs when the Jewish state was established here. There was no way of avoiding these wrongs, perhaps, but they were still wrongs. That's all I'm saying. I'm sorry if I haven't been completely clear."

"And *you* are wrong!" said Uriel. "That's what we are saying. I'm sure we've been completely clear!"

"Yes," I answered heatedly, "completely clear."

The whole thing has gotten out of hand, I thought. Uriel and several others were heading towards the door, cursing loudly as they stalked off.

"Look," I said to the rest of the class, now gathering my papers and trying not to show my anger, "I think we'd better call it quits. It's getting very late."

They all nodded. I thanked them for their time, and said — though at the moment I didn't feel it — that they had been a fine group. I then snatched my papers and left.

Neeli and David came up behind me.

"You're heading for lunch now, aren't you?" asked David.

"Yes, I am."

"Can we join you?"

"Yes."

We walked for several minutes in silence and then Neeli said: "You know, our class once paid a visit to a high school in Nazareth. It was two years after the Six-Day War. We tried to talk to them openly, to have a dialogue, and it all ended just like now. All they would say is what they read in the Arab newspapers — you know, that we must return to the pre-June '67 borders, that we must resettle the refugees before there can be peace. That's all they would say."

"Really," said David, "that's the way it was. They had learned their arguments well and they stuck to them."

"And you?" I asked.

"Yes, we have learned ours, too," said Neeli. She forced a laugh. "I know it's no good, but that's the way it is."

"The thing that bothers me, though," I said, "is that I'm not an Arab from Nazareth. I'm a Jew — a Jew here in the kibbutz, and still you people argue this way."

"It's not arguing just for the sake of arguing," said David. "You don't seem to understand. We believe what we say."

"You see," said Neeli, "You are still an outsider. Jew or not. Even though you're living here, you're still an American journalist. The things you say are the same things that some of the Americans who support *Al Fatah* say."

We entered the dining hall and the man pushing the food cart steered us to some empty seats. A young woman was sitting at the table alone. Neeli said hello to her as we sat down, and then she resumed: "You see, we assume you don't think like those New Left Americans, but still your arguments are the same."

"It's not that you are a hundred per cent wrong," David said, "but what you say is grossly exaggerated."

"Or just let's say, one-sided," added Neeli.

"Politics. I smell politics," quipped the young woman sitting at the table. She spoke with a British accent. "You should have sat at the other table."

We all smiled.

"Seriously," Neeli continued, "what you say about our buying land from the effendis and causing some Arabs to leave, is true. We know that."

"But it's only part of the story," said David. "And a small part, at that. Or what you said to me in class about Ramla and Lod; you made it sound like we deliberately went in and threw them out, without the slightest provocation. Remember, there was a war at the time. A war that we didn't start or want."

"I know that," I said. "I thought I made it clear that I thought of these Arabs as war victims, war casualties you could say."

"You did," admitted Neeli. Then to David: "He did say that, David."

"All right, so he said it," said David irritatedly. "The problem is not with any single thing he said; the problem is with all of it, the point of view. I mean, why bring up Deir Yassin?" He looked at me squarely: "Why bring up *that*?"

"Because you didn't."

"You didn't expect us to go bragging about that, did you?"

"No, but I thought you could have mentioned it."

"I know what he means," said Neeli to David. "If we don't mention it, Michael thinks we don't know about it, or that we have forgotten it. He thinks we see ourselves as made of gold."

David shook his head knowingly and sighed. Then he said to Neeli: "You know who Michael reminds me of a little? Victor."

"Oh hell!" blurted out the young woman in English. Then in Hebrew: "You're not going to drag in Victor, are you?"

"That's right," David said to her. "He was a friend of yours."

The woman said nothing.

"Who is Victor?" I asked.

"Linda can tell you better than we can," David said.

"Come on, David," said Neeli. "You can see she doesn't want to go into it."

"Then I'll tell you," said David. The young woman, Linda, looked over at David, more disgusted than angry. "I'll make it brief: Victor was once a member here . . ."

"He still is," interrupted Linda.

"All right, he still is. Anyway, he hasn't been here for about a year. He's been in England studying poultry raising. He'll never come back . . ."

"That's your opinion," interrupted Linda again.

"Better get to the point, David," Neeli said gently.

"The point is that Victor held opinions that were extremist."

"*Rakah*," said Neeli, naming the more left-oriented of the two Israeli Communist parties.

"I don't know if he was a member of *Rakah* himself . . ."

"What does it matter?" challenged Linda.

David ignored her. "But those were his opinions. He received all the Communist party literature, put it in the reading room for everyone to see, and talked about it with anyone who would listen. He never shut up. Even during the Six-Day War, while we were in the shelters, and while all the men here were away at the front, he was saying how Nasser was right."

"He didn't have to fight," said Neeli. "He was diabetic."

"So what did he do?" said David. "He stood here and shot off his mouth."

"It wasn't just what he said," added Neeli, "but how he said it. And *when* he said it. Some of the things you say are similar to what he said, but really, you're not at all like him."

"A pity!" said Linda in my direction. "He's a very fine man."

"I don't know about that."

"I'm not surprised," said Linda.

"Come on, David," said Neeli. "You know he wasn't such a bad guy."

"Who cares?"

"He wasn't a bad guy at all," said Neeli to me. "Actually, quite a few people liked him personally."

"*Just* personally!" repeated Linda, mockingly.

"Yes, that's right!" said David, angrily. "What did you expect? For us to also go around shouting praises while he sat here saying Nasser is right?"

Linda waved her hand in disgust at David. "To hell with it!" she said in English. Then in Hebrew: "I don't even want to talk about it."

"All right, let's not!" said Neeli. "Let's drop the whole thing."

And we did.

Liverpool Lady

The next time I saw Linda was about a week later. She was sitting by the pool in a blue bikini, her feet dangling in the water, her head tilted up to the sun. In one hand she had a pair of sunglasses, and in the other a cigarette. The transistor radio at her side was playing softly, a Mozart piano concerto. The pool was almost empty. Except for a few teenage boys who were tossing around a large rubber ball, Linda sat there alone. She seemed very peaceful.

I jumped into the water and began swimming my usual ten laps. The water was lukewarm, which was the way it got just before the algae came to the top, and it began to stink. When this happened, Yehudah, the old German, would empty the pool out, curse the kids and volunteers who he said urinated in it, then he would fill it up again. Emptying and refilling took three to five days, depending upon Yehudah's mood, and in the interval you could either go to the Sea of Galilee or take cold showers. Yehudah suggested cold showers.

"Why don't you come out and cool off," Linda shouted in English, as I rounded my seventh lap. I was surprised to hear her.

"Just a few more laps," I shouted back, and began to swim a bit more quickly.

When I finished the laps, I came over to the side of the pool where Linda was still sitting, her feet kicking gently in the water. She looked beautiful. She was blond and fair-skinned, and much better shaped than I had expected from seeing her in the dining hall in her work clothes. Unlike a good many other kibbutz women in their mid-twenties, her body had not yet begun to muffin over into doughy rolls of fat, giving that settled and rooted look. Not her; she was still slim and pliable, and in that bare blue bikini, she hardly looked settled. I surely wasn't.

"You're not bad," she said as I sat down next to her. You're not bad yourself, I almost answered, but she was wearing a wedding ring — I had just noticed — and besides, that would have been lousy for openers.

"My dog-paddle, you mean?" I said over-modestly. It felt good to speak English.

"Your butterfly stroke. You're not bad at all."

"Not very good either. I'm out of shape."

"Still, you're pretty good."

"Well, thank you. How about you? Do you swim?"

"I sunbathe."

"Yes, I've noticed."

She smiled. "It's the best time. Just after lunch. Nobody is here."

"I usually go just before sundown. Or in the morning, on *Shabat*."

"Really? I think it's awful then. It's filled like a bathtub on *Shabat*. You can't move without bumping into somebody."

"Yes, I know."

"You don't mind?"

"No, I'm from New York. How about you? Wait, don't tell me, London!"

"Wrong. Bilat."

"No, really ... Wait, let me try again ... Born in London, converted to Bilat."

"*Converted*!" She laughed loudly.

"Am I close?"

"Hundreds of miles off."

"That far?"

"Yes."

"All right, you tell me."

"How's born in Liverpool, converted in *Moledet*, living in Bilat."

"*Moledet*? I don't exactly follow." *Moledet* is the Hebrew word for "homeland."

"*Moledet* — the moshav. Haven't you heard of it?"

"Oh! I thought you were being poetic. I thought you meant, converted in your homeland — Israel."

She laughed again.

We began to talk about Moshav Moledet (a cooperative farm in the Lower Galilee), and Linda explained how she and another British girl had been sent there shortly after the Six-Day War. Actually, they had tried to come to Israel as volunteers in those hectic weeks just before the war broke out. But, there had been such confusion, with all the Israelis in London who were trying to get back to Israel then, that she and her friend didn't make it until after the war. Both of them were Zionists; not the religious type, but cultural Zionists. If they hadn't come then, she imagined they would have come later; certainly by now.

Anyway, it was almost three years since they had been in Moledet, and while her friend had quickly moved to the city, she had stayed. Linda had loved the life on the *moshav* — the farm work, the people, everything about it. The only problem was that most of the people there spoke English fairly well, and it was impossible for her to learn Hebrew. She was not very good at languages, and really quite lazy. So, after about a year in Moledet, she went to the Jewish Agency and asked to join a kibbutz *ulpan* (a 6-month program in which you learned Hebrew part-time, and worked part-time). At that time, Bilat was about to start such a program. So she came here.

At first, she didn't like the idea of being on the border with all the shooting that was going on, and she thought she would leave. She was no hero. It was one thing to live in Israel, but quite another to live on the border. But she was enjoying herself. She had a handsome boyfriend from the kibbutz, and one thing led to another, and soon he was asking her to marry him. She liked him very much but she didn't really want to stay here. She thought it over for several months, began living with him, and soon they were married.

"And that's the story," she said. She smiled weakly. "Short, sweet, and they all lived happily ever after. You know my husband, Ami, don't you? He works in the vineyards with Menachem. Ami's the good-looking one."

"I don't know either of them."

"No? How about Zakkai and Rachel, Ami's parents?"

Zakkai was the man with the Yemenese accent who read from the Bible on Passover, but I had never met Rachel. Linda was surprised; she thought everyone knew Rachel. She was, after all, "the most exotic looking woman in the kibbutz." Zakkai had met her in Syria when he was working with the Jewish underground, and he smuggled her — and Ami, who was then six years old — into Israel. He later married Rachel, and adopted Ami.

"So Ami was born in Syria?" I asked.

"Right. In fact, his younger brother, Itzy" — Linda pointed to a tall long-haired boy at the other side of the pool — "is the only one in the family who was born in Israel."

I nodded.

"So, of course, he's the rebel in the family." Linda chuckled to herself. "Take a look at him, with the hair down to the shoulders. I think it looks lovely, but try telling one of these kibbutz conservatives about *that*. They almost spit at you. A real shame because once you get to know Itzy, you realize what a wonderfully gentle and sensitive boy he is. Loves nature and art. In fact, he wants to study art, but the kibbutz has told him no. Oh, they give him one week in the summer to go to art school. But he's unhappy with that, he wants to study art full-time. So what happens? He winds up doing nothing in the kibbutz school — won't do his homework, skips classes, argues with the teachers, everything. It's a real waste of talent. A shame . . ."

"Well, what about Ami?"

"He's a bit of a rebel himself. Nothing like Itzy, but he's learning." Linda laughed loudly, and splashed her feet in the water. "He used to be a very nicely behaved boy. Or so they keep telling me."

"And then?"

"And then he met me!"

We both laughed.

"And I brought out the best in him. He began to see things a little clearer."

"How so?"

"*How so?*" she repeated mockingly. "All right, I'll draw it nice and neat for you. Let's see . . . I think the best way to put it is that Ami was never very happy here, but he didn't know it." She was serious now. "Oh, he'd say little things like 'I wish the food were better,' or 'Why do we have to see all these damned cowboy movies,' but when it came down to really criticizing the kibbutz, really seeing all the pettiness here, he'd look the other way. He didn't want to see it. You see, he had to be this way. He's always been an outsider here. He didn't come here until he was six. He missed all the early years with his group, and was never really accepted by them. So, he's always been on the defensive, always trying to prove himself to them. In a way, you know, I think that's why he married me. I mean he loved me and all that, but still he wanted to show them that he didn't have to take just a kibbutz girl, or just a *sabra*. He could get somebody from the outside."

"Wait," I interrupted, "I'm not sure that makes sense. I mean, it seems he should have *wanted* to marry a kibbutz girl, just to be more on the inside, to get in with the rest of them."

"Yep!" she said, shaking her head knowingly. "That's what seems to make sense, doesn't it? But that's not the way it works. I know, because I've spent a lot of time thinking about it. You see, by marrying me he was able to show them that he was at least as good as they are. And at the same time, he managed to stay an outsider."

"Which is where you think he really wants to be?"

"Right! That's the point."

"Does he know this? I mean, does he know your analysis of the whole thing?"

"Well, yes and no. He knows that I think he is unhappy here."

"Does *he* think he's unhappy here?"

"Yes, of course. That's what I am saying. He's come around to seeing it. The why and wherefore of his unhappiness, no, I haven't discussed it with him. He wouldn't appreciate it. Kibbutzniks don't go in much for psychological explanations, you know."

"Yes, I've gathered that . . . But let me ask you this. Are you two going to leave?"

"Well, that's the question. We don't know. I've tried to get Ami to move to Moshav Moledet. That way — assuming we were accepted — he could continue with farm work, which is really all he has been trained for. Personally, I'd rather live in the city. I've changed my mind about living on the farm, but I don't want to press this point with him. First, I just want to get away from here. I'm twenty-six now, and I want to get on with having a family. Kids, I mean. I want lots of them. But, I don't want to start now. Not with the way things are."

"You mean, here in the kibbutz?"

"Right. I don't want to start here. It wouldn't be any good." Linda paused and lit a filter cigarette, the kind you couldn't get in the kibbutz, but had to buy in Tiberias. "You know, it's strange," she continued. "I never expected to feel this way . . . About raising kids in the kibbutz, I mean. I used to think the kibbutz was the ideal place to raise children. You just have to take a look at them to see it, right? They're big, healthy, smiley, and they play so beautifully with each other. Not all those interpersonal problems that you find in English kids. But, then you take a closer look at them, and you see what's really happening to them.

"I've worked in the children's houses for two years now — a real charwoman, that's me — and I've seen it up close. I don't know how much of it is being on the border, and how much of it is just being on the kibbutz, but these kids are becoming tough as nails. You see it in the way they play. Three- and four-year-old boys — that's the age of my group — go around yelling, 'I'm Daddy, the tank commander,' or 'I'm going to shoot you, you dirty Arab!' Or the girls, what do they play? Not 'House,' like we used to play, but 'Shelter.' That's right, they make little shelters and put little chairs and mattresses in them, and pretend they're hiding out from the Arabs. Or else they play games like 'Bombing' and they want you to get under the bench so you won't get hit. I bet you haven't heard about things like that?"

"Well, some of it. I spoke to the psychiatrist from Jerusalem when he was last here. But these strike me as problems of being on the border, not of being in a kibbutz."

"Wait! Let me finish. It's not just a matter of being on the border. At least, I don't think so. Even if there weren't a war these kids would be very tough. You see it in all the kids who were raised here when there was no border war. It's what Bettelheim wrote about kibbutz children in *Children of the Dream*.

"His point is that kibbutz children grow up tough, incapable of deep emotional ties. They get along with each other, they don't have the same interpersonal problems that other kids have, but they don't have the same emotional depth, either."

"And you think it's true?"

"Yes, more or less. There are exceptions. I think Ami is an exception. And there are others. But, most of the exceptions are people who weren't born here. They've only spent part of their childhood in the kibbutz."

"So what are you saying? That even without a border war the kids would play these games, and they'd be tough?"

"Yes. Maybe I'm wrong about the games. Maybe I just see them as a sign of everything else. But I'm sure that if you raised the kids in the house with the parents, even with the war, they would turn out all right; they wouldn't be such thick-skins. That's what I've come to feel. It may be very simple and bourgeois of me — that's what the kibbutzniks will say anyway — but that's the way I see it." Linda put out her cigarette on the stone walk next to the pool, and put it back in her cigarette case. Two of the boys who had been tossing around the rubber ball at the other side of the pool, swam over to our side, and the tall, dark one, Itzy, said: "How about a cigarette, Linda? Just one."

"All right," she answered. "Take one." She handed Itzy the cigarette case, and a small box of matches.

"Just one more, for Uri?" The boy next to him smiled.

"All right, take another one. But don't go around advertising it!" The two boys swam off. Then, turning back to me, Linda said: "I'm not supposed to give it to them. Not until they're eighteen. They're not supposed to smoke. Many of them do, but they do it discreetly. If anyone came along now and saw me giving them cigarettes, there would be talk — not just against them, but against me. I suppose you've noticed that: the rumor mop here, they swish it through everyone's life."

"Yes, I have . . ." I stopped short. It seemed like a good time to bring up something that had been on my mind since I first met Linda — Victor. "Speaking of the rumor mop, what was all that talk between you, David, and Neeli; remember, when I first met you?"

"What talk?"

"About Victor."

"Oh!" She paused. "It's not worth going into."

"It sounded important to me."

"It is. It *is* important. I'd just rather not go into it. Anyone else will be glad to tell you. They just love raking him over the coals. But keep me out of it. The whole thing makes me puke." Linda lit up another cigarette.

"You know, that's really the thing that stinks most here. The talk. All the lousy, cheap talk. People don't have enough to occupy their minds with. So they let the filth fly. About everyone and everything. Take what they were saying about me for a while. One morning I answered a knock at the door, with only a towel wrapped around myself. I was alone in the house, and I had just finished taking a shower. It turned out to be my neighbor, Adena, and she seemed surprised to see me that way. I told her to come in, but she apologized for disturbing me, and said she'd come back later. She left, and I got dressed. No sooner did I have my clothes on, when our friend, Noah, came into the house. He sat down, we chatted awhile, maybe a half-hour, and we were just leaving the house when Adena showed up again. She sort of gasped, and went off. Then the next day — mind you, only one day later — it was common knowledge in the kibbutz that Noah and I were sleeping together. Can you imagine that?"

"What did Ami say to all this?"

Linda let out a sigh: "That was the worst part. That was the part that almost made me leave altogether."

"What did he say?"

"He asked me if it were true."

June 5th

Exactly three years before, I had sat in the plush living room of my parents' home in White Plains, New York, and listened to the first televised reports of the Six-Day War. Nobody knew, of course, that the war would last just six days, and, in fact, nobody was sure Israel would make it out alive. But everyone was praying for them — my father, mother, two brothers, and the three or four neighbors who had come to watch with them. They were all pulling for them, invoking the assistance of the Almighty, who they usually had contact with only on *Pesach* and *Yom Kippur*, but who they now assumed to be listening in.

I had no such illusions. I had long ago broken off whatever contact I once had with Jehovah, and moreover, for the past two years, I had been arguing adamantly that the Arabs were right. Most of these disputes, or the most heated of them I should say, took place in my parents' living room. My mother remained calm through it all, simply pointing out that my position struck her as "a bit too adamant." But my father, who was able to sit through all my other revolutionary talk in silence, became unnerved when I began to focus it on Israel. "Look, my budding Che Guevara son," I remember his saying on one of these occasions, "if you must make your revolutions, please make them outside, not in the house!"

For my part, I was always annoyed and upset after these sessions, yet I was never sure whether it was just because my parents were narrow-minded and bigoted, or also because I was "a bit too adamant."

I never brought it up with them, but I knew that I was still attached to the kibbutz. I had never forgotten my time in Hazorea, and I knew that if a war came, it would be a war for survival, and if I was with the Arabs, then I was against the existence of Israel, against the kibbutz, against my friends in Hazorea. But I also knew that that was what it meant to be a revolutionary; you had to make impersonal choices. I felt I could do it and I was eager to try.

The June war was that test for me. And at first, I was pleased it had come. However, as the week continued, and all those who gathered daily in my parents' home to listen to the televised reports became more and more ecstatic, I became more and more miserable. And somehow I sensed that I felt lousy, not just because the Israelis were winning on all fronts and the Arab armies were proving weak and inefficient, but because somewhere seeping through my philosophical architecture was the feeling that, yes, I wanted it that way. It didn't come out like that. It never came out like that. And in fact, by the time it had solidified into statement, and I coughed it up for all those Israelphiles to hear, it was something very different, something alien to all of us: "I wish to hell they'd throw the damned Israelis back. They've got no business invading Arab lands!" It was the fourth day of the war, and everyone looked at me aghast. Nobody said anything for several minutes, and then my father rose out of his armchair and for the first time ordered me out of his house.

"Don't just stand there at the door," shouted Bierman. "Come in!" He was lying on the sofa listening to the radio.

"Good to see you," said Hannah. "You remember Uzi, don't you?"

"Sssh! Listen to this!" said Bierman loudly. His ear was only a few inches away from the blasting radio.

I listened, but I probably wouldn't have understood if I didn't know that it was June 5th, and the Israelis were celebrating the third anniversary of their victory. The radio announcer was reading off a list of nonsense names and colors — things like "lion's eye" and "blue bandana" — which I assumed to be the code names of army reserve units; that was one of the ways the army called up men for duty during an emergency situation.

"You hear that?" said Bierman. "That's how it was just before the war." He looked over at his nephew. "Uzi wasn't in the army then, but he remembers too."

Uzi nodded in agreement.

"Bierman, why don't you explain what you're listening to?" Hannah said. "Tell Michael the name of the program, at least."

"Remembrances of the Six-Day War. Wait . . . Listen to this!"

The announcer's voice trailed off and someone began shouting in flawed Hebrew. There was a lot of static and I couldn't make out what it was.

"Radio Cairo," said Hannah softly. "Did you ever hear such rot?"

"Sssh!" said Bierman. He put his ear next to the radio. His mouth was open and he held up his hand like a traffic cop, halting any further conversation. Uzi was deadpan. Hannah continued knitting.

"You hear that one? Did you hear it? Listen! Listen closely!"

Bierman turned the radio up and I caught ". . . vermin into the sea!" Then there was a break in the static and the Israeli commentator resumed speaking.

"That's how it was! The Hebrew language broadcasts from Cairo during the war. Tell him what they said, Uzi."

Uzi blushed. "War promises from Cairo. Nasser was sending us his best wishes."

"No, tell him exactly," Bierman insisted, evidently annoyed by Uzi's sarcasm.

"'Haifa is in flames! Tel Aviv has been taken!'" Uzi said with mock excitement.

"Can you imagine it?" said Bierman, turning to me. "Here they are with their entire Air Force wiped out . . ."

"We didn't know it then," interrupted Uzi.

"No, we didn't know it, but *they* sure did. And so did our commanding òfficers! Their entire Air Force, hundreds of Migs, destroyed on the ground, and they were trying to scare us with their propaganda. 'Haifa in flames!' 'Tel Aviv taken!'"

"'All the filthy Jews shall be cast like vermin into the sea!'" added Hannah.

"'Destroy them and leave no trace!'"

"'We'll take the land and all their women!'"

"Hold on," said Bierman gently. "*That* they didn't say on the radio."

Hannah shrugged. "Well, you *know* that's what they would have done."

"Yes, that's what they would have done, but they knew better than to say it."

He turned the radio back up, and we listened to a description of the capture of Jerusalem.

"Why don't you turn it off," said Hannah. "You've heard it a dozen times." Then to me: "He's got the whole record album of the Six-Day War. He knows it by heart."

"Sssh!" said Bierman, and turned the radio up louder. The announcer was now describing how the Israeli Army encircled the Old City of Jerusalem, and then fought a house-to-house battle that cost scores of lives. They could have captured it far more quickly, he said, but that would have meant destroying it with artillery, and there was never any question of doing that.

"And they tell us to give back Jerusalem after that!" said Bierman shaking his head angrily. "Can you imagine it?"

"Why don't you take a rest from it?" Hannah said. "I'll go get you something to eat." She went into the pantry. Uzi went into the bathroom. Bierman turned off the radio.

"Two thousand years we have been saying it," Bierman continued, turning slowly towards me. "'Next year in Jerusalem, next year in Jerusalem.' And now we are there, and they are telling us we have to give it back. U Thant and the U.N. telling us what to do. They couldn't even stand up straight at Sharm-el-Sheikh when they were supposed to, but now they have the right to tell us what to do. Jerusalem goes back. Settled and finished!" He slapped his hands together in a gesture of finality. "Jerusalem goes back!"

"So let them talk," said Hannah, returning with a tray of refreshments. "What do we care?"

"So what do we care?" repeated Bierman, heatedly. "We care because we have no choice. Until the Americans take a clear stand, we cannot be sure what will happen. That's what the Russians have done to us."

"Here, Bierman, have something cool," said Hannah, handing him a glass of lemonade, and a slice of ice-box cake that appeared to be made with matzohs and chocolate cream. "Uzi! Come in and join us!"

"I can't. I just started shaving," Uzi shouted back. There was the hum of an electric razor in the bathroom.

"It'll take him twenty minutes to cut off those porcupine quills," whispered Hannah. "I think he does them one by one."

"Never mind," said Bierman. "He's a fine boy."

"Of course he's a fine boy," said Hannah. "He's my brother's son."

"A quiet boy," continued Bierman. "Doesn't like to talk much. He's had it rough." Bierman suddenly seemed quite somber.

"He was on the Canal," said Hannah. "Until he got wounded about a year ago. They've restationed him in the Jordan Valley. He never says much about it. At least not to us."

"They've all had it rough," said Bierman. "Some more than others. They don't talk about it, but we know it just the same."

"A few of them *did* speak about it right after the war," corrected Hannah. "There was a get-together of the entire kibbutz, and a few of them spoke. Some of the older boys, like Reuben Ben Zvi, Baruch Torka . . . ."

"Baruch from the olives? Ofra's husband?"

"Right. Do you know him?"

"Yes."

"He was one of the best. Wouldn't you say, Bierman?"

"He was good. He likes to talk more than most of the boys. The rest don't like to."

"How about the older people?" I asked. "They seem to talk more freely."

Bierman nodded.

"We haven't been through what they have," said Hannah. "Not lately anyway." Then turning towards the bathroom she shouted: "Haven't you finished in there yet? How long does it take to shave one face?"

"Go ahead and start without me," Uzi shouted back. "It'll take me a few more minutes."

Hannah turned back to us. "See! What did I tell you? One by one he cuts them off."

Bierman ignored Hannah and continued: "It's easier for us to talk. We're more used to it. We've seen these things before."

"We've been Jews longer," added Hannah.

Bierman smiled. "You get used to it," he said. "You get used to everything."

"Besides, it hasn't been so rough on us here," said Hannah. "It's not like on the Canal. We've had it quite easy, everything considered. Even during the Six-Day War it wasn't bad."

"It's true," said Bierman. "We had a very easy time here during the war."

The Syrian tanks, Bierman said, were sitting right above the Sea of Galilee, and once the war started, everyone expected them to come pouring down into the Jordan Valley; that's what they had done in '48 until they were stopped by Molotov cocktails in Kibbutz Degania. As for the Jordanians, their tanks were waiting in the villages just across the Yarmuk, and when you went out on patrol you could see them down there. They were the tougher army, the Jordanians, and once the war broke out, everyone figured they would try to come roaring into Bilat.

But this time Bilat was better prepared than in '48. In '48, they had nothing — only a few old single-shot rifles, not enough for everyone. But now, they had equipment: anti-tank guns, Browning recoilless rifles, Uzi sub-machine-guns, and more. They didn't have the men, though. All of them had been called up, except for those under eighteen and over fifty, and since you couldn't use high-school kids in the front-line defense, all you really had were the grandfathers.

"And the women," Hannah added.

Well, no — said Bierman — not on the front lines. True, the women did whatever work had to be done in the kibbutz: they cooked, cared for the children in the crowded shelters (there were only twelve at the time), milked the cows and fed the chickens. But when it came to handling machine-guns, no, they couldn't be counted on.

"Anyway, we used to be in the front lines," said Hannah.

"That was awhile back," retorted Bierman. "Even in '48 we evacuated most of the women from here."

"Some of the younger women were in the *Palmach*," corrected Hannah.

"But only a few," Bierman persisted.

"Orna was," said Hannah to me. "And so were a few others who aren't here anymore. Remember Sarah, Bierman?"

Bierman wasn't paying any attention. He was looking out of the window.

"Remember Sarah?" she repeated.

Bierman turned back. "Remember who?"

"Sarah."

"Yes . . . " He stopped short and looked out of the window. He seemed to be listening for something.

"She was one of those who fought in Jerusalem. It was besieged for several months. Finally, in the . . . " Hannah jumped. *Fsooosh . . . . Boom*! *Fsoooosh . . . . Boom*! Katyushas. The windows shook.

"I knew it!" said Bierman. "I knew it was starting." He stood up quickly. "Come on, get into the bathroom. Away from the windows."

The three of us rushed into the bathroom, squeezing by Uzi as we entered. Uzi was still working away on his chin.

"Come on, Uzi, knock it off!"

Uzi didn't answer. He unplugged the razor and took it out into the pantry, and began shaving there.

"Uzi!" shouted Hannah. "Stop being such a hero." Her voice was loud but not insistent.

"It's too crowded," he shouted back. "I'm almost done anyway."

There was a short silence and Bierman resumed his account of the war. He was leaning now against the sink, and next to him sitting on a straw-topped stool, was Hannah. I was standing under the shower. The whole situation seemed absurd.

"We had a couple of weeks to get ready for the war," said Bierman. "Everyone knew it was coming, it was just a question of when. You see, once Nasser closed down the Straits of Tiran — May 22nd or 23rd, I think it was — there was no alternative for us."

"You didn't think there was any chance the Big Powers could have intervened and stopped it?" I asked.

"Intervened then?" Bierman laughed. "You sound like Eban. That's what he told us: 'It is advisable that we first confer with our friends before taking any further, independent measures.'" Bierman said this in a professorial, flowery Hebrew, which I assumed to be his imitation of Abba Eban. "So what did Eban do? He went traveling. First to De Gaulle, who told him that what Nasser did wasn't very nice, but France could do nothing about it. And then to Wilson who said yes, it was horrible what Nasser did, but please sit tight and don't start anything. And finally he went to Johnson, and again he heard it — with a few ifs and maybes on the side, but that was the message: hold your guns until the other side fires first. That's what Eban brought back from the Big Powers."

"Not much, was it?" said Hannah, shaking her head.

Fsoooosh .... Boom! Fsoooosh .... Boom!

"Uzi!" shouted Bierman. "Get in here!"

"All right. All right. I'm finishing."

"Now! Right now!"

The hum of the electric razor stopped, and Uzi came into the bathroom shaking his head, irritatedly. He sat on the toilet seat.

"We don't need any heroes in *this* house," said Hannah. "You stand out there endangering yourself for what? A few whiskers?"

"Forget it," said Bierman. "You see he's here." Then to me: "So, Eban came back with nothing, just as we expected. And then the war started. The rest you know, I'm sure."

"What happened here," I asked.

"Nothing," Bierman answered. "Nothing happened here. We sat in the trenches and nothing happened. Not a shot fired."

"Were *you* in the trenches?"

"Who else? Just the grandfathers, like I told you."

"Not all the time," said Hannah to Bierman. "Remember, you weren't in the trenches all the time. Not at the beginning, you weren't. Tell Michael about the beginning, when you got the news from Tel Aviv."

"How about telling about it outside in the living room," interrupted Uzi. "I'd like to finish up."

"Not yet," Bierman said curtly.

"Uzi, please sit still for once," said Hannah. "Remember, no heroes in *this* house."

"At the beginning of the war," said Bierman, ignoring Hannah and Uzi, "I had a shipment of chicks to go to market. We couldn't vaccinate them because we didn't have the time, and besides, Dodik and Pinchas were in the trenches. So I called Tel Aviv, and they said they would take them anyway. They sent a boy to pick them up. He had something wrong with his arm — that's why he wasn't in the

Army. It was the first few hours of the war when he got here, and after he picked them up, I called Tel Aviv again just to confirm that we had shipped them off. That's when I heard about it: the destruction of the Egyptian Air Force. The fellow in Tel Aviv told me they had just found out. I couldn't believe it. Ten, twenty, fifty destroyed planes, *that* I could believe; but not *one hundred and fifty*. It was as ridiculous as those broadcasts from Cairo. In fact, when I brought the news to the trenches, nobody else would believe it. It was too good to be true. Only later that night, as we sat up — nobody could sleep — and listened to the news reports, did we really believe it was true. The Egyptian, Iraqi and Jordanian Air Forces had been knocked out in the first hours of the war. You cannot imagine what happiness we felt. We felt so wonderful that right then in the dark, right there in the trenches, we took out a map and began planning our future boundaries. We'd keep Gaza and Sharm-el-Sheikh, and Jerusalem once we got it; that was for sure. We'd also keep the Golan if we could get it. We didn't know then whether we would try to capture it, but we all hoped so. And as you know, a few days later it was ours. When was *that* exactly?" Bierman looked at Uzi.

"The fourth day. Look, I'm going to finish up shaving. There haven't been any shells for ten minutes."

"All right," Bierman confirmed. "It's safe now."

We returned to the living room, and Uzi then took his razor back into the bathroom.

"Those were the good moments," said Hannah. "The first few hours, the first day of the war. We brought wine to the trenches that night and toasted. We toasted life."

"We had more toasts in the next few days," said Bierman.

"Two more toasts," said Hannah. "When we found out that we had taken Jerusalem. And later, when we took the Golan . . ." She hesitated, and began shaking her head slowly. "But by then we already had the news about Hanoch."

"He was killed going up the Golan," said Bierman. "A piece of shrapnel through the neck." Bierman jabbed his neck with his thumb.

There was a pause, and I asked whether he was the only one Bilat lost during the war.

"No," said Hannah. "Esther Pinsky's son, Mota, was killed, too. That was awful. We didn't know about him for days. There were several others we didn't hear from until after the war, but eventually they managed to let us know that they were alive."

"The boys phoned or sent messages through friends," added Bierman.

"But from Mota we heard nothing . . . Or what really happened is that we *supposedly* did hear from him. That was the awful part. Someone who had been in Sinai with him — not in his battalion, but some other one — would say: 'Oh, Mota. He's the one with the dark hair and big smile, right? Sure, he's all right, we saw him in Gaza.' We got a couple of messages like that until we finally got confirmation from the Army. They never notify until they are sure. His half-truck, they said, had received a direct hit. They identified him by his watch."

"Hey, how about talking about something happier than this," said Uzi, as he finally emerged from the bathroom massaging his face. The smell of after-shave wafted through the room.

"Uzi's right," said Bierman.

"Absolutely right," agreed Hannah. She got up from her chair and began gathering the dishes. Then, sniffing at the air, she said: "Uzi, do you have to wear that awful stuff?"

"The girls like it," said Bierman.

"*I* like it," announced Uzi.

"Well, I don't," said Hannah. "I would never fall for a man with a smell like that on his face."

"Tastes change," said Bierman. "That's what they like now — the perfumey stuff."

"Why don't we leave my face alone?" said Uzi.

Hannah shrugged. "All right, we'll say no more. It's your face, do what you want with it."

"Thank you."

There was a short silence, and Bierman turned to me: "*Nu,* my friend, what else would you like to know?"

Fleeing the Coop

For the past month I had wanted to tell Bierman that I would like a different job, but I knew he would take it as heresy. The *Lool* was his place, his creation almost, and if there was one thing Bierman didn't like it was "complainers." They are like paratyphus germs," he once said. "Small, dirt-loving creatures, and if you don't catch them in time, all the animals are sick." So I had kept my criticisms to myself, or mostly to myself, and only on those occasions when I visited Lea, did I reveal them fully. She was, I could see, glad to hear them. She didn't seem to like Bierman — though she always avoided any direct criticism of him — and she told me that Orna had made a mistake in letting me work in the *Lool*. I should be working with young people, people my own age — not with Sadie ("Around her mouth, I wish I didn't have ears"), and Pinchas ("He has never forgiven God for resting on the seventh day"), and Dodik ("I haven't spoken to him for years; maybe he's changed"). They were difficult enough to live with in the same kibbutz, but to work with them, too, was beyond the call of duty.

I agreed. And I was finally building myself up to explain this to Bierman, when a situation occurred that brought it all out. It happened one day while we were vaccinating chickens — Sadie, Pinchas, Dodik and I. As usual, Sadie's monologue was running at full sail, spiriting along on her favorite topic — the kibbutz. We were all trying to ignore her, but I, at least, was having no success. Perhaps it was my recent conversation with Linda, or perhaps it was just my own discontent with some things I had been noticing in the kibbutz. In any case, Sadie's plaudits for "the most decent, honest way of life" were unusually hard to listen to that day, and so I committed the cardinal sin of not only interrupting her, but also contradicting her.

"I haven't found that to be true," I stated matter-of-factly, as she rounded the turn about kibbutzniks being selfless, and never thinking about money. The room was suddenly quiet, and Sadie stared at me.

"What?" she said accusingly.

I knew I had started something. "Some people do think about money. The young people, for instance."

"Sadie is talking about the majority," said Pinchas, diplomatically.

"*Who* thinks about money?" Sadie said, ignoring Pinchas.

"The young people," I repeated. I began to describe my conversation with the high-school students, especially David's complaint about the kibbutz taking away almost all of the army severance pay.

"*Who* told you that?" Sadie demanded to know.

"One student said it. Several others seemed to agree."

"I know who said it: Hassan. The long-haired one. We know about him."

"No, it wasn't . . ."

"Don't bother with him," interrupted Dodik. "He doesn't know what he's talking about. He can't see clearly; the hair gets in the way." Sadie laughed loudly and Pinchas smiled.

"He thinks he's Samson," Pinchas added, and laughed loudly at his own joke.

"Every place has its complainers," Dodik continued. "Don't pay any attention to him."

"Who else agreed with him?" Sadie demanded.

"I don't remember."

"Nobody agrees with him. Nobody at all. He tries to corrupt everybody, but he can't get away with it. The children know he's a bad seed." There was a short silence and Sadie immediately continued: "That's the best thing about the kibbutz. We've brought the children up to see life dedicatedly, reverently."

"That's true," said Dodik, now seeming to take an interest in the conversation. "Look at the army. Thirty per cent of the pilots are kibbutzniks. And what are we? Just four per cent of the country. Or, look at the casualties in the war: a quarter of them came from the kibbutz."

"And why's that?" asked Sadie rhetorically. "Because the children are raised to see life dedicatedly. They volunteer for the toughest jobs and the riskiest assignments."

"And who are the officers in the army?" said Dodik. "Kibbutzniks. Look around you here. Open your eyes and you'll see. All the men here are officers."

"My sons," said Sadie. "Two lieutenants and a captain."

"Who's the captain?" asked Dodik, evidently surprised.

"Yitzchak."

"I thought he was a major."

"Almost. Later this year, he thinks."

"Anyway, do you hear that?" Dodik said, turning back to me. "Three sons and two of them are lieutenants and the other is almost a major."

"If they were career soldiers," said Sadie, "they'd all become generals. But no, they know their place is here in the kibbutz with the rest of us. That's what we mean by dedication."

"It's not like the city," said Dodik, "where you have slackers and wild donkeys who race around in sports cars with girls."

"And never work."

"And wear long hair, and make demonstrations, and think they know better than the government what to do."

"The cities breed corruption."

"And laziness."

"And crime and rape and murder," said Sadie, concluding this litany of evils. "Tell me, when have you ever heard of someone committing a crime in a kibbutz?"

"That's something to think about," said Dodik. "Two hundred and something kibbutzim, and not one crime. Not one policeman in any of them."

"That's what the kibbutz is," said Sadie. "An honest way of life."

"But do you know what?" said Dodik, his eyebrows raised. "Not many people can live in kibbutzim." Sadie stared at *him* now. "It's too honest."

"What do you mean?" Sadie asked uncertainly.

"It's *too* honest. Most people cannot live that honestly. It's too hard for them."

"Right!" said Sadie, finally catching on. "People want to be slackers . . ."

"Nobody wants to work anymore," agreed Pinchas.

"Most people are selfish," said Dodik. "They like to make lots of money and exploit the next guy; take advantage of him if he has no money, no property. That's the way it has always been down through the civilizations."

"Capitalism," said Pinchas. "The highest stage of exploitation.

You see it all around you, throughout the world."

"In America," said Sadie. "That's where it has become the worst. I bet you didn't realize that. It's the worst there. That's why there are no kibbutzim in America."

"That's not why," I said flatly, feeling disgusted at the triple-dose propaganda. It was the thickest I had ever tasted.

"Then you tell me why," said Sadie belligerently.

"Because America doesn't need them," I blurted out, and no sooner had I said it when I realized I had thrown down the gauntlet. What I meant by the comment was that America was a developed country, not surrounded by hostile neighbors; and therefore, unlike Israel, it didn't require border agricultural outposts. This explanation of Israeli kibbutzim was debatable enough in itself, and no doubt would have provoked *some* criticism, but nothing like what I invited by stating baldly that America didn't need kibbutzim.

"Did you hear that, Dodik?" Sadie's voice was heavy with anger. "America doesn't need kibbutzim."

"I heard it."

"Two presidents killed in the last ten years, gangsters running the Wall Street, and he says America doesn't need kibbutzim."

"Only one president . . ." I began.

"He doesn't know what he's talking about." Dodik was angry, too.

"Wait a minute!" I said. "You don't understand what I mean."

"What *do* you mean?" asked Pinchas. Even he seemed irritated.

I decided to skip the border-outpost stuff, and say what was really on my mind. "I know that kibbutzim are a special way of life," I began. "I've always thought that . . . It's just that, special as kibbutzim are — or were — I've come to feel that the people in the kibbutz, are not so very different from those outside. The problems here are the same as anywhere else. Children and parents don't see eye to eye. Husbands and wives don't get along better here than elsewhere. And then," I knew it would be taken badly, but I felt I had to say it, "I don't see that kibbutz people are any more open-minded or big-hearted than anywhere else."

"You don't know what you are saying," said Sadie, now more shaken than angry at my words.

"Listen to him! The kibbutz is the same as anywhere else," Dodik said mockingly, with an American accent. "And how about Israel? I suppose it's just a country like anywhere else?"

"I didn't say that."

"No, you don't have to. I know your kind."

"Forget it." Pinchas said to Dodik.

"An American author!" Dodik said, staring at me. "What do you know?"

"How to talk to people with respect."

"To hell with your respect. To hell with all your damned American respect!"

"Come on! Come on!" yelled a voice from the next room. It was Bierman, and he was coming quickly towards us, wearing a wide, appeasing smile. "What's all the arguing about?"

Nobody said anything; we all continued vaccinating the chickens.

"*Nu?*"

Dodik looked up abruptly. "They don't know a damned thing," he blurted out.

"Who doesn't?"

"These damned Americans."

"What Americans?"

"Our friend here," Dodik said, nodding in my direction. "The *author*."

"What did you say?" Bierman asked me.

"I was comparing kibbutz life to outside life."

"He doesn't know what he's talking about," said Sadie.

"Americans!" said Dodik. "Who needs them?"

"Unfortunately we do," said Bierman. He smiled sadly in my direction to indicate that he meant no offense. "We may not like everything they say, but we do need them." Then turning to Pinchas: "What was it, exactly, that you were arguing about?"

"Nothing much," answered Pinchas. "Michael, here, was just saying he thought kibbutz life was no better than life anywhere else."

"I see," said Bierman. The muscles in his face tightened. "Well, Michael is new here. He's learning. He's an American Jew who's just beginning to learn what life is in a kibbutz, and what life is in Israel. All beginnings are difficult." Bierman nodded his head slowly, contemplatively, then added: "Not everyone loves kibbutz life, and not everyone is able to live in a kibbutz. It's a difficult life. But the question of living in Israel or not, is another matter. It is something every Jew must examine with both of his eyes open. Michael is examining it. He is learning." And with that Bierman left, and we were all silent again.

We were sitting in the office — Bierman, Zelda, and I — drinking coffee before going home, and Bierman was looking me over carefully, as if for the first time. After what had happened in the *Lool* that morning, I had no intention of working there again, and I could tell by the way he was eyeing me that Bierman knew it.

"That was a bad scene this morning," he finally said, somberly.

"I know," I answered.

"I have known Dodik for twenty-five years, and I have never seen him that upset."

"He was very upset," said Zelda.

"I tried to cool him off, just before he left," Bierman went on, "but he was still on fire."

"He looked awful," said Zelda.

"I wasn't very happy about it myself," I said.

"No, I can see," Bierman said. "But I hope you learned something from it."

I didn't answer.

"Let me tell you something," he continued, "Dodik is a simple man."

"Very simple," said Zelda.

"But what he says is important. It is important because a simple man will tell you outright what he thinks. A more cultivated man will think it, but not say it. And to be frank with you, there is a lot of anger against the Jews who come here — particularly the American Jews — and spend a few months vacation, and then go back home. Sure there is anger. What do you expect, that we should feel just love in our hearts for them? For us, this is no vacation resort. For us, this is no game. We are not free to fly about and spend vacations here and there. We need to be here to protect the Land. And we must pay for this."

"Bierman is right," said Zelda. "That's the way it is for us."

"Look, just the other day a boy from Ma'agan was killed."

Bierman pointed in the direction of the border kibbutz a few miles up the road. "And yesterday, a boy was wounded in Ihud."

"Who's that?" interrupted Zelda, shocked.

"The Luria boy. Amos Luria."

"I thought he just got nicked in the arm."

"Nicked? The shrapnel came down through his shoulder," — Bierman traced an arc through the air and came down hard on his right shoulder — "and tore out most of his right lung and liver."

"Oh, my God!" said Zelda.

"Anyway, you see, Michael, it's not a game for us."

"I understand."

"You can go back. But we must stay. You can send money. But we must live here, never knowing what will be the end. That's why there is anger. That's why Dodik lost his temper and said whatever he said to you."

"Sometimes he has a bad temper," said Zelda. "He doesn't mean anything by it."

"I'm not saying you have to like him for it," Bierman continued. "I'm only saying it is important for you to understand him."

"I think I do."

"Good," Bierman said. "Whatever you do is your business. But I wanted to make sure you understand."

"I do."

"Good. Let's go home."

"Right. Let's go home," said Zelda. "It's been a long day."

Some Bug or Other

That same evening I began to feel ill. At first, I figured it was nothing more than a headache from the argument in the *Lool*, but when the aspirins left me feeling no better, I went to bed, hoping the whole thing would be gone in the morning.

But it wasn't. If anything, I felt worse, and I decided to visit the infirmary. It was a small building, tucked away on the opposite side of the kibbutz, and a long walk from where I lived. That morning it seemed especially long, and I felt strange going there in my sweater and jacket, as the morning sun poured down through the date-palm trees. When I arrived, there were two or three patients in front of me, all old people. The assistant nurse, Hava, told me there would be at least a half-hour wait before the doctor could see me. She handed me a thermometer and told me to take my temperature.

Finally, the doctor — a young man, no more than 30 years old — called for me. He didn't seem at all surprised by my fever, which was now 103 degrees Fahrenheit. There was "some bug or other" going around, he said. Still, he checked my throat, my stomach and my chest, and as Hava stood there sternly taking notes, he assured me there was nothing to worry about. He didn't know what the bug was, but he felt sure it would be gone in a few days or a week at the most. He would be back in Bilat in a couple of days; if I didn't feel any better by then, I should come and see him. He smiled. Meanwhile, the best cure was to rest and drink lots of fluids. Hava would bring around my meals, and she would also have something to ease my headache. Aspirin should do the trick.

". . . No wonder you're sick," boomed a voice just above me. I looked up, groggy and disoriented. "What?"

"I said, with a room like this, no wonder you're sick." Hava's big masculine body was swaying there above me. She had a tray in one hand, and with the other she was pointing angrily at the corner of my room.

"What time is it?" I asked weakly, ignoring her anger.

"Dinner time. I've brought you some salad and tea. Nothing more tonight."

"That's fine." I reached for the tray.

"Wait!" she said, pulling the tray away. "Don't you think you should clean yourself up before you eat?"

"All right."

She sat the tray down on the table by my bed. "I don't know how you expect to get well with all this filth around."

"It's not very neat," I admitted. I began to get out of bed.

"Not very neat?" she repeated, mockingly. "I don't understand you."

"No?"

"No! Your clothes on the floor. Newspapers, pencils, books all over the place. One would think you never learned to clean up after yourself."

"I'm sorry, I wasn't exactly expecting company."

"I shouldn't think so with the way this place looks."

"I'll have it more presentable when I'm feeling better. Now, if you'll excuse me . . ."

"A little fever, and the place looks like a pigsty."

"I'm going to wash." I walked out of the door and Hava followed right on my heels.

"You'll never get healthy living like this," she called after me. "Garbage on the floor, clothes not hung up, papers and books . . ."

I didn't hear the rest because I was, at last, inside the bathroom and had the water running good and loud.

The next morning, I was feeling slightly better. The fever was down some, the chills were gone, and I was able to sit up in bed. I did not, however, feel up to straightening out my room or myself, so I prepared once again to fail Hava's inspection. And, of course, I did. Though somewhat less irritable than the previous night, she nonetheless repeated that she just didn't understand where I had acquired such poor living habits, and that if I took a look in any kibbutznik's room I would never see such chaos. Nor would I see any kibbutznik, sick or not, lie about in the same bed clothes for three straight days. I admitted that I probably didn't look very presentable, and agreed to shave that day. She seemed relieved by my decision, and as a reward she went outside, brought back a broom, and swept out every crack and crevice in the room. I thanked her, and when she left, she smiled and told me that already I was beginning to look healthier. I could have visitors now, if I wanted.

Nobody came, however, until that evening. Then just after dinner, as I was dozing off, there was a knock at the door and someone greeted me in a loud, cheerful voice; "So how's the invalid coming along tonight?"

It was Orna, smiling and suntanned, with a bowl of fruit in one hand and some newspapers in the other. "So how are you feeling?"

"Much better." I propped myself up against the wall.

"Good to hear it. I just heard that you haven't been feeling well the past day or so."

"No, I haven't."

"You must have caught it — the bug that's been going around."

"I guess so."

"It's a rotten bug. Hits like an explosion inside the head, right?"

"Yes."

"Then goes away. It takes a few days."

"I guess. I feel much better."

"You'll be completely over it in a day or so. I'm sure of it."

She handed me the newspapers and fruit, and went over to the corner of the room to get my armchair. She dragged it over and sat down in it. Her face was suddenly quite serious. "There's something I want to discuss with you," she said. "Unless you're too tired and want to sleep."

"No, I'm fine."

"First, I would like to know how long you are planning on staying here."

"In bed?"

"No." She laughed. "In the kibbutz. I want to know how much more time you think you will need."

"I see. Well ... "

"Please don't think that I'm rushing you. I'm not; not at all. We are glad to have you here. It's just that originally we spoke in terms of three months, and I want to know — for various reasons — if that is still your intention."

I wasn't sure what she meant by "various reasons" but I had an idea. Anyway, I explained to her that I would like to stay in the kibbutz an extra couple of months, through the summer, and that I was hoping to see a little more of what was going on.

"That's a good idea," she answered. "You want to get the full picture, I am sure."

I nodded.

"Well, that's what I had in mind. To be more specific, I was wondering if you wouldn't want to try working in some other branch of the kibbutz. Outdoors, for instance. I remember you enjoyed working in the olives last year."

"Yes, I did." Orna was diplomatically suggesting I move out of the *Lool*.

"The only problem is that the olive harvest doesn't begin for

another month. But in the meantime, you could work in the
vineyards; they are just beginning to harvest now. You could work
with them, and then in about a month, switch over to the olives.
How does that sound?"

It sounded great. But did she think there would be any problem in
the *Lool*?

"No problem," she assured me. "I've already taken it up with
Bierman." "He, of course, will still be your family. He's very
interested in you, you realize, and he is sorry to see you move to
another branch of the kibbutz. So, please, do me a favor, keep in
touch with them. You know, go there on Friday nights and
holidays."

"Of course."

"Good. Oh yes, one more thing. As soon as there is an opening in a
new room, a better room, I think you can move out of here."

"Why?"

"I'm going to find you a new room, over where the members live.
I have my eye on one right now. I just don't want to promise it to
you yet."

"Well, thanks. For everything."

"Not at all. I'm glad to do it. But don't forget about Bierman."
And she left.

I was still thinking over what she had said when two more visitors
knocked at the door — Lea and Neeli.

They came in slowly, glanced around the room (It was the first
time they had been there.), and then Lea sat down in the armchair.
She apologized for not visiting sooner, but she didn't know I was sick
until just a few minutes ago, when, by chance, she had bumped into
Orna. Orna told her all about me, that I was almost over whatever I
had, and that when I was fully recovered there were going to be
some changes in my life. She had heard "vaguely" about my
argument at the *Lool*, and quite frankly, she wasn't at all surprised.
She had warned me before that I didn't belong there, and, knowing
me as she did, it was only a matter of time until something like that
happened. As far as she was concerned, it had all worked out for the
best. I was sure to enjoy myself much more outside and among
young people. Neeli agreed and said, in her polite and feminine
way, that she was looking forward to seeing me out there. In another

week, school would be over, and she would be working full-time in the vineyards. They said they would be back again the next day if I weren't better and, oh yes, if Moshe happened to come by, I should tell him they went on to the exhibition hall. This was the last night for the exhibition of paintings and sculptures by Jordan Valley artists, and they wanted to see it before it closed. They smiled again and left.

Moshe arrived about ten minutes later. He sat down in the armchair beside the bed. It was obvious that he had something on his mind, but it was also obvious that he didn't want to talk about it. Instead, he began directing the conversation at me. He asked how I was feeling, how life was going in the *Lool* (He seemed surprised, though not at all interested, that I was shifting to the vineyards.), then how much longer I was planning on staying in Bilat and Israel. He appeared rather disinterested in my answers until the last part, the part where I mentioned that I was planning to prolong my stay. This perked him up. He looked at me closely, stared out the window, then looked back, and in a serious voice, said: "You know, I've been meaning to talk to you about something, ever since you had that meeting with my class. There are certain things I think you ought to know."

"Fine," I said. I wasn't sure what he meant, because the truth was, we *had* talked after his class, and at considerable length. For the most part, we had agreed as to the mistakes and prejudices of the students, but while he was quite willing to make explanations or excuses for them, I was not; or not, at any rate, to the extent that he was. And so, we had ended on an unpleasant, mutually self-righteous, note. It was hard to figure why he wanted to bring it up again at this time.

"I don't want to rehash what went on in class," he continued, "or even what we said about it that other time. I'd rather discuss it on a more personal level, if it's all right with you."

Moshe took out a package of kibbutz cigarettes, offered me one, then remembering that I didn't smoke, he apologized and lit one up for himself. "A foul habit," he said. He inhaled, got up and brought back the wastebasket for an ashtray.

"I think the most instructive way to say what I want, is for me to tell you a little of my own background."

He was born, he said, "some sixty years back," in the eastern part of Germany, but due to the invasion of the Russians during World War I, he and his family fled to Berlin. His father was a successful businessman who quickly established himself there. It was only later, when the world-wide depression hit and Hitler came to power, that his father lost all his money and the family suffered its tragedy.

"I do not like to recall such things," he said, "but it is important for you to hear it. You see, in many ways, I was like you. I remember that evening, the first evening you and I met at Lea's, and how you talked about your family not celebrating any of the Jewish holidays, and how you barely considered yourself a Jew. It may seem strange to you, but in many ways I was once like that myself. My parents were not Reformed Jews like yours; we were Orthodox, and we celebrated the holidays and lit candles on Friday nights. But I, personally, never believed in any of that. I was, and still am, an atheist, and I only went along with these family traditions to please my parents. Intellectually, I never accepted any of it. In fact, my father and I used to get into long arguments over the Jewish question. He would insist that I was above all else a Jew, and I would argue that I was first and foremost a German. Couldn't he see the evidence? We lived in a German neighborhood, not a Jewish ghetto; I went to a German high school with other Germans, not a yeshiva with only Jews; and I did not limit my friendships to Jews, but liked all kinds of people. I thought this made perfectly good sense, and on intellectual grounds it did. The problem was that deep inside, I knew there *was* something to what he said. I knew I felt closest to Jews and that my best friends were Jews. Of course, I would never admit it, and I just sloughed it off when he'd carry on about how we Jews were a people unto our own, a nation whose real loyalties were to Palestine. But, in my heart, I knew he wasn't completely mistaken."

"Why didn't your father emigrate to Palestine?"

"Unfortunately, like so many of your American Zionists, he was too comfortable and too settled to ever seriously contemplate coming here. It was something to talk about, to educate your children with, but not something to act upon. So, of course, the children never really took it seriously. I realize your parents are not Zionists, or not the way my father was, but they did insist that you have some religious education, and they do hold a kind of special attachment for Israel. That, if I remember correctly, is what you told me.

"But, lest you miss the importance of what I am saying to you, I want to tell you a little more thoroughly what happened to my father and the rest of us. I will not tell you all of it; just enough to give you an idea."

Moshe lit up another cigarette. "By 1933, most of us had a good idea what direction Germany was taking. You didn't have to be a Zionist or an intellectual to see it. Hitler made it obvious. To me, once he became Chancellor, the situation had become irreversible. Only a miracle could save us. I remember that day exactly, the day he became Chancellor: January 30, 1933. I remember it so well because on that very day when he was sworn in as Chancellor of the German Republic, I was also sworn in as a lawyer intern, working for the state courthouse. I had just finished my studies, and I had a two-year internship before I would receive my law degree. I knew that I would never get it, that it was only a matter of time until I, and all other Jews, were released from their positions. I knew this, in my blood I knew it, and still I hoped that I was wrong.

"Then two months later I got the letter. It was a form letter sent to all Jewish government workers, and it said that there would be a temporary lay-off. It didn't say why, it just said 'for the time being' there will be a lay-off. When I received this letter, I knew at last that the end had come. I said farewell to my supervisor, a judge, and he said 'I'll see you in a few days.' I looked at him for a few seconds and then I answered: 'No, this is for always. We will never see each other again.'

"What happened next was what happened to so many Jewish families. We split up. I was the youngest of the three children, so I got to leave first. That's the way my father wanted it. I went to the Zionist pioneering office, enlisted in their training program, and was sent for a short while to the Sudetenland. There were Jewish farmers there — it was the first I had ever heard of them — and they took us on and trained us, until we got certificates (legal permission) to go to Palestine. I went this way, and so did my brother and sister. But my parents were another story. They stayed in Berlin and while waiting for their certificates, they were arrested. My mother was allowed to stay in Berlin, but my father was sent to Buchenwald. He was lucky; he was one of those who survived."

Moshe paused and looked at me squarely. He seemed a bit shaken. "Now, why have I gone into all this with you?" he asked. "Why should I be so concerned that you hear it?

"Because just like you I would never have believed that any of this could happen. Not to me, not to my family, not to ... not to my country. I never intended to come here. I never intended to be an Israeli, a Zionist, or a man who can sit here now and tell you, from the depths of his being, that he is a Jew."

Moshe's eyes were watering now, and he could barely control his voice. He stopped again, got up and paced around my room, and then without sitting down he resumed: "I was in my mid-twenties then, about the same age as you are now, and I thought I knew. I thought I had it figured out. I was a German, not a Jew, and I had a whole set of arguments to prove that I was right. A real intellectual, I was. Nobody knew better than me what my religion was and what my country was, and what really mattered."

Moshe was beginning to make me uncomfortable. It wasn't just his words and the obvious suffering behind them that were hard to listen to, but the fact that beneath it all was the same old argument about anti-Semitism. And no matter how often or how convincingly I heard it, it never really hit home, and I always resented the person who said it.

"But I wouldn't waste my time or yours," he continued, now in a calmer voice, "if I thought you would dismiss all that I have just told you as just another German Jew's story. I want you to look deeper and see what was behind my intellectual attitude. And hopefully, if I am not mistaken, you will see what is behind yours. You see, at the heart of my self-deception was not simply a loyalty to Germany, but also a belief that I could decide my own fate, my own identity. I thought that I could rise above what other people said I was, that I could choose which of my feelings was most appropriate to act on, that I could decide to be German, and not a Jew.

"Now, in a very real way you have done the same thing; you are suffering from the same illness. You may have no deep love for America, but you are just as arrogant as I was in thinking that you can rise above your own identity; that you can avoid the facts of your birth and ignore those emotional ties which you find awkward or uncomfortable. You cannot do it. You cannot get away with it. *You* cannot decide to be a Jew or not. It may turn out that you, in *your* lifetime, will never have to pay the price that we German Jews did. But you will pay another price, I assure you. In fact, from all that I know of you, I am sure you are already paying it. And that is, by refusing to accept that you are first and foremost a Jew, and that Israel is your place, you remain a *luftmensch:* a man of the air; a man who has no real place, no real future; a man who says what he says, not from the heart where it really counts, but from the head where all is thought out and simple." Moshe began tapping his chest, and he smiled sadly. "I know your illness, Michael. I know it because I have suffered from it myself, and by now I have seen enough other cases of it, so that I recognize the symptoms. You have, Michael, that special Jewish heart disease known as Intellectualism — arrogant, self-deceiving Intellectualism. It is what makes us think that we can somehow figure out an identity for ourselves, without paying attention to what our feelings tell us is really us and really ours. It is an awful illness and it is common to Jews of the Diaspora." He smiled again, this time warmly, and he tapped the bed once or twice. "I can only pray that you will be over it soon."

New Job

4:00 A. M.: The sky a swollen gray, the air still damp with night.
"Ami! Where's Menachem?" an old-man's voice yelled.
"He went to get the tractor and cart."
"Where? In Haifa?"
"Jerusalem."
"Fifteen minutes to get a tractor and cart! If he moved any slower, he'd be standing still."
"Never mind, Elisha. Go drink some tea in the meantime. It's healthy for.you."
The young man, Ami, smiled, and the old man, Elisha, went off to

the kitchen. I followed after him to the back room of the kitchen, where there was a cauldron of steaming tea and a table piled with bread and a bucket of jam. I ladled out a glass of tea for myself, and made a jam sandwich to go along with it. There were about twenty others moving in and out of the room, some of them kibbutzniks and some volunteers from the Hebrew University, and they were all dressed in work clothes and looked as groggy as I felt.

"Let's go, comrades!" Ami's grinning face peered at us through the window. "You can finish your picnic out in the vineyards. We're ready to go."

"A half-hour you wait for *them*," said Elisha, to nobody in particular, "and then when you've got the tea poured, they come yelling that *they're* ready to go."

"Right!" said Ami. "Ready to go. Bring it along with you, Elisha. It's healthy for you."

The ride out to the vineyards was bumpy and beautiful. About thirty of us were seated on the flatbed cart, and except for Elisha and one or two other old-timers, nobody had any burlap bags to cushion the bumps. The vineyards were about a mile northeast of the main kibbutz buildings, and the asphalt road was pitted all the way. But you didn't feel it so much if you were big-butted, or thick-skinned, or if you ignored it, which was easy enough to do if you happened to be on the right side of the cart and you had a view of the flaming orange sun coming up from behind the thin gray line of the Gilead Heights, lighting up the Valley and the vineyards where the grape leaves, still wet, reflected the orange all over.

"A scorcher today!" said Elisha, as the tractor stopped in the middle of the vineyards and everybody climbed off. "A half-hour to fetch the tractor, and we have to begin in the sun."

"Never mind, my good man," said Ami. "You're tough, you can take it."

"You're going to make raisins out of us."

"But such sweet raisins!"

"Baach!" Elisha waved his hand in mock disgust at Ami, and went to pick up his grape-cutting shears.

Ami winked at me, and in a voice loud enough for Elisha to hear, said: "Why is it that the best workers are always the biggest complainers?"

"Baach!" repeated Elisha, but obviously pleased.

"Thirty years he's been working out here," continued Ami, still in the loud voice, "and every day a new complaint. A very creative man, our Elisha."

"Baach!" Elisha waved back again.

"The flesh and blood of the vineyards," Ami said, now talking just to me. "The voice of the vineyards, too." We both laughed. Then, extending his hand, Ami said: "We haven't met yet. I'm Ami. Linda has told me about you. I'm glad you're going to be out here with us."

"So am I, from the looks of things."

"Good. Very good."

We walked over to the spot where some people were still choosing their shears, and Ami picked up a few pairs, tried them out, and handed me the one that worked best. Then he asked whether I had ever worked in the vineyards before, and when I told him "no," he suggested I go along with Elisha. He was a little "mouthy," of course, but more than anyone else, he knew what he was doing.

Elisha was altogether lost in a grapevine by the time I found him, and only his large straw hat was visible. Already he had filled the better part of one newspaper-lined crate with bunches of yellow grapes. He didn't seem to welcome my intrusion.

"What? You don't know how to cut grapes?" he asked, as he went on working.

"I've never done it before."

"Never cut grapes before?"

"Never."

"Well, all right." He came out from under the vine. "Look here, it's simple." He took hold of a bunch of grapes, pulled it away from the surrounding leaves, and snipped. He then placed it delicately, stem up, into the wooden crate. "There's nothing to it. Just find them, cut them, and pack them. Only thing you want to be extra careful about is not to pick the green ones."

"Like these?" I asked, pointing to a large bunch of greenish grapes. "Right. Those you leave. But these, here" — he took hold of a greenish-yellow bunch — "you can cut. They'll be ripe by the time they get to market."

"I see."

"No problems, right?"

"I don't think so."

"Fine. Why don't you take the row across from me. You see a bunch you're not sure about, give me a shout. Don't pick it. Shout."

We worked like that for the next hour or so, Elisha on one side, I on the other. Far from being "mouthy," Elisha was too absorbed in the work to say anything. In fact, the only time he talked at all was when he saw, or thought he saw, a green bunch in one of my crates. Then he came over, held the bunch up to the sun to see whether the light went through the grapes, and passed judgment accordingly. It was important not to make mistakes, he said, because each bunch weighed an average of one kilogram, and each kilogram brought the kibbutz one Israeli pound and thirty *agorot:* so, ten mistakes and thirteen Israeli pounds would be lost.

Such was the extent of our conversation until the break at six o'clock. Then, as we sat there in a group, passing around the thermoses of water, he told me about himself. He had come to Bilat, he said, straight from Russia; the first group that started the kibbutz. He and his wife had come together, they had three sons — only one was still in the kibbutz — and he had worked all his life in the fields, mostly the vineyards. At his age — he was sixty-four — it was a little difficult to work like this and the sun sometimes got to him. But still he planned to stay out there, and do what he could; that was really all that mattered.

I then started to tell him a little of my background, but I soon saw that he wasn't very interested. The fact that I was an American, and a volunteer in his kibbutz, seemed a common enough story to him, and he asked no questions. The only thing he did finally question, was the remark I made that this was the first time in a couple of years I was having the chance to eat grapes. He didn't understand this. So I explained how there had been a grape-pickers strike in America, and those of us who supported it, hadn't been eating grapes. He still didn't understand.

"Most Americans," I said, "have continued to eat grapes. But some have not. And this has produced a surplus on the market and lower prices. Eventually we expect the vineyard owners will have to come to terms with the Mexican-Americans who do the picking. They will have to raise their wages."

"The *who* do the picking?" he asked.

"The Mexican-Americans. People from Mexico who come to pick the grapes."

"Ah yes! I see what you mean. And the vineyard owners, who are they?"

"Native Americans, I believe."

"Yes, yes, I understand. They exploit the American-Mexicans."

"Right. We feel they are exploited."

"You're right, I'm sure. That's the way it always is. Except, not here in Israel. Here, Jews own, Jews pick and Jews eat." And with that, he stood up and motioned for me to come back to work.

By 8:30 A. M., Elisha and I had together filled about three dozen crates, and we were wringing wet. Elisha's face was red and beaded with sweat and his body seemed to sag under the weight of the sun. Still, he wouldn't stop; not even when Ami came over and told him that breakfast was ready. He had to finish the row. And, as his sidekick, I had to stay with him.

When he finally did finish, we went to the irrigation ditch that carried water from the Yarmuk to the vineyards, and we washed ourselves. I dipped my head deep down into the water, letting it lap against my neck and shoulders, and when I came up Elisha was shaking his finger at me.

"You want to make yourself sick?"

"Sick?"

"Yes, *sick*. One minute hot, the next minute cold. The body doesn't like to have tricks played on it. *Shpritz* a little. It's good for you. At your age, you won't wilt."

We walked over to the large wooden shed where about fifteen people were eating breakfast at two picnic tables. About half of our original group had left. Menachem had driven them back to the kibbutz dining hall for breakfast, and they would not be returning until tomorrow. They didn't have the rest of the day off, of course; they worked elsewhere. The volunteers from the Hebrew University went out to the banana groves to chop leaves until lunchtime. Kibbutzniks went to their regular jobs to work for another six or seven hours.

The crew that remained in the vineyards packed the grapes for market, and as a special reward for being the regulars, we received a luxury breakfast. In addition to the usual salad-herring-olive stuff, there was honey, cottage cheese, sardines and fresh-cooked omelets. *Protexia,* Ami called it, using the Hebrew word for "pull," or "influence." "You've got to know somebody in the kitchen," he said, "and you've got to speak up. Otherwise, you can go on eating tomatoes and cucumbers the rest of your life."

When breakfast was over, after a half-hour or so (Only Elisha was paying much attention to the time.), we all headed for the long shed, where we began to pack the grapes for market. Menachem and Ami tractored in the crates of grapes from the fields. Shmuel, a short bald-headed man, took the crates and placed them on a conveyor belt which delivered them to the ten packers. And the packers pruned, cleaned and sorted them, and packed them neatly into two kinds of cartons (the best grapes into fancy white cartons for France and England; the "second best" into drab brown cartons for Tel Aviv). Then these cartons were sent down another conveyor belt where I covered them, stamped them, and arranged them into separate piles. My job also consisted of picking up the empty crates, bringing white and brown cartons to the packers, and placing the boxes of "third best" grapes, the greenish and broken ones, into a pile of their own; these were the grapes that went back to the kibbutz and showed up on the dinner table.

None of these tasks was especially enjoyable. Still the constant running about gave me a chance to chat briefly with many of the packers, all of whom were women except for Elisha. Also, since I moved quickly I was able to take a short break every half-hour or so. Ami and Menachem seemed to have the same work strategy, because they would race in from the oven-hot fields with a load of crates, unload them quickly with Shmuel, and then we would all sit together and drink water and eat cookies.

"A lazy bunch of Arabs is what you guys are," a dark-haired girl yelled, as we sat there taking one of our breaks. "The women work and the men sit!" She seemed to be joking.

"You're welcome to change places with me any time you want, Aviva," shouted back Ami.

"Big shot!" said the dark-haired girl, Aviva. "How about using your muscles to bring me over a glass of water!"

"Yes, my lady." He didn't move.

"Bring a glass to Elisha, too."

"Never mind," said Elisha. "But do me a favor: come weigh this carton." Ami got up and took the white carton over to the scales. It was supposed to weigh 5 kilograms.

"Too much, Elisha," Ami said. "Don't be so generous. Remember, this batch is going to France."

"How much over?" asked Elisha, ignoring the joke.

"Three hundred grams."

"Baach! You can't win. Three hundred grams too much and you're a fool; three hundred grams too little and you're a thief."

"Better to be a thief," said Ami curtly.

"Where's my water?" called Aviva again.

"Coming, dear."

"Skip the affection. Just give me the water."

"Yes, dear." Ami delicately placed a cup beside her and then, as if he were a *maitre d'* pouring out his restaurant's finest wine, he trickled a few drops out of the thermos and into the cup. "See if it is to your taste," he said solicitously. Menachem and Shmuel were enjoying the performance, but most of the women didn't seem to find it very funny.

"I ought to toss it in your face," said Aviva.

"You ought not," said Ami, threateningly. Aviva held out her cup for more and Ami filled it. "To your health!" he said, and went over to the tractor, and with Menachem, drove back to the fields.

Shortly after they had driven off, I happened to be collecting empty crates next to Aviva's chair, and I overheard something she was saying about Ami. She was talking with an older woman, not very loudly, but still loud enough so that the two packers sitting nearby could hear it. The packers were trying not to look at her, yet one could be sure they were lapping up every word of it; the stuff was too good to ignore.

"It's not exactly *his* fault," Aviva said, popping a large yellow grape into her mouth and pausing momentarily. She had just finished saying that Ami had always been a bit of a wise-guy, ever since she had known him. (He had come to the kibbutz when he was in second grade, and she was in kindergarten.) Still, he had a certain charm about him, and if he had married a better woman, a more stable type than Linda, he wouldn't have become "such a wise-guy." Aviva popped another grape into her mouth and spat out the pits behind her. She wiped her mouth off with her sleeve. "I've got nothing against her personally," she continued. "She can do what she likes. It's not my business. It's just that she's not doing Ami any good. I don't know whether it's true or not what they say about her and Noah. Maybe she is, and maybe she isn't...." The older woman snickered knowingly, but said nothing. "Well, what does it matter anyhow?" Aviva went on. "To me? To you? What does it matter? She's free to do as she likes. But for Ami it's no good. You can see it's beginning to get to him."

I moved away to the other end of the conveyor belt, pretending I was just going about my work; so I heard no more. Yet, what I had heard was enough to start me thinking about Linda, and all that she had told me that time at the poolside. I had liked and trusted her immediately, and I had believed what she said about Ami and herself. I had also believed her when she cursed the "rumor mop" of the kibbutz, and insinuated that the business about her and Noah sleeping together was nonsense. Now I was not so sure. The "rumor mop" was, as Linda had said, "filthy and cheap", but it was also, more often than not, accurate. It had taken me a few months and a few dozen rumors to figure this out, but I had come to see that on such personal matters as sex, the mop swished with special thoroughness, picking up all the dirt. So, perhaps Aviva was right after all. You couldn't be sure.

Sabra Soldier

Two children stood at the eastern-most perimeter of the kibbutz, their heads tilted up towards the sky, their hands cupping their eyes to ward off the late afternoon sun.

"It's a *Phantom*," said the small boy, pointing to a bird-like speck that was heading for Jordan's Gilead Heights.

"No, stupid, its a *Skyhawk*," said the second boy. He was Ilan, Ofra and Baruch's son. "*Phantoms* move faster."

The two boys argued without taking their eyes off the speck. Then they became silent and their mouths hung open as if they were watching a tight-rope walker approach the last few feet of his act.

"Now they dip!" said Ilan excitedly. "Now they go get 'em!"

And sure enough, the jet began to nose-dive towards the Heights, coming down hard upon them like some earth-bound angel. Five seconds, ten seconds, it kept diving, and when it was just above the ground it looped suddenly upwards, releasing its load of bombs, and the earth shook. The Gilead Heights trembled and the children broke into laughter.

"Ilan! Get over here!" shouted a husky voice. It was Baruch. He was standing just outside his apartment about a hundred feet away.

"Wait a . . . " Ilan began to answer.

"Over here! What do you think this is? A circus?"

There was another loud explosion and the children jerked their heads back towards the sky. A second jet was heading for the Heights, and the Jordanians were trying to knock it down with anti-aircraft fire. This was a dangerous business for the kibbutzniks because the anti-aircraft fire could come plummeting down into the kibbutz.

"You better listen to your father," I said to Ilan. He paid no attention.

"Ilan!" Baruch shouted again, now coming quickly towards us. He motioned for me to take hold of the boy.

"Come on, Ilan," I said, putting my hand on his shoulder, but he shook away.

"Can't even have a little fun," he sulked.

When Baruch reached us, scowling and breathing hard, I was sure he was going to whack Ilan. But instead he stood there, his hands on his hips, looking down menacingly into the boy's face. "So you need a special invitation, Mr. Big Shot?" Ilan didn't answer. "What did I tell you about standing outside during an attack?" Ilan still didn't answer. Baruch stared at him for a long moment, and then in a gentle voice, said: "What am I going to do with you, Ilan? A few years ago I couldn't get you to come out of the shelter, and now I can't get you to go into one. What am I going to do with you?" Ilan shrugged and Baruch hoisted him high in the air and plopped him down on his massive shoulders. They began walking to the apartment. Baruch told me to come along with them.

Baruch and Ofra lived in the last row of flats, the ones next to the barbed wire fence which separated the main kibbutz area from the beginning of the banana groves. Only young couples lived in these flats, and the deep green lawn in front of them was usually crowded at this time of the day with small children who ran around half-naked as their parents sat there watching and chatting. On that afternoon nearly everyone was inside.

This was the first time I was visiting them since Baruch had come home from the reserves about three weeks before. We had met several times in the dining hall, but on these occasions Baruch had been uncommunicative. He refused to talk about reserve duty ("Not now, we'll spoil our dinner."), and when he joked, his humor was not light and cynical, as I had remembered it, but hard-edged and bitter. "There are two kinds of Arabs, right?" he asked one night as we were eating dinner. I nodded my head, thinking he meant what the kibbutzniks usually told their children — that there were some bad Arabs and some good ones. "Glad you agree," he said, a smile darting across his face. "Just two kinds: bad ones and dead ones." Ofra winced and I said nothing, and Baruch didn't say another word for the rest of the meal.

Ofra was washing dishes in the pantry when Baruch, Ilan and I entered. The two girls, Hedi and Hagar, were playing with dolls on the yellow living room sofa. They were completely oblivious to the thundering explosions outside.

Ilan ignored the harsh look his mother was giving him, and instead ran over to the bookcase and snatched one of the model planes which was sitting on top of it. "A *Skyhawk!*" he said, waving the model plane at Baruch. "That's what it was, daddy, wasn't it?"

Baruch nodded.

"I knew it was!" continued Ilan. "Rami said a *Phantom*. But *Phantoms* are different. Bigger wingspread, right?"

Baruch nodded again, and Ilan returned to the shelf and took down all the model planes and began playing with them. There was also a model of Apollo 11, with the *Spider* module and Armstrong on a white, pitted lunar surface, but Ilan didn't bother with it.

"Sit down," Baruch said, motioning me to an oriental cushion in the corner of the living room. He went into the bedroom and brought out another cushion, and he sat down across from me, his legs buckled under him in a yoga-like position. He then shooed all the children into the new reinforced concrete room. "Bastards," he said, in a low voice.

I looked at him in surprise, thinking he meant his children.

"No, no, not them," he said, glancing at the new room and chuckling. "Our neighbors, I mean. Our goddamned Arab neighbors."

"Hey!" Ofra shouted from the kitchen. "How about some fruit?"

"Fine," Baruch answered. "And heavy on the grapes for Michael!" He laughed hard at this one, and we began talking about the vineyards. Baruch told me that he had worked out there himself for the first few years when he was back from the army. That was ten or twelve years ago, when Elisha was "king of the grapes." He didn't get along with Elisha (The man "has a sense of humor like a sour grape."), and since Elisha was not about to leave the vineyards until they carried him out, Baruch chose the olive groves.

"Here, have some," Ofra said, handing me a colorful straw platter of fruit. There were no grapes, so I helped myself to a pear from the red and yellow platter. "It's a beautiful thing," I said, examining the platter. It looked like something you might find in the Old City of Jerusalem.

"War booty," Baruch said, flatly.

"What?"

"War booty. Or if you prefer, a gift from our neighbors."

"It's lovely, isn't it?" Ofra said.

"Yes," I agreed. "But where did you get it? Or shouldn't I ask?"

"You shouldn't," said Baruch, "but I will tell you anyway. I brought it back from the Golan. A souvenir."

It wasn't from the Six-Day War, he said, because he had refused to bring anything home from the war. It was a policy of the Israeli Army that there could be no war booty, and the soldiers in his battalion were forced to discard everything they took. Except for trinkets; they were allowed to keep small mementos if they wanted to. But, at the time, he, personally, wanted no souvenirs. He was happy enough to bring himself back.

However, about a month or so after the war, he was again on the Golan, this time not as a soldier, but as a farmer. Virtually all of the Syrian farmers had fled to the Syrian side of the cease-fire line, leaving behind them a plush wheat crop that would have gone to waste if someone didn't come along and harvest it. So, the kibbutzim in the Jordan Valley decided to "turn their swords into plowshares." Two men and a combine were sent from each kibbutz. Baruch and Edo went from Bilat. They worked twelve-hour shifts, night and day for a month, and each had earned for the kibbutz the equivalent of three hundred Israeli pounds per day. It had been exhausting work, and as a small reward for his labors Baruch had decided to bring home this Syrian fruit platter which he found in a one-room house just outside of Kuneitra. The family had obviously been quite poor, but he was sure they wouldn't miss it. "You see, they are never coming back there."

Bar Mitzvah

The invitations had been sent (about 150 of them), the caterer had been contacted, and the main ballroom of the Roger Smith Hotel in downtown White Plains had been reserved. Everything was set. Everything, that is, except me, the Bar Mitzvah *boy. I was nowhere near ready. In fact, with a month to go, I had not begun to learn the fifty-seven lines of Hebrew that I was supposed to read for the congregation. And what made matters worse, I had no idea how I would ever learn them, because after two years of Hebrew school, I could still barely read this mysterious language.*

"You're just getting nervous," my father said, when I confronted him with this problem. "The big day is approaching, and you're getting nervous. But don't worry. If you need some help, then help you'll get. Just don't worry." And so, with about twenty days remaining, some help was found. Her name was Mrs. Shapiro, a hefty peroxide-haired woman who once taught Hebrew school, and for a fancy price — my mother was "pained" to say just how fancy it was — she tutored me in my assigned reading from the Haftorah. *Twelve one-hour lessons is what it took. Every other day for three weeks, and during the final week a telephone call each night, in which I recited the whole passage for her, including the small*

explanation in English that I was supposed to make before reading the Hebrew. On the night before my Bar Mitzvah, *she assured me I would be "just great."*

I wasn't so sure. I was still nervous, knowing full well that if I got lost anywhere along the way, I might blank out completely. I had, after all, only memorized the stuff. I couldn't read it. "But who will know, anyway?" my father reasoned with me, as we were driving to Temple, the morning of my Bar Mitzvah. *"Who, besides you and the rabbi will know if you make a mistake?" He was right, of course, but it still didn't help much. "All you have to do," he continued to advise me, "is pretend that everyone out there is naked. That's right, pretend they're all sitting out there with no clothes on, and they're all just as embarrassed and scared as you are. It'll work."*

So I took my father's advice. And as Rabbi Schwartz was concluding his portion of the reading, I stared out at my relatives and friends, and I undressed them — everyone except my mother and two grandmothers; them, I left fully clothed. Then, as the organ music stopped, I strode up to the satin-covered podium, and like the confident patriarch of the congregation, I delivered fifty-seven lines of flawless Hebrew.

"A big night," Bierman said, poking a piece of cake into his mouth. Hannah, Yael, and Eton were standing next to him, and along with everyone else, they were *noshing* on the pastries and small sandwiches spread on the long, white-clothed table.

The entire lawn next to the high school was covered with rows of benches that led up to a wooden stage at the far end. The area was lit by strings of light bulbs dangling from the trees at the edges of the lawn. "She's the one who planned it," Hannah said, putting her arm around Yael's waist. "Every year she does it. Right, Yael?"

"It's no big deal. Michael's been to a *Bar Mitzvah* before, I am sure."

"Not like this. I'm sure he hasn't been to one like this. Not in America, anyway."

"No, I haven't."

"Come, let's go sit down," Bierman said, taking Hannah's arm. "I'm sure they want to begin."

We all followed Bierman to the front row, and when we got there,

Eton began explaining to me what *Bar Mitzvah* meant. He spoke like a school-teacher, or worse, like a Jew explaining something to a gentile; he assumed I knew nothing. "Traditionally," he said, "*Bar Mitzvah* has been a religious celebration. A boy reaches the age of thirteen, and he is accepted into the community as an adult. He is expected to take up his religious duties like all other men. That's what *Bar Mitzvah* means: son of duty."

Bierman looked over to catch what Eton was saying. He smiled but added nothing.

"Yet, what meaning can a religious celebration have for kibbutz children?" Eton asked rhetorically. "That's the question our fathers had to ask themselves. And what they decided is that *Bar Mitzvah* still applies. Instead of religious duties, there are other duties — to the kibbutz, for instance. Or to the country. And also, since we are a society where men and women count equally, boys *and* girls celebrate together."

Much of the celebration is symbolic, Eton continued. For a month or so prior to the *Bar Mitzvah* date, the boys and girls performed tasks — thirteen altogether — which symbolized their coming of age. Some of these tasks were simple: working a full-day instead of the usual two hours per week; or writing a letter to a member of the Knesset — Israel's parliament — and receiving a response. But other tasks were more unfamiliar: for example, using money to take a bus into town — Tel Aviv or Haifa — and spending a night alone with some family. "All of this may seem a little silly and unimportant," Eton concluded, "but to us, to the children involved, it's a big moment."

The audience, seated now, was quiet. Yael, standing off to the side of the stage, waved to the back benches and the *Bar Mitzvah* children — seven boys and five girls — began marching up the aisle. They were carrying long torches and their faces, very serious, glowed in the flames. Everyone craned their necks to look as they paraded up to the stage and lined up in front of it. Then, at Yael's signal, all the children turned suddenly about-face, jabbed their torches into the ground, and went running off behind the stage.

After such a dramatic introduction, the rest of the program seemed rather routine. A couple of children sang, a few read poetry (Yael helped them write it, according to Hannah.), and everyone danced. The only thing that was at all unusual was the last part of the program. A thick rope, about twenty feet long and ten feet off the ground, was strung tightly between two eucalyptus trees at the side of the stage. A second rope was strung some six feet above it, which each child held as he crossed. Still, it didn't look easy, especially the final bit, in which one let go of the top rope, bent quickly, caught hold of the bottom rope, and swung to the ground. "A symbolic act," explained Eton, as the last girl leaped from the rope and everyone applauded loudly. "The difficult journey from one stage of life to another."

Afterward, most of the kibbutzniks returned to the refreshment table or went into the classroom where the *Bar Mitzvah* children had an exhibit of handicrafts. It was a large display of hand-made jewelry, pottery, dresses, aprons and wood carvings, and it was all laid out carefully on blue-and-white tables. The kibbutzniks picked up the objects, held them to the light, and passed them around admiringly to one another. "Thirteen years old and they make things like these," marveled Hannah, showing me a hand-woven apron with an Israeli flag on it. "Can you imagine it?"

I held the apron up in front of me, and looked for the name on it.

"Oh, you won't find a name on it. That's a secret. You're not supposed to know."

"I don't understand," I said, handing her back the apron.

"No? Well, that's the whole point of our *Bar Mitzvah* here." She folded the apron neatly and replaced it on the table. "Everyone celebrates together. It's the group that is *Bar-Mitzvahed*."

"Lvov in 1919 was as poor as a beggar's boot, and still my father insisted I have the usual *Bar Mitzvah*." Bierman paused and sipped his lemonade. We were sitting outside their apartment, on a blanket underneath the jacaranda tree. The sprinkler was turned on for the rose bushes, and the crickets were rubbing their backs against the night. Bierman stared momentarily out at the darkness, then took another drink of lemonade, and asked: "You have been to a Hasidic *Bar Mitzvah*, Michael?"

I shook my head no.

"Well, I was once a Hasid, you remember. I've already told you about that, haven't I?"

"Yes."

"Good. So you can understand now why, poor as we were, my father still demanded I have the usual *Bar Mitzvah* celebration. The *gantseh mishpocheh* (the whole family) had to be there. From all over Poland. Even those relatives who didn't have the money to buy a newspaper, my father insisted upon bringing. To this day, I still don't know where he got the money."

"His wife gave it to him, of course," joked Hannah.

Bierman laughed. "Who knows? Anyway, they were all there. Maybe two hundred people, including all the friends and important people in the community. It was on a *Shabat*, of course, and the small wooden synagogue was packed. The men, in their caftans and fur hats, on one side of the synagogue, and the women, in simple dresses and kerchiefs over their heads, on the other — everyone there to hear me deliver an oration."

Bierman smiled and wiped his forehead with a crumpled, white handkerchief. "It seems a little strange to look back on it, but then it was a serious matter. It was something every boy began to think about, to dread almost, from the time he knew how to read. *Bar Mitzvah* — what did it mean? It meant you had come of age. You had become an adult, and your father was no longer responsible for your transgressions. Now, *you* were. You, who still didn't know how to shave, were suddenly a man in the eyes of God. Think of it!"

"Don't bother," interrupted Hannah. "It's a waste of time. The whole thing was a lot of nonsense."

"Listen to her!" Bierman said to me, nodding towards Hannah.

"What? I don't know about such things?" Hannah asked, in mock anger.

"Yes, you know about such things."

"My father wasn't a rabbi?"

"Your father *was* a rabbi."

"So I know what was nonsense and what was not nonsense."

"Yes, you know. But Michael doesn't. So, why not let me finish the story?"

"All right, finish the story, then."

Bierman turned back to me. "So where were we?"

"The meaning of *Bar Mitzvah*," I said. "You became a man in the eyes of God."

"Right. In the eyes of God and the eyes of the community. You became an adult. And to symbolize this fact, to demonstrate your coming of age, you prepared a long oration on some passage from the Talmud. You recited the passage, and then you recited the various commentaries on it. You know what is *pilpul*?"

"No, I don't."

"Really? I'm surprised. Well, anyway, to put it simply, it's a form of scholarly argument. For instance, you read the passage, and then you have to say what Rabbi So-and-So of, say, Vilna, gives as its meaning. Then, you say what Rabbi So-and-So of Kharkov had to say about the interpretation of Rabbi So-and-So of Vilna."

"Fascinating, isn't it?" interrupted Hannah, a smug expression darting across her face.

Bierman ignored her. "And that's the way it goes on. The more interesting and challenging the Talmudic passage, the more Rabbi So-and-So's you have to discuss. And the more you discuss, the better you sound."

"The work of geniuses!" Hannah said, sarcastically.

"Yes, *some* were geniuses," said Bierman calmly, but seriously. "And some just sounded like geniuses. Like me. That's what I did. I took an extremely difficult passage and then spent months memorizing all the commentaries about it. Very impressive. My chin barely reached the podium, and my voice cracked as I spoke, but oh, how I spoke! In Hebrew, in Yiddish; citing this rabbi, citing that one. Oh, how I went on! A couple of hours maybe, and in the end, everyone was very impressed."

"They didn't understand one word of it," Hannah said softly.

"Some did," corrected Bierman. "Some understood it. My father, and the rabbi, and a few others. But not me." Bierman forced a laugh. "That was the nonsense of it. I didn't really know what I was saying. I had just memorized the stuff."

The Rogers Proposals

For the volunteer in Bilat, there was also something resembling the *Bar Mitzvah*, or a "coming of age." It was not a formal ceremony, of course, and in some cases, I had been told, it could take a year or so to happen. But, eventually, no matter who you were — whether you spoke Hebrew or not, or even whether you liked Bilat or not — you started to become a member of the society; you became "one of them."

There were all sorts of indications that this was happening. You might, for instance, take a trip away from the kibbutz for two or three days, and then when you came back, many people, even those to whom you usually said no more than "Shalom," would approach and ask where you had been. They hadn't missed you in the sense of wishing you were there; but somehow *your* face had become part of *their* scenery, and they knew it when you were gone. This, of course, worked both ways; you began to know all the faces, and if one were missing for awhile, you sensed it. It was what sociologists might call a "group consciousness," and it was a strange thing when you started to become part of it.

There are other things that began happening, too, but these were less mysterious in nature. You began to receive, for example, more invitations to "drop over some time," and people began talking more freely to you. You found out who was respected and had power in the kibbutz, and who they wished would pack up and leave; or, who was sleeping with someone else's wife, and who had just received a bundle of money from an uncle in Tel Aviv but wasn't talking to anyone about it. In other words, the gossip got richer. You began to know something about everyone, and as a price, everyone began to know something about you. "There are no secrets in a kibbutz," is the way Lea put it. "Here, we wash our dirty linen in public. And, either you learn to live with that, or you leave."

For me, this was of little concern: I figured I had a great deal more to learn than to lose from the gossip. But there was something else that was happening to me as I became "one of them," which *did* concern me. And that is, I sensed that I was rapidly becoming, just like almost all of them, prejudiced against the Arabs. In a way, of course, I should have expected it. I had chosen to live on the border, chosen to sit under *Al Fatah's* attacks, and so, in a way, I had invited it. But now that it was happening, I was bothered. It went against everything I had ever believed in, and yet there could be no doubt about it: I was becoming bigoted. I no longer tried to see the Arab point of view; I looked suspiciously at the Arab laborers in the kibbutz; I laughed at anti-Arab jokes (the lighter ones), and I even began feeling that they should all go bug off and stop making problems for us. That's right, *us*. Leave *us* alone. Stop shooting at *us*. Who the hell did they think they were, shooting at innocent civilians? What the hell right did they think they had to Palestine, anyway? It surged through me. The questions, the feelings, the bigotry. And in the end, what made it so difficult to accept, so difficult to reconcile with all that had gone before, was the awareness that something in me liked it this way. Something in me liked disliking the Arabs, liked the bigotry, and liked it all for the simple, ordinary reason that it made me "one of them."

This awareness that I was becoming "one of them" was further heightened by the events of late June and early July. It was during this time that U.S. Secretary of State Rogers made his proposals for peace in the Middle East (June 25th), and every Arab country in the area snarled and sputtered accordingly. The Palestinians and Syrians dismissed the plan outright. The Lebanese were cautious. Hussein was troubled. And Nasser — the one everyone was listening to — blustered that "we will make no concessions regarding one inch of Arab territory."

For Israel, these weeks were extremely difficult. The proposals — calling for an immediate ninety-day cease-fire — had come at a time when Egyptian pressure along the Canal was intensifying. The Bar-Lev Line was under constant artillery fire ("You couldn't even go outside the bunker to take a shit," one kibbutz soldier told me.), and the main defense on the line, the jets, were now under the growing threat of Soviet missiles. The situation was serious. And yet, there was hope because as long as the Soviet missiles (the SAM 3's which were effective at roof-top level) didn't get brought into the Canal zone, you could still continue the saturation bombing attacks on Egyptian artillery, and you could still hold the Bar-Lev Line without too many casualties. At least, you hoped so, anyway.

Of course, to the outsider sitting in New York the situation must

have looked nearly hopeless, and the Rogers proposals must therefore have seemed like a saving opportunity for the Israelis to catch
their breath (for the last time?), and maybe to make peace. But,
sitting as I was in Bilat, this is not how it seemed at all. On the
contrary, it seemed like a sell-out. The Americans were asking —
even demanding — that Israel hold its fire for ninety days, with no
promise of further support, no agreement to sell the 125 jets which
Israel had for months tried to buy, and no guarantee that Nasser and
the Soviets would not move their missiles into the thirty-two-mile
belt along the Canal. It was a sell-out, pure and simple. And almost
all of us were hoping that Israel would have the guts to turn it down.

"We've got to turn it down," Rafael said. "There's no other way.
If someone puts a pistol to your head, you don't have to oblige him
by pulling the trigger." We were sitting on a bench next to the
swimming pool — Rafael, Edo and I.

"Can't turn it down now," said Edo tersely. "Can't." He took off
his terrycloth robe and went over to the edge of the pool. "I thought
so myself at the beginning. We'll turn it down. Very simple . . ."

"Of course it's simple," interrupted Rafael. "You just pick up the
telephone, dial Washington, and tell them to go shove it."

"Can't now," repeated Edo. He dived into the pool and Rafael
waved his hand after him in disgust.

"Like hell you can't," Rafael muttered. "What are we, anyway?
Puppets?"

I didn't answer him. He seemed to be talking to the air. We both
knew that Edo was politically savvy, and if he made such a
statement, there were surely reasons for it. So we said nothing more,
and instead took off our shirts and sandals and followed Edo into the
pool.

We swam several laps, about twenty minutes altogether, and
carefully avoided re-opening the discussion. Edo stayed at the deep
end of the pool, treading water, while Rafael and I raced each other.
Then, as the sun started to go down, and the air outside the pool
turned cool, Rafael and I returned to the bench to towel off. Edo was
already there, and I could see by the severe look which Rafael gave
him, that he was going to bring it up again. But he didn't get the
chance. Edo raised it first.

"I know what you're thinking, that I've overestimated America's power. That I'm looking at us as their satellite."

"Something like that," Rafael said coldly.

"But you're completely wrong," Edo said. "We are still free to do what's best for us in the long run. But for the moment — *just* for the moment — we'll have to go along with them."

"Why's that?"

"Look what's going on now," Edo answered, somewhat pedantically. "Nasser has been in the Soviet Union for a week and he is going to stay longer."

"So what? He's got diabetes. He doesn't trust the Egyptian doctors."

"Forget his diabetes. It has nothing to do with it."

"How do you know?"

"Take my word for it. At a time like this, you don't go for rest cures."

"All right. So Nasser is in good health, and just for the fun of it, he has decided to hang around with his Russian buddies."

"He has to. Something is cooking in Moscow, and he has to stay around and taste it."

"All right, chef, what is it?"

"Well, *you* figure it. If you were the Russians what would you be cooking up?"

"Blintzes."

"Come on, seriously!" Edo paused, and when nobody answered he went on: "Well, you want the Canal, right? You want the route to the East, and you'll take it any way you can get it. Of course, the easier you can get it, the better. You don't want to fight Israel if you can possibly avoid it; you'd lose too many men. And then, too, you might have to face the Americans."

"I doubt *that*," said Rafael.

"You may be right," agreed Edo. "But, then again, look what Nixon said the other day, comparing the Middle East with the Balkans before World War I. He knows the two superpowers could be drawn into a confrontation any minute."

"Nixon talks out of both sides of his mouth."

"Maybe," agreed Edo. "Maybe he means it, and maybe he doesn't. The point is the Russians can't be sure. So for them, the best and safest way to get the Canal is through diplomacy. Make a deal. Give the Americans something in Vietnam. Get something from the Americans in the Middle East."

"Hell, that's just what I'm telling you," said Rafael. "The Americans are screwing us, and you're saying go along with them."

"No, I'm not! Let me finish." We began walking back toward our rooms. We were all living in the same row of flats. (Orna had found me a room with shower over in the "singles" section of the kibbutz.) "All I'm saying," Edo resumed, "is that we have to accept the proposals. Tell the world we accept them . . . "

"And then not go along?" I interrupted.

"Yes, go along for a while. Until the cease-fire is broken."

"In the first minute," said Rafael. "They'll break it in the first minute."

"Of course," said Edo. "That's the way the Russians will get Nasser to go along: they will promise him that he can move the missiles up into the Canal zone, after the cease-fire begins. This is what he wants. His casualties have become enormous. He can't cope with our planes. So he has to go along even though it hurts him in the eyes of the Arab Left, and probably also in the eyes of his own people. He has no choice."

"Then if Nasser goes along," I said, "and Israel still refuses, she looks like she doesn't want peace."

"Right!"

"Then let it look that way," said Rafael.

"No need to," said Edo. "We could, but there's no need to."

"To hell with world opinion," said Rafael. "Who needs it?"

"It's a factor," said Edo coldly. "But more important, the Americans are probably making their arms sales dependent upon our acceptance. They could get nasty."

"Screw them! They need us as much as we need them."

"Why test it? I don't trust them any more than you do. But why, as long as it can still be avoided, should we put them to the test?"

Rafael shook his head slowly, but he said nothing more. There was a long silence, and then Edo added: "The only thing I wonder is, what happens once the Americans see the cease-fire broken. We know what *we'll* do, but what will *they* do? How will *they* respond? That's what I'm not so sure of."

Woman in Love

The first Israeli woman I ever met was a lieutenant. In 1963, I had just stepped off the Israeli liner, *Moledet*, on my first trip to Israel, and there she stood at the end of the gangplank, barking out instructions. "Welcome to Israel! Customs that way!" Her arm shooting out to the left, her voice blasting away, she was everything I had come to distrust and dislike in Jewish women, all rolled up in khaki.

"You're silly," Neeli said, a coy smile flickering at the corners of her mouth.

"I was young," I said.

"Not young. Silly. Look at us. Do we bark?"

"I was young," I repeated, smiling. "That was the stereotype. I guess I was just looking for it."

"And you found it. You always find what you're looking for. If you thought we still walked around like Eve, in a fig leaf, you would have found that too."

"You promise?"

She waved her hand in mock disgust at me, and went back to picking grapes. For a quick second I wished that I was seventeen, and she was still available.

But she wasn't. She had made that clear a few weeks ago, when we first started working together in the vineyards. She had a boyfriend, she said. A sergeant with the commando forces. And they were planning to be married as soon as she finished her military duty. Only twenty months from September — May 1972. She had figured it out already.

"You don't happen to know the exact date?" I had asked her joshingly.

"May 14th," she answered promptly. "Independence Day. I want to be married on Independence Day."

"Oh, she's a romantic," Lea said. "Just like I was at her age." Lea smiled wisely, and turned off the air-conditioning. She then went into the pantry and came back with my favorite peach cake. "Neeli made it. A present for you."

She leaned back slowly in her chair, and became silent, brooding. I was sure it had to do with Neeli; either her, or one of her sons who had left the kibbutz. I had seen Lea like this before, and always it turned out to be something about her children. A real Jewish mother, I thought. Thirty years in the kibbutz, and still a real Jewish mother.

"What's so funny?" Lea asked, irritatedly. "You've got a robber's grin all over your face."

"I'm sorry. It's just that I'm enjoying the peach cake."

"Well, I'm not. Not one bit."

I didn't say anything. And Lea resumed her silence. She sat there for a minute or two more, thinking, almost talking to herself. Then, finally, as if the thought had just come to her, she blurted out: "What's the use of raising children, anyway? You raise them, give them everything you can, and then they go make the same mistakes you did. You're not a mother, you wouldn't know. How could you have any idea what it's like to see your child heading for the same trap that you once stepped into, and there you are on the sidelines, powerless to do anything for her.

"Someday maybe you'll have a daughter and you'll know. You'll have the same frustration." Lea paused and started to pick up her plate of peach cake, but put it down and pushed it off to the side. She took a long swallow of coffee instead. "At 17, you think the world is spinning in the right direction. Everything will end in rainbows. That's the way I was. That's the way Neeli is. She's just like me. That's what makes it so hard. I listen to her tell me about this boy, this soldier, and how they are planning to get married when she gets out of the army, and I try to smile. I try to share her happiness with her, to say nothing of what I'm thinking. But it slips out. I can't help it. Two years waiting, two years of army duty in between, and she talks as if it were tomorrow. It's so completely unrealistic. So, so . . . blind."

Lea stopped and massaged her eyes with her thin, white hands. She looked up at the door as if she were expecting someone. "I remember when she first told me about it . . . about a year ago. I already knew that she was chumming around with this soldier boy. She told me about it herself, but I had no idea how serious it had gotten. Then, one night she came here as I was about to go to sleep.

The lights were off, and she came bursting in and scared me half to death. Her face was flushed and her hair was rumpled and wet. I knew immediately what had happened.

"I knew because I was once young myself, and I know what that look on a girl's face means. She had slept with him. When she finished telling me all about it, I felt deeply sad. I tried not to show her; I tried to share her excitement, but I was sad. No, not about the sex. I'm not a prude in that way, and Neeli knows it. I suppose that's why she could tell me. But I was deeply worried about what it meant to her. She's a serious girl — I'm sure you know that — and I knew that if she slept with him, she must be serious about him. And she was only 16. It was too young . . . much too young."

Lea sighed and leaned back in her chair. She was silent for a moment or two, as she massaged her eyes again, and then she sat forward and looked at me. She seemed to be asking for a reaction.

"How do Neeli's friends look at it? Do they see it the way you do?"

"Of course not, they think she's lucky. They wish they were in her place."

"Getting married?"

"No — not getting married. Having a boyfriend. Having a love affair."

"Is that uncommon?"

"At sixteen, seventeen? Sure it's uncommon!"

I was surprised. I had always thought kibbutz kids started their sex and love lives early. That's the way it had seemed at Kibbutz Hazorea, where the boys and girls lived together in the same rooms until they went off to the army. And while the set-up was somewhat different in Bilat — they stopped sharing rooms once they reached puberty — I didn't suppose the outcome was any different. There was, after all, nobody to watch over them at night, and as Ruthy had pointed out during my visit to the high school, they were "free to do what they wanted."

I told this to Lea and she looked at me, startled. How could I think that just because there was nobody there to watch over them, they "necessarily got into trouble?" It was my American background, she said, that made me think like this. It blinded me. And, as a matter of fact, there was very little "fooling around" among the children. That was the whole point of what she had just told me about Neeli. She slept with this boy not as a lark, but because she loved him. And besides, he was not a boy from her class, or even from Bilat. He was from another kibbutz, and he was already in the army when she met him.

"In fact," Lea continued, "maybe if he were from Bilat, and in her class, I wouldn't worry so much about it. Maybe it would work out. There are several couples here who have had it work out that way."

"Baruch and Ofra, I know ... "

"And several others. Reuben and Shoshi. Eton and Yael. Many. Six or seven. But that's not the point. The problem is that he's different from her; he's had many girlfriends already ... " She hesitated and then said: "He still has many."

I looked at her, amazed. "You *know* this?"

"Yes, I know. I found out. I have friends in that kibbutz."

"Does Neeli know?"

"I'm not sure. If she does, she hasn't told me."

"And you haven't told her?"

"I can't. I want to tell her but I can't. I just can't."

"Of course, they play around," Rafael said. "What do you think this is, a convent?"

I turned around and looked again at the group of high school students and soldiers sitting in a circle at the edge of the soccer field. One of the soldiers had a guitar and was sitting in the middle, leading the singing.

"You want to go join them?" Rafael asked.

"No, I'd rather go swimming," I said.

"All right. Suit yourself."

We continued walking. Rafael was silent for a moment, and then he picked up the thread of conversation. We had just begun talking about sex, particularly extracurricular sex.

"So you want to know a little of the smut?" he teased.

"I'll even settle for some of the clean stuff," I joshed back.

"Sorry. No clean stuff."

"Then make it smut."

"I'd love to."

We broke into laughter. An old woman who was walking by gave us a suspicious look, but we just went right on laughing, sobbing away like drunkards, completely out of control. By the time we got to the pool we were wet with tears.

Later, when we were sitting at the edge of the pool, after swimming several laps, Rafael began talking again. "Actually, I was just kidding you before," he said, smiling. "There's not really that much smut to tell. No more than anywhere else. In Tel Aviv, you've got the same thing. Even in Jerusalem. I don't care where you are, people are people."

"Even in the kibbutz?" I joked.

He laughed. "Yes, even in the *kolkhoz.*" There was a short silence as Rafael toweled off his hair. Then he said: "The only difference between here and anywhere else, is that here everyone knows what is going on."

"Like a small town?"

"Right. Same thing. You can't avoid it. Sooner or later, no matter what you've done, everyone knows it."

"Sounds embarrassing."

"It is ..." He hesitated. "It is, and it isn't. That's the strange thing about a place like this. People here get on each other's nerves all the time and they're always arguing. But you take things like screwing around, things that would become a scandal anyplace else — might even have some shootings or stabbings because of it — and here it is overlooked. It's just gossiped about, and then it's usually forgotten."

"I hadn't thought of it that way."

"I'm not saying it's so nice to be talked about, but it's a hell of a lot better than a shoot-out."

I agreed.

Rafael looked slowly around, as if he were suddenly concerned about being overheard. "Though, sometimes even in the kibbutz, there are scandals. Not often. Very rarely, in fact. But sometimes it happens."

He looked around again, just to make sure. "Don't ever let anyone know I told you this. It would be bad if it got out. I'm only telling you because you know the Biermans, and I know it'll interest you. But don't tell anyone.

"It happened a year ago. Right in the apartment house where we are living. The room next to yours. The guy who used to live there was a fellow named Eliezer — one of Elisha's sons. He was a real Casanova. I think he had a permanent erection. Anyway, he used to bring girls there all the time — volunteers from the Hebrew University, army girls, British girls, American girls, all kinds — and nobody thought very much of it. It was his way, they figured. Only his old man, Elisha, used to give him a hard time. Thought he wasn't serious enough; wasn't taking his responsibilities the way Elisha expected him to.

"But that didn't stop Eliezer. He went right on screwing around. And always he was smart enough to get someone from the outside; not to mess around with anyone from the kibbutz. So he didn't have any real trouble..." Rafael paused as a woman and her two children passed. "Not until last year did he have any problems. Then he finally overstepped the line. He got in trouble with a kibbutz woman. A virgin, we figured. That's what it sounded like anyway. You'd hear the moaning and the banging through the walls, but you never saw her come in or go out. So, one night we decided to stay up and see who it was. Me and another guy. We waited all night in my room looking out of the window, and then about 3:00 A.M. we saw Eliezer's door open, saw him give her a quick little good-bye pat on the ass, and then when she looked up, we got a full view of her. It was Yael.

"That's right, Yael. We were surprised too. But Eton was away in reserves; and Yael must have gotten bored. Still, we were surprised. We didn't think she was like that, and we decided to keep our mouths shut. Not to tell anyone."

"But Yael couldn't leave well enough alone. Once Eton got back, instead of forgetting about Eliezer, she kept sneaking over. I saw her several times myself. She'd come about five o'clock in the morning, wearing her work clothes, and then she'd spend an hour or so making it with Eliezer, before going off to work. And he, the *schmuck*, didn't have sense enough to keep her away. So, eventually, of course they were discovered. And you know, they still didn't stop. Everyone knew about it — Eton, Bierman, Hannah, the whole kibbutz — and still they kept carrying on.

"It became a scandal. Eton was on the verge of breaking up with her, and Bierman was beside himself. And as you know, Bierman is not one to sit back and let the shit fly all around him. Eton, yes. But not Bierman. So, he went to the *Masceeroot*, to the Secretary of the kibbutz, Drora, and he tried to get them to stop it. But what could they do? The kibbutz is not a kindergarten. So, then he went to Eliezer. Bierman demanded that he stop it; he told him that he was breaking up a family, there were children involved, and that either he stopped it himself, or he, Bierman, would stop it for him."

Rafael suddenly stood up and motioned for us to go. We began walking away, and he became silent.

"So what happened then?" I asked impatiently.

"Well, Yael and Eton are still together, aren't they?"

"But where's Eliezer?"

"In South Africa. The kibbutz has sent him there as an agricultural expert. A volunteer. And he won't be back until next year."

"Did Bierman do it?"

"Your guess is as good as mine."

I didn't say anything, and Rafael added, philosophically: "These things have a way of working themselves out. They blow over. Even the worst scandals blow over. That's one of the strange things about living here."

Linda. The lady from Liverpool. The lovely lady from Liverpool. In a way, you had to admire her. She must have known that rumors were flying like bats all around her, but she never showed it. She continued to pal around with Noah, continued to walk around in her blue bikini, and continued to flirt with any man in the kibbutz that caught her fancy. Yet, with all this she somehow managed to keep Ami from throwing her out, or even treating her with anger in public. I couldn't understand it.

"But what's there to understand?" Linda asked, unbelievingly. "What the bloody hell is there to understand?"

We were sitting alone in her small, cramped apartment, eating some fresh dates she had brought back from Tiberias. Ami had left a few days ago for reserve duty, and she had invited me to drop over. After a few minutes of chit-chat, I finally asked her whether she wasn't worried that there would be gossip about my coming over, now that Ami was away. I told her I thought she was gutsy, but I just didn't understand why she wanted to make problems for herself.

"What problems? How do you figure I'm making problems by inviting you over? Look, if I were sleeping with you, that would be one thing. But simply to invite you over — what have I got to be ashamed of?"

"Nothing," I said flatly. "Nothing at all."

Linda stood up and went over to the bookshelf, where she had a small stereo set. It was a present which her parents had brought her from England. She put on the Beatles' "Abbey Road," and got some ice cubes, soda, and a bottle of Gordon's gin from the pantry.

"You drink gin, don't you?" she asked.

"Only when I'm thirsty."

"Good. You look thirsty."

She poured the drinks, handed me one, and leaned back in her sheepskin chair. There was a short silence, and then I broke it by telling her that I would like to ask her some questions. She looked at me curiously. So, I explained how in the past week I had talked with Rafael and Lea, and they had given me a few generalizations on the "sexual mores" of the kibbutz. Her mouth curved into a smile at the expression "sexual mores," but she remained silent. What I wanted to know from her, I continued straight-faced, was some specific information — that is, "if she happened to have it."

She laughed. "Happen to have it?" she repeated teasingly. "You put things so delicately. All right. Go ahead. What would you like to know?"

She gave me a bored look, but I figured I'd ask the questions anyway.

"Well, first of all, I'd like to know something about the sex education here. What age it begins, what is said — that kind of thing."

"Sort of a bird's-eye view," she said tongue-in-cheek.

"Right."

She smiled and took a long swallow of her gin and tonic, tinkling the ice cubes between her teeth as she drank.

"It's not bad, in fact, it's one of the few things they do really well here. The kids grow up healthy. Without all this guilt and perversion like you see in England."

"They start them early here. And they don't hide anything from them. For example, you take my group of four-year-olds — the ones I work with. Already they are asking questions. You take them to see a cow giving birth, say, and they want to know how it happens. These are farm kids, remember. You can't hide things from them. So you tell them everything. How the bull puts the seed into the cow, and how the seed grows into a baby cow. Even how it happens in human beings. You compare it for them."

"Do they understand?"

"Some more, some less. One or two even come back to the children's house and want to try it out. But, of course, we tell them not to. It won't work. You have to be grown-up for it to work — mommies and daddies, we tell them."

"And they listen?"

"Well, we have no problems. The pregnancy rate among the four-year olds in Bilat has been most acceptable." She grinned, and picked an ice cube out of her glass and put it in her mouth.

"How about among the older children?" I asked. "Are there any problems with the boys and girls living together?"

"They don't live together, you know."

"They share the same apartment house, don't they?"

"The same apartment house, yes."

"And there are no problems?"

"If you mean, do they sleep with each other, the answer is no. They're more like brothers and sisters; it would be almost incestuous for a boy and girl of the same class to sleep together. However," she raised her finger, "if you mean, because nobody is there to watch over them, they are free to make it with someone *not* in their class, the answer is yes. They fool around. Many of them."

"Most?"

"I couldn't say. At fifteen or sixteen — no. But, by seventeen, eighteen, many of them have begun. Usually with someone from another kibbutz, or from the Army."

"Doesn't anyone ever get pregnant?"

Linda smiled widely, as if she had been expecting this question.

"Here's where practice begins to depart from theory. On the one hand, the kibbutz handles these things very well. I've got to hand it to them. They give the kids a good sex education. When the kids are about thirteen, Mical, the nurse, speaks to them about the mechanics of sex, on the biology — the what goes where sort of thing — and also on contraception. Pills, diaphragms, prophylactics — the lot. In theory, anyone who wants to, can have contraceptives. All he has to do is go to Mical and ask for them. But figure it for yourself. If he went to her, and he was, say, fifteen, Mical might tell his parents. Get him into trouble. So, if he wants to fool around at that age he depends on his luck, or as they call it here — the 'careful' method."

"How about at seventeen? Do they feel free to ask for contraceptives then?"

"Not then either. They have no guilt about sleeping together at that age; in fact, most of them think it's perfectly lovely to have a love affair when you're still in high school. But again, what would happen if the nurse knew about it? She might tell the parents. Remember, this isn't some sort of health clinic — it's a kibbutz."

"So they use the 'careful' method, too?"

"Unless they want to spend their money on contraceptives in Tiberias."

Linda stood up and went over to the stereo set to change the record. "It gets even more interesting when they *do* slip up; when one of the girls does get pregnant. That's what you asked me originally, right? Well, here's what happened to one high school girl about two years ago — shortly after I got here. It was the talk of the kibbutz. The girl — never mind who — was going with this Indian boy . . ."

"Indian boy?"

"Yes. A Jewish boy from India. There was a whole group of Indian Jews here, then. Very dark skins, if you've seen them. Bilat tried to assimilate them, but it didn't work out, and they eventually left. Anyway, one of these Indian boys was going with this girl, and he got her pregnant. The girl got scared, and didn't tell anyone for about five or six months. By then, it was too late to have an abortion."

"Are abortions legal here?"

"Not really. But the government closes its eyes to it. There's a doctor in Tiberias who does it for 150 Israeli pounds. Very good, very cheap. The kibbutz uses him when they have to. And with this girl, they surely would have used him. But as I said, they didn't have a chance . . ." Linda bit lightly at one of her fingernails. "The girl was really a mess. She didn't want to marry the boy, he didn't want to marry her, but she *wanted* to have the baby — and to keep it. The kibbutz didn't like the idea. So she wound up having the baby — a big healthy baby, too — and then giving it up for adoption."

"She couldn't keep it?"

"There was too much pressure on her to give it up. She couldn't take it. She gave in . . . She gave in, and she's been a mess ever since. Screws now with any boy that asks her. The whole army in the Jordan Valley knows about her by now."

Linda shook her head and her whole face tightened with anger. "It really gets me, the way they deal with these things here. All right, maybe she shouldn't have had the baby. Maybe she wouldn't have been a good mother to it. But, who knows? And, what the hell business is it of theirs if she wanted to keep the child? Who the hell are they to tell her what to do?"

She refilled the glasses, and then in a calmer voice said: "It's things like this that make me sure I can't go on here. They happen all the time. The kibbutz sits on you and tries to make you into one of them. And, you know, it succeeds. It bloody well succeeds. Either you leave in time, or it molds you into one of them. I can feel it happening. Every day, I can feel them swishing their slimy, rumor mop through my life, feel them pinching and poking at me, trying to tell me what to do. But I won't have it. It's my life, and I'll do as I please with it. If I want to invite you to drop over, it's my business. If I want to chum around with Noah, I'll go ahead and do it . . . " She paused to catch her breath. She looked at me closely.

"And Ami?" I asked, softly.

She didn't answer, but went on looking.

"Does he agree?"

Her eyes pulled away from me, and she stared down at her glass. She pulled out a huge ice cube, held it up to the light, and then poked it into her mouth. "I don't know," she said coldly. "I don't know, and at this point, I almost don't care."

The Olive Groves

"You call *her* a woman?" asked Rafael, kiddingly.

"Hell no!" answered the bald-headed guy, Shmuel. "Not the way *she* works."

"You guys are terrible!" said Edo, disgustedly. "Three kids, a good husband, and you talk all this crap about her."

"Her husband's a queer," said Shmuel, jokingly.

"You're nuts!" Edo answered, his face flushed with anger. He picked up his empty glass and left.

Rafael, Shmuel and I continued to sit there, under the datepalm tree, next to our apartment house. There was a long silence after Edo stalked off, and I was sorry the question had ever come up. "You still working in the vineyards?" Rafael had asked politely, to make conversation. I answered that tomorrow I was shifting into the olive groves to work with Baruch. "And Charna!" Shmuel had added, with a grin. When I asked who she was, Edo explained that she was a new boss in the olive groves: Baruch used to be the sole boss, but now that he was spending so much time away on reserve duty, Charna had moved in to help him. She's "a fine person, a fine woman," Edo had said.

"A lieutenant, too," Shmuel added. "In the woman's army."

"Charna?"

"Right. Your new boss. She runs the olive groves like a military camp."

"Let's forget it," Rafael said softly. "Let him find out for himself, tomorrow."

"You ever work out there with her?" Shmuel persisted.

Rafael shook his head no.

"Makes you see that a woman's place is in the home — the kitchen," Shmuel said, smiling. "Seriously, I worked out there with her once myself — before she was boss — and one day was all I could take. Her poor son-of-a-bitch husband, Motti, was out there too." Shmuel chuckled to himself. "You should have seen the way she treated him. Poor son-of-a-bitch was on the ground picking up olives — the ones that had fallen — when she came by. 'Up on the ladder!' she told him. Just like that. 'But there's many on the ground, dear,' he answered her in that soft little voice of his. 'Never mind. Get back on the ladder!' And the poor son-of-a-bitch jumped right back up there. She probably would have beat his ass if he didn't."

It had to be her. 4:00 A.M., and she was ushering everyone out of the kitchen, away from the hot tea, and out into the damp dawn where the truck waited to take us to the olive groves. I didn't remember her from the year before, though I surely would have. She was tall and sinewy, and in those tight blue shorts and white tee-shirt she looked like a track star, sure and sexless.

"What are we waiting for?" she barked at David, who was sitting in the cabin of the truck.

"Baruch," David answered flatly. "He's not back yet, Charna." She stood there, hands on hips, looking around. The pickers, mostly high-school kids, were climbing slowly onto the trunk, grunting and groaning as they sat down.

"He's still on the telephone?" she demanded.

"He was having trouble with the connection."

Charna pursed her thin, colorless lips, and shook her head knowingly. I wasn't exactly sure what was going on, but I had an idea. Baruch had told me about it last year. The olive groves, he said, were scattered through many areas around the kibbutz: some were next to the swimming pool, some bordered on the long road that led up to the kibbutz (I had worked in these), and many were interspersed in small patches among the banana groves. These latter groves were the dangerous ones, and you couldn't work in them without first checking, by telephone, with the army. "It makes the work interesting," Baruch had quipped. "The Arabs are kind to us in this way. They know how dull olive-picking is, and they try to liven it up for us."

"*Nu?* What's the word?" Charna shouted, as Baruch came walking from the direction of the *Masceeroot*. The high school kids turned toward him expectantly.

"Sad news!" Baruch yelled cheerfully. He was looking at the kids, not at Charna. "The Arabs have let you down today. The groves are clear. No bombing!"

The kids groaned, and smiled along with him. Charna stared at them, her dark eyes serious and challenging.

"All right! Let's get going," she said loudly. She climbed up into the cabin of the truck, next to David. Baruch got into the driver's seat, and we drove off.

The haze was just lifting from the valley when we arrived, some ten minutes later, at the edge of the olive grove. The tall grass was still wet, the mosquitoes still out, and you could hear the Yarmuk River not more than 150 yards away.

I had never worked this close to the border, and had only been down there once, the year before. Jordan's Ghor Canal (which carried Yarmuk water to Jordanian fields) was within hollering distance. Only a couple of months ago, several of us had stood on the kibbutz water tower about a kilometer away, and watched the Jordanians repairing the Canal which the Israelis had destroyed in retaliation for the border bombings. Then, presumably due to American urgings, the Israelis agreed to permit the Jordanians to rebuild it. But, *Al Fatah*, denouncing any cooperation or bargain with the Israelis, threatened to disrupt the repair work. Thus, you had this absurd scene in which Jordanian laborers were working on the Canal, as Israeli tanks and cannons stood nearby protecting them from *Al Fatah*. Once the Canal was repaired, the Jordanian Government and *Al Fatah* evidently patched up their differences, and the attacks on the kibbutzim were resumed.

"Come on, what are you waiting for!" Charna shouted, as the kids slowly climbed off the truck. None of them bothered looking at her. "Grab a sack, and pick a tree. Two to a tree, and remember . . . " She stopped short and stared at a dumpy little girl who was hobbling over to the pile of sacks. "What's wrong with you, Danit?"

"Nothing," the girl muttered.

"Then, let's get a move on it!"

"My toe hurts."

"Then, sit down. But, for God's sake, don't hobble!"

The girl sat down and Charna went over and ministered to her. The rest took sacks — wide, semi-circular bags that hooked around the waist and shoulders — and started picking. Baruch, with a ladder on each shoulder, asked me to go with him.

"Better work with me awhile," he said. "Work in the tree all day and you'll go crazy."

We walked behind the last row of trees, over to an embankment where there was a stack of aluminum ladders. "Take as many as you can carry, and follow me."

I grabbed two ladders and followed Baruch through the sticky knee-high grass to the end of the row where some kids were lying on the ground.

"Excuse me for disturbing your sleep," Baruch said good-naturedly. He set the ladders up against the trees, and jostled them to see if they were standing securely.

"All right, rest is over," he said firmly, noticing that nobody was moving. "No more excuses for being on your butts."

"I've got one," snickered a long-haired boy.

"That's one too many," answered Baruch, and we walked off.

We continued setting up ladders for the next half-hour or so, trudging through the grass, as the mosquitoes tailed after us. When we finished, Baruch had something he wanted to show me. Circling a cement-lined irrigation ditch, we entered a second olive grove, where the olives were dark, almost black, and the trees more widely dispersed.

"We pick these next month," Baruch said. "If they are still here. You see anything unusual?"

We approached one of the trees, a small one that had several lower branches broken off. "See that? Happened two nights ago. About thirty trees hit like this. One right after the other. Just lucky we weren't here."

"Jesus Christ!"

Baruch smiled. "Not him this time. Another friend — Mohammed."

When we returned to the grove where everyone was working, I was assigned — with Baruch's "deepest apologies" — to an olive tree. The sun was already simmering overhead, and the whole area was as muggy as a greenhouse. The kids, however, seemed oblivious to it now, and were plucking away at the large green olives.

"No, not like that!" Charna corrected a thin, pimple-faced girl beside me. "You don't pick olives one by one. You milk them." She climbed quickly up the girl's ladder, grabbed a full branch of olives, held the branch over her sack, and then in one downward swipe of her fingers she pulled about twenty olives into her sac. "Milk them, see?"

The girl nodded and climbed slowly back onto her ladder.

"How about you?" Charna looked in my direction. "You're Michael, right?"

"Yes."

"You know how to pick, don't you?"

"Sure."

"Good. And remember. Four boxes today. That's the quota. You should finish by breakfast. Assuming you *do* know how to pick!" She flashed me a smile and hurried off.

The girl beside me followed her with angry eyes. "You forgot to salute her," she said in mock seriousness. "Assuming you *do* know how to salute!"

"What the hell is this — an army camp?" muttered the boy sitting next to me. He stuffed a piece of halvah into his mouth, and rose from the table.

"Come on, let's get going!" repeated Charna, looking at her wristwatch. "Anyone who can't eat breakfast in thirty-five minutes, doesn't deserve it."

"Take it easy," Baruch said gently to her. He was sitting at the table near Charna, and had just started making a salad. "I want to eat in peace."

Charna looked at him indulgently, and left. Baruch glanced over to see if I was watching, then winked, and motioned for me to join him. I poured myself another cup of coffee and moved over to his table.

"Can't let her get to you," he said matter-of-factly, as I sat down. He shoveled a spoonful of salad into his mouth. "Heat, flies, Arabs — same thing. Got to learn to parry them."

"Any suggestions?"

"Training. Takes training." Another spoonful into the mouth. "And understanding. Can't do anything till you understand them."

Charna reappeared and called me, but Baruch nonchalantly waved her off with his spoon. She protested — something about my receiving "special treatment" — but Baruch went right on waving, and she stalked off.

"Soft as jelly, once you get to know her," Baruch said.

"Perhaps."

"Not perhaps. Definitely." He smiled broadly, and with a piece of rye bread brushed the flies away from his plate. "Hell, what could you know about her, anyway?"

"Nothing much. Just what I've heard today."

"Lies. All lies. She's soft as jelly, believe me. Everything she does is a show. A bluff. Believe me."

I shook my head unbelievingly and Baruch began explaining what I didn't know about Charna. She was not born in Bilat, he said, but came here when she was about twenty. She didn't really want to come. He knew this because he was friends with her husband, Motti — they were from the same class — and the two of them had discussed it. Motti felt he had to stay in Bilat, his family was here, and the kibbutz needed him as an economic planner. Charna, on the other hand, came from an established kibbutz in the Jezreel Valley, and wanted to follow her brother to a new kibbutz in the Negev. Motti and Charna argued about it, and in the end — as was usually the case — the man won. They stayed here.

Charna was slow to fit into the kibbutz. At first, she was very shy, very nervous. She didn't make friends easily, and was really something of a problem. Motti got worried about her and decided that it would be best, after all, if they went to the Negev. But now Charna refused. One member of her family in the Negev was enough, she said. So they stayed here. And slowly, after a few years, she began to slip out of her shyness. She had a few kids, began working outdoors — instead of in the laundry — and made a few friends.

"I wouldn't say she was the happiest person who ever set foot in Bilat," Baruch continued, "but she got along. That's the point. About four years ago, she decided that she wanted to move from the vineyards to the olive groves. I was head of the olives then, and she asked how I felt about it. She was a good worker and I was glad to have her. And she really worked out well. In the first year, she designed a new *tarmeel* (olive-picker's sack), and it doubled the amount of work we were able to do in a day: other kibbutzim have picked up the patent. She also designed those push-along ladders we use, and reorganized our work schedule to include the high school kids. And best of all, she took over for me whenever I was away for reserves or something like that. She was terrific. Wonderful. There was never any of this lieutenant stuff that she dishes out now. That's only a recent development."

Baruch hesitated and looked over in the direction of the groves. He got up from the table, and wiped his hands on his pants. "The last year or so she's gotten like that. I think it's her brother. Poor devil got killed two years ago in an accident, got pinned underneath his tractor and was crushed to death. In the Negev. Early in . . ." Baruch stopped short. Charna was walking quickly towards us, her dark eyes angry, threatening.

"Dammit!" she said loudly. "Nobody is working today. You guys take an hour for . . ."

Baruch held up his hand. "We're coming."

"Well, it's about time!"

"I was just telling Michael you'd be along any minute . . ."

"Glad I didn't disappoint you."

" . . . and you'd invite us back to work . . ."

"Sure!"

" . . . and that, deep down, you were the easiest, most soft-hearted boss he would ever have."

"Cut the crap, Baruch."

"It's true."

"Cut it, I tell you. I've had enough for one day. Cut it."

Baruch shrugged nonchalantly, and we walked off to the olive trees, as Charna stood there watching us, her hands on her hips, the sweat pouring down her face and onto the clinging, white tee-shirt.

An Attack

That same evening, after my first day's work in the olive groves, there was a mortar attack. It happened about 8:00 P. M., when most of the kibbutz was in the theater watching, of all damn things, *High Noon*. I had seen it about five times, so I decided to pass it up. Instead, I was sitting in the the kibbutz *Moadone* (clubroom) reading a three-week-old copy of *Life* and sipping a glass of lemonade. Hardly anyone else was there. Only the soft whir of the fan and the occasional ping of a moth that flew into the screened windows, disturbed the stillness.

Then, I was running. Through the six-foot deep trench outside the *Moadone,* around the dining hall, scared like never before. Running without thinking, the stones at the bottom of the trench slowing me down; the bombs shattering above me.

"Take it easy! Take it easy!" The barrel-chested man at the entrance to the shelter held up both his hands. It was Saul, the shoeman.

"Sorry, sorry," I mumbled.

"Go down there. Relax."

I nodded, trying to catch my breath, but didn't move.

"Damned close," he said seriously. "In the kibbutz. Must have landed inside." He looked out at the darkness, seeming to sniff the air. "Find out soon enough."

I nodded again, and went down the double flight of steps, through the heavy iron door, and into the shelter. It was like entering someone's living room. Five or six people were sitting there on the thin-mattressed beds, their eyes glued to the T.V. set. They barely noticed me come in. Only a little girl, who was fidgeting in her mother's arms, watched as I sat down. I tried to smile at her, but she turned away and hid behind her mother.

" ... *Meanwhile there has been mounting tension between the Jordanian Army and the terrorists,"* the crisp, young news commentator was saying on the T.V. *"There were reports last night of new shooting incidents in the Jordanian capital, and the terrorists today charged that King Hussein is — quote — no longer fulfilling his commitments according to the July 14th pact' — end quote. The July 14th pact, it should be remembered, gave the terrorists a virtually free hand in their military operations in Jordan. However — according to political analysts here in Jerusalem — should King Hussein go ahead and make a positive response to the nearly month-old proposals set forth by U.S. Secretary of State Rogers, he would then be inviting almost certain reprisals from the terrorists; reprisals which, in the opinion of several analysts, could topple his shaky regime ..."* The commentator paused.

"Lovely people," muttered the thin, gray-haired woman sitting next to me. The old man at her left said nothing, but continued watching the T.V. "One day they shoot at each other, the next day they shoot at us."

"Sssh!" said the man. "Weather forecast."

"Excuse me," she answered. Then she turned to me. "Lovely people. I wish them luck on the days they shoot at each other." She smiled gently.

The T.V. commentator began talking about the weather in the same well-brushed tone that he had just used to describe the political situation in Jordan. Cool tomorrow in Jerusalem. Hot in Beersheva. Mild in Haifa. Hot in Tiberias.

"*Oy!*" said the woman. "The heat, it never stops." She looked at me with her watery-blue eyes. "It's worse than the bombs."

"Sssh!"

The woman cupped her pale, bony hands around her mouth. "Worse than the bombs. The heat hits *everyone*. Isn't any way to ..." She stopped short as the heavy iron door leading into the shelter suddenly flew open and banged against the cement wall. Saul stood there, his eyes wild.

"Hassan's been hit!" he said excitedly. "Hassan and three or four others!"

"My God!"

"How bad?"

Saul walked a few steps into the shelter. The old man turned off the T.V.

"Nobody knows yet," Saul said. "They took Hassan away in the ambulance."

"Oh my God!"

"The others?" asked the old man, his voice shaky. "Who are they?"

"Volunteers. They came yesterday."

"My God!" sighed the woman again. Then to me: "Children. Teenagers. They come for vacation on the kibbutz, and look what happens."

I didn't answer. Instead I asked Saul if he knew what was doing outside. "Clear," he said tersely. "No word yet from the security people, but it looks clear. Nothing for the last ten minutes."

I got up and started to walk towards the door.

"Don't go!" the woman shouted after me. "Not yet. Wait!"

Saul walked over to her and said something softly which I didn't hear, and I left.

Over by the theater, three or four soldiers were walking about slowly, their flashlights trained on the ground. Several kibbutzniks stood by watching them. I couldn't, however, see who they were because it was very dark and nobody was talking.

"Check the walls, too!" yelled the officer in the rear.

The soldiers beamed their flashlights on the outside walls of the theater, looking for shrapnel marks. I walked a bit closer to the half-dozen kibbutzniks who were milling around, and I recognized one of them — the Argentinian boy who was in Hassan's class. I asked if he knew what had happened.

"Yes," he answered without looking at me. His eyes remained on the soldiers.

"Was Hassan hit bad?" I persisted.

"In the back. Yes. Bad."

"The others?"

"Nicked. Legs, arms, nothing bad." He moved away.

The soldiers had turned their flashlights away from the theater walls and back toward the ground. They were walking in our direction.

"I don't think anything hit here," said one soldier to the officer. The officer signaled for his men to follow him, and I saw, for the first time, that he was carrying something in his hand. I moved closer to see what it was.

"82 mm. job," the officer said matter-of-factly, holding the broken end of a mortar up in front of his flashlight.

"Where did it hit?" I asked.

"Up there," He pointed to the path in front of him, in the direction of the dining hall.

"Is that where they got hit?"

"Couldn't say. I wasn't here."

The soldiers filed past us. "Have to come back tomorrow," said the officer as he passed the kibbutzniks. "Can't find a damn thing anymore."

The kibbutzniks nodded, and silently went home.

The following morning, we waited until 7 o'clock before leaving for the olive groves. Charna said she didn't want to go at all, but Baruch told her she was being ridiculous. How would the kids feel if we didn't work because of what had happened last night? Sure they were afraid, sure they were thinking about Hassan — he knew that, but it wouldn't do any good to sit up in the kibbutz and wait for the news. It would only make things worse. Finally Charna agreed. It was better to work, she said. That way nobody would think about it.

And so, we spent the morning picking olives, nobody paying much attention to the work, and everyone speculating what had happened to Hassan. "He was the last one out of the theater," said Danit, as we were walking back to the trees after breakfast. "I kept telling him to move. But not him! 'I gotta see the ending,' he kept saying. If they hadn't shut the movie off, he would have gone right on sitting there." The boy walking in front of her turned around abruptly, and added: "And he never would have gotten hit!"

The Wedding

"How could it be *worse?*"

"If we hadn't gone along."

"I don't see it."

"Then open your eyes, Uzi. The Americans say no *Phantoms*, no *Skyhawks*. The world says Israel deserves what it gets. The Russians try to cross the Canal. There is war. And the Americans watch."

"They will watch anyway."

"Don't be so sure."

"And you, Bierman, *you* are sure?"

"No, I'm not sure. Who can be sure?"

"*I* am sure." Hannah smiled diplomatically, and pushed the dishes of ice cream at Uzi and Bierman. Uzi pushed his dish to the side angrily, and ran his thick fingers through his hair, and then down around his face. "I'm not hungry," he said. He stood up. "I'm going to shave."

Hannah raised her eyebrows, but said nothing. There was a long silence as Bierman slurped up his ice cream, and Hannah sat there staring at him.

"I told you, Bierman, not to start with him." Hannah's face was flushed with anger, and she was shouting at Bierman in a whisper.

"He talks nonsense. The cease-fire has already ..."

"Don't cease-fire me. *You* cease fire!"

"All right, calm yourself."

"I told you not tonight."

"Let's forget it."

"Any other night, but not tonight. He doesn't need anything more to upset him."

"All right, let's forget it."

Hannah stood up huffily and left for the bedroom "to get ready." Bierman watched her leave, shaking his head in exasperation, and then turned to me. "The boy talks nonsense, and she wants us to sit here and listen to it. Anyone who cannot see that we had to go along is blind. Foolish."

Bierman looked at me closely, waiting for my reaction, though he already knew I agreed with him. We had discussed it just two evenings before when Golda Meir announced that the cease-fire would begin at midnight. It was sooner than we had expected, and most of us were — in spite of our voiced apprehensions — still convinced that the government had made the right decision. A month earlier, of course, we hadn't felt this way: we hadn't wanted Israel to go along with the Rogers proposals. But once Nasser had returned from the Soviet Union and said yes, and then Hussein went along too, there seemed to be no alternative. We had to accept the proposals. We had to accept them, and we had to sit tight now and wait for Nasser's next move (We all expected Egypt to soon violate the cease-fire agreement.), and we had to listen to all those right-wing critics in the government — and the kibbutz — who told us that we were trying to sell Israel down the river.

"Now we are going to have some new fireworks," Bierman had predicted that evening. "As soon as there is a cease-fire with our neighbors, we start fighting among ourselves. It's an old Jewish tradition."

"Bierman!" Hannah called from the bedroom. "Don't tell me you are planning to go like that?" Bierman was wearing his baggy tan pants, and white tee-shirt.

"No, I'm just keeping Michael company."

"Well, come in and get dressed. I'm sure he won't get lonely."

Bierman shrugged apologetically, and went into the bedroom. Uzi was still in the bathroom shaving, primping for the wedding that he didn't want to attend. I couldn't blame him; not if what Hannah told me was true. According to her, Uzi had been in love with Aviva — the girl from the vineyards — and he was secretly hoping to marry her once he finished his military duty. However, in the meantime, Aviva had met another boy — a volunteer from The Hebrew University who spent a month in Bilat — and before Uzi knew it, she had dumped him and announced her wedding plans. It had been a terrible blow to him, coming as it did right after he was wounded at the Canal, and Hannah was worried about him. Particularly tonight.

"Uzi, dear!" Hannah called to the bathroom, as she and Bierman came out of the bedroom. "I know you want to have a nice shave, but please ... Seven-thirty, it begins."

"Just about done," Uzi answered.

"We are all waiting for you."

"I'm coming."

The hum of the electric razor stopped, and Uzi exited from the bathroom, buttoning up his white shirt.

"Hmm!" sighed Hannah. "You smell wonderful. You must be using new after-shave lotion."

"It's Bierman's."

"Ah, no wonder!"

"I thought I'd try it."

"Go right ahead," said Bierman. "Keep it if you want."

"No thanks."

"Really, it's yours if you want it."

"Go ahead, keep it," added Hannah. "On you it smells wonderful. Even better than on Bierman."

Uzi forced a smile, and tucked his shirt into his pants. Hannah stood there for a long moment nodding her approval. Then as if she were a sergeant leading her squadron off to battle, she motioned for us to follow her to the wedding ceremonies.

Underneath the avocado trees that grew alongside the apartment house where Aviva's parents lived, a small crowd had already gathered. Most, of course, were kibbutzniks, well-scrubbed and simply dressed, but there was also a large contingent of guests, distinguishable by their suits and ties, coiffed hair, jewelry, and one blue-haired lady that stood in their midst, cradling in her arms a fully-dressed pink poodle.

"The groom's relatives," Hannah commented, nodding towards the pink-poodle people. "The groom's father is supposed to be a *macher* in Tel Aviv. Lots of money."

"We can do without the explanations," Bierman said curtly.

"It's not true?"

"It's not important."

"We will see!"

Hannah smiled knowingly at me. A week before, the same evening she had told me about Uzi and Aviva, she had also commented on "Uzi's replacement." Personally, she said, she had nothing against him. He evidently was a smart boy — an engineering student — and he had informed the kibbutz that once he and Aviva were married, he wanted to live here and work in the new, electrical parts factory which was starting next year (Bilat's first factory). However, said Hannah, "I'll believe it when I see it. A boy with a college degree and a businessman father in Tel Aviv ... Well, we'll see how long he stays with us."

Now Hannah grabbed my arm. "Over there! Coming out of the door!" I turned my head toward the apartment house where Aviva's parents lived. They were coming in our direction — Aviva in a knee-length white dress and white hat with a veil, and the groom in black slacks and an open-necked white shirt. Behind them, chatting as they walked, were Aviva's parents, the groom's parents, and a red-bearded rabbi. The rabbi was carrying a black book in one hand, and the traditional *chupah* (four poles with a cloth canopy) in the other.

When they reached the crowd of kibbutzniks and guests, they faded into it. Aviva and the groom were surrounded by young people — soldiers, students, Aviva's friends. Bierman suggested to Uzi that he join the young people, but Uzi wouldn't budge, and Hannah told Bierman to leave him alone. Bierman shrugged, and went over to chat with the rabbi.

Several minutes later, after Bierman had rejoined us, the rabbi called everyone together beneath the avocado trees. Four men — two soldiers, Aviva's brother, and her uncle — held the *chupah* over the heads of the bride and groom. The rabbi was in front of them, and all of us gathered around them.

"*Baruch Attah Adonai...*" The prayers began, the rabbi's red beard moving up and down. Menachem, the pudgy kibbutz photographer, brought over a wooden stool, stood on it, and began photographing the ceremony. *"Elohaynu Melech Ha'olam..."* Aviva's cherubic face looked up at the rabbi, then across at the groom, then up at Menachem. Flash! "Caught it!" Menachem whispered excitedly, leaning back on the stool; and no sooner had the words left his mouth, when the stool teetered, a leg split, and Menachem tumbled to the ground, his camera and flash-attachment landing on top of him. Everyone turned around abruptly. *"...V'Anachnu Ha Yom..."* But not the rabbi; he continued as if nothing had happened.

Five, ten minutes more, the rabbi prayed onward, the black book open in front of him, the red beard bobbing up and down. Aviva was smiling uncontrollably now. And Menachem had gotten back on his feet, and went over to get a more sturdy chair. He came back just in time to photograph the rabbi pouring wine into the glass. Aviva drank first, and then the groom drank. (Uzi looked away.) The rabbi wrapped the glass in a white cloth napkin, and placed it on the ground. The groom smiled once more at Aviva, then lifted his right foot off the ground and stomped on the glass, smashing it to bits. Everyone cheered and the new kibbutz couple embraced. (Uzi was gone.)

"I don't know where he is," said Hannah, trying to appear calm. "He'll get over it. I'm sure he'll get over it." She handed the soup tureen to Eton, and continued looking at Yael.

We were sitting now in front of the dining hall where the tables were set up in six long rows, and covered with white tablecloths. As usual, we were eating chicken. The lawn was lit by strings of light bulbs, and at the far end there was a make-shift wooden stage that stood immediately in front of shelter 24. A five-piece band from the neighboring kibbutz was playing bauble-like music.

"Of course, he'll get over it," Yael confirmed. "He's no baby."

Hannah looked at her coldly.

"Better to learn about such things when he's young," Yael added, for good measure.

"Your soup is getting cold," Bierman said to her, curtly.

Yael quietly ate her soup. Hannah was busy watching the goings-on at the edge of the lawn.

"Look at them, Bierman!" Hannah said excitedly. "Oh, wonderful!" she started clapping in time with the hora music.

The band stepped up the tempo, and the soldiers who had spontaneously begun to dance, tried to keep up with them — their heads thrown back, their black Army boots shining, "... *Ooh! Ooh! Ooh-rokdeem v'lesameach...*" Everyone was singing, laughing, clapping with them. Bierman up on his feet clapping, Hannah on her feet, "...*Ooh-rokdeem v'lesameach, Ooh-rokdee ... ee ... eemm ...,*" the circle of khaki still swirling, still yelling and singing, "*v'lesameach ... a ... ach,*" until the music burst, and suddenly it was over.

Hannah was dripping wet as she sat down, and so was Bierman. The two of them looked at each other and laughed — laughed like they were sixteen years old, and had just met.

"Oh, wonderful!" sighed Hannah again, returning to her cold soup.

"Soldiers," said Bierman. "Leave it to them!"

At the edge of the lawn now, standing on the wooden stage and tapping on the microphone, was the kibbutz gym teacher, Hanasi. "One, two, three, testing ..."

"Jackass," mumbled Yael, looking up at Hanasi. "He doesn't have enough sense to let people finish their food. No, he's got to start already with his miserable jokes. And look at him, like he's going for a swim."

Hanasi was wearing sandals, white shorts, a short-sleeve blue pullover, and his usual toothy smile. He had a reputation for lousy jokes, and nobody could remember how or why he had become the unofficial emcee for such occasions.

Our corner of the table more or less ignored Hanasi as he made a welcoming speech to the groom's relatives (Hannah said there were at least two hundred.), congratulating them on behalf of their "comrades in Bilat." We continued eating, polishing off the chicken, fruit compote, and the chocolate ice cream bars that the high-school kids passed out. As the meal ended, Hannah and Bierman stood up and excused themselves; they were part of the evening's entertainment, Hannah said.

"What?" I asked in astonishment.

"You will see," Hannah said teasingly, as she and Bierman were leaving. Then to Yael: "Don't tell him. Let it be a surprise."

Shortly after they were gone, the band started up again, this time playing "Jerusalem of Gold." Hanasi, still at the microphone, boomed out that the bride and groom were coming, "softly making their way towards us, ladies and gentlemen, Aviva and Aron in their luxury coach, ladies and gentlemen..." He flung out his left arm towards the asphalt road behind the stage and the shelter. There, chugging in our direction, seated snugly in an improvised love-seat that was six feet off the ground in the jagged-toothed mouth of the kibbutz bulldozer, was the new kibbutz couple.

"Ladies and gentlemen, the bride and groom — Aviva and Aron ..." The couple sat there, smiling as though they were on television. Then, the love-seat was lowered to the level of the stage, and Aviva and the groom got out and casually brushed themselves off.

The rest was anti-climactic. Drora congratulated the couple. A little girl dressed in white gave them a bouquet of red, kibbutz-grown roses. And each of the newlyweds delivered a short thank-you speech. When this was over, Hanasi again returned to the microphone and introduced the first bit of entertainment — songs by Ruthy's class.

"So what do you think?" Eton asked, talking to me for the first time that evening.

"A typical Jewish wedding it isn't," I answered flippantly.

"How do you know?" Yael challenged.

I didn't answer.

"Actually," she continued, a slick smile flitting across her lips, "I'd expect you to be familiar with this kind of thing."

I looked at her questioningly, not sure what she was driving at.

"Money. Jews in America don't have money? They don't throw big weddings?"

"So?"

"So, look at our *honored* guests this evening. That woman with her stupid little dog."

"She seems out of place."

"The whole *bunch* of them are out of place!"

Yael took a long swallow of iced-tea, looked for a moment at the children on stage, then looked again at me. She seemed slightly calmer. "I told Uzi, when he first began with her, I told him he was looking for trouble. Aviva was only playing with him. She didn't give a damn about him. She wanted money. Money and a chance to leave the kibbutz. That's the way she's always been."

"It's not worth discussing," said Eton, putting his hand lightly — too lightly — on Yael's shoulder.

Yael looked at him disgustedly, and then, in a sarcastic voice, continued: "Boy from the city meets girl from the kibbutz. Boy has money, girl has none. Boy marries girl, comes to kibbutz; brings record player, hi-fi set, fancy furniture. Boy spends year in kibbutz. Very polite. Boy takes girl back to city. End story." Yael smiled nastily.

"Who cares?" said Eton feigning indifference.

"I do!" answered Yael. "I do, because it damn well isn't fair." She tossed her head back, flinging her long brown hair out of her face. "When we were married, what did we get? Fancy furniture, hi-fi sets, record players? Hell, no. All we got was seventy pounds from the kibbutz to go on a honeymoon; seventy pounds, and another twenty for the ring." Yael thrust out her left hand for me to see the thin gold band on her wedding finger. "We didn't have big-shot relatives in Tel Aviv to give us hundreds of pounds cash for a luxury honeymoon by the sea, or fancy furniture and all that other stuff."

"What does it matter?" interrupted Eton.

"It matters, dammit! It matters. If they have a right to those things, so do I. So do you. So does Michael ..."

"Sssh!" said the old couple sitting a few yards away from us. "We want to hear!"

Yael looked at the old couple, then added in an angry whisper, "It matters, dammit. I tell you, it matters."

On the stage, Hanasi was turning his Ed Sullivan smile on the group of high-school kids who had just finished a series of folk dances. Then, with a joke about some "religious visitors from the Old Country," Hanasi introduced the next, and last entertainers. The band started up, softly, almost plaintively, and coming out of the shelter, one by one, was a row of black-clad figures. They ambled up to the stage, dancing now, and you could see them more clearly. Bierman and Hannah, Talik and Zelda, Zakkai and Rachel — five couples in all — dressed as Hasidic Jews, with black caftans, black hats, fake beards and side-curls on the men, and black dresses and kerchiefs on the women. The music became louder, gayer, like something out of *Fiddler on the Roof,* and the five couples whirled around, shouting and singing in Yiddish. Everyone stood up to watch, all six hundred of us, standing on the chairs and benches, clapping our hands, as the band played for all it was worth.

"Look at Bierman!" said Yael, laughing. "Look at my father!"

The ten black figures came dancing down off the stage, one after the other, with Talik leading them. They circled around Aviva and Aron, their hands waving wildly in the air, still shouting in Yiddish, still laughing.

"Look at my father!" repeated Yael. And there he was in the back of the line, everyone else whooping it up except him — Bierman the Hasid, Bierman with the long side-curls and grandfather's beard, Bierman with his arms folded across his chest, his legs kicking stiffly, his face as stern and unsmiling as a Polish winter, Bierman the Hasidic Jew at the wedding of *apikorsim.*

Guard Duty

Every man who could fight had a weapon in his room. It had begun in late '67, shortly after the first intrusions of *Al Fatah.* Rushing to the padlocked ammunitions storeroom wouldn't be quick enough, they decided, so weapons were passed out. Usually it was an Uzi, but sometimes it was nothing more than a single-shot rifle with fifty or a hundred rounds of ammunition; and sometimes it was a Russian *Kalachnikov,* the superb long-range rifles that *Al Fatah* used, and that a few of the Six-Day War veterans now owned, but wouldn't tell you about.

Even I had a weapon, at one point. Rafael gave it to me, since he had two. It was a single-shot job with fifty rounds of ammunition, and it was the first weapon I had owned since I was eleven years old and lost my slingshot. However, kibbutz and military regulations being what they were, Shimon, the kibbutz security chief, soon confiscated it. "But don't worry," Rafael had consoled me, after

Shimon removed the rifle from my room, "if you want to catch *Al Fatah*, I have a much better method. Foolproof." And with that, he tacked up on my wall a long strip of yellow flypaper.

At the time, it was a good joke — a racist joke perhaps, but still a good joke — and Rafael had carried on for the next hour or so about the military ineptitude of the terrorists. But several nights later when the mortars had exploded inside the kibbutz, and Hassan almost got killed (as it turned out, he lost a kidney), the flypaper on my wall didn't seem so funny. Nor did it amuse us, that while Nasser and Hussein had agreed to a cease-fire, *Al Fatah* repeatedly vowed to continue their "war of liberation."

We knew what that meant; or at least, we thought we did. Sooner or later, *Al Fatah* would have a show-down with Hussein, and we all expected it to take the form of an open flaunting of the cease-fire by *Al Fatah,* or in other words, increased attacks on border kibbutzim. Evidently, military people in Tel Aviv had the same expectations, because when I went there in the early part of August and tried to get permission to go out on a night patrol down by the Yarmuk, I was strongly discouraged. It was far too dangerous; now, more than ever.

So, if I wanted to have a look at what went on down by the Yarmuk at night, I would have to do my looking from the kibbutz gates — with the permission of the guards. This was a little disappointing, but not a complete letdown. I had been out on guard duty the year before, when I came to write a magazine article, but I had found out almost nothing. They had been very suspicious. "Is your article going through the army censor?" was the first thing they wanted to know. When I told them it wasn't, they didn't want to let me go. Then, by the end of the week, they reluctantly allowed me a quick peep, with the apology that, "You never can be sure. Spies could come by here anytime without our knowing it." The whole thing was understandable, but still unpleasant (especially considering all the olives I had picked), and I was relieved this time when Shimon told me, "There's no problem at all. I'll arrange it for you tomorrow with Zakkai. No problem at all."

We met outside the dining hall at 7:00 P. M. The sun was just going down, and a few late afternoon swimmers were clopping by in their rubber sandals, flicking their towels at each other. Zakkai was walking right behind them, his Uzi draped casually over his left shoulder. As usual, he was singing to himself. When he noticed me sitting there on the bench, he waved in a kind of half-salute, and greeted me — "Comrade Gorki!"

"How is our great Russian novelist doing this evening?"

"Tired."

"A pity. We'd better go have some coffee."

We went into the kitchen, drank a cup of stale coffee, and chatted briefly about his son, Ami, who was still away on reserve duty — "in a safe spot now: the Canal." Then, leaving by the rear door, we walked towards the kibbutz front gate where Zakkai was on guard duty. When we were almost there, he veered off behind some huge bushes that stood protectively in front of a padlocked room.

"I'm sure you want to have a look at this," he said, flipping a key ring out of his pocket. "The ammunitions storeroom."

He opened the heavy iron door, and we entered the room — an arsenal really — that was stacked from floor to ceiling with a wide variety of hand weapons.

"Not like in '48," he said laughingly, as we left. "Let them come pay us a visit sometime and find out." We returned to the main driveway that led towards the kibbutz front gate. It was dark when we got there. A soldier was waiting for us, and he shined his flashlight in our faces as we approached.

"*Erev tov*, Benjy," Zakkai boomed out, in his guttural Yemenese accent.

"Who's this?" the soldier answered suspiciously. He flashed the light in my face.

"Comrade Gorki. He's going to be spending the night with us. At least, until he falls asleep."

"Who is he?"

"A friend, Benjy. A Jew. Now give me your damned flashlight and go eat your supper."

The soldier said nothing, but handed Zakkai the flashlight and left.

"Security precautions," Zakkai said, after the soldier was gone. "They've gotten very careful now, since those boys from the Rotary were shot. Can't really blame them."

He removed the Uzi from his shoulder, laid it down on the bench (he kept the clip in his pocket), and went over to make sure the front gate was shut. He turned his flashlight on the sandbag-lined trenches next to the bench, and called over to me: "See these trenches, here?"

"Yes."

"The guard was sleeping here ... Excuse me, he was guarding here — I just assume he was sleeping — and he woke up, got scared, and fired at point-blank range at the Rotary boys who were coming from over there." Zakkai flashed his light up the road that led to the cowshed. "Boys never had a chance. A real shame." He turned off the flashlight and came back to the bench.

"What ever happened with the guard?" I asked. "I remember the police took him away."

"I don't really know. I don't think his case has come up yet. No, not till the end of the year, I think I heard Shimon say."

"What do you expect will happen?"

"They'll put him away. A year, maybe two."

"That much?"

"Oh yes. Hell, yes. He's lucky if he doesn't get more." Zakkai reached for his Uzi, and slung it back over his shoulder. "Can't kill a man just like that and get away with it. Hell, no."

I didn't really agree with Zakkai, but I saw no point in arguing with him. Instead, I asked a few general questions about guard duty, and why it was that he, Zakkai, had a reputation for loving this night-watchman's job.

Zakkai laughed. "Who told you that? Well, whoever told you, has good information. I do love it."

He took a package of cigarettes out of his folded shirtsleeve, offered me one, then lit up one for himself. He drew deeply, and pointed with the cigarette towards the sky. "The night — look at it. Who can help loving it?"

He drew again, and started telling me about his "love affair with the night." He hadn't always loved it. In fact, he used to be afraid of it. His parents came from Yemen, and they brought with them that Arab superstition of the night. As a boy and even as a young man, he was afraid of darkness. However, when he came to Bilat in his early twenties, they assigned him to the night-watch-man job, and he was too embarrassed to tell them he was afraid of the dark. He would sit out there on his horse, rifle in hand, "waiting for them — wolves, jackals, Arabs, anything — to come charging out of the bushes.

"But soon I grew used to it. There were no wolves or jackals, or even Arabs. Oh well, maybe once in awhile the Arabs would come rob some vegetables — a few tomatoes, bananas. But all you had to do was fire a shot into the air, and they'd go scampering away like rabbits. Very simple." Zakkai snuffed out the cigarette, and chuckled to himself. "The whole job was very simple. Very simple, and very beautiful. Riding around through the banana groves at night, looking at the sky. The calmness, the night air .... Well, look at it. Who could help falling in love with it?"

Zakkai tilted his head toward the sky, then turned abruptly towards the kibbutz driveway, as a set of headlights was coming quickly in our direction. He went to the gate, shoving the clip into the Uzi as he walked. Then, seeing that it was an army truck, he unbolted the gate and let them in.

"What's the hurry?" he asked the young driver.

"Nothing, pop. Amos, here, has to take a crap."

"Tell Amos to learn some control."

"Thanks for the advice, pop."

The truck sped off. Zakkai returned to the bench, shaking his head and smiling. He took the clip out of the Uzi and put it back into his pocket.

"Where were we?"

"The night. Falling in love with the night."

"Right." Zakkai took out another cigarette and lit up. "The *Palmach*. I also learned to love the night in the *Palmach*." The *Palmach* was the "striking force" of the *Haganah*, the illegal Jewish defense organization during the time of the British Mandate.

"Did you know that one of the first *Palmach* camps was here. Started in '41, if I remember right."

"I thought the *Palmach* began before that."

"No. The *Haganah*, maybe you're thinking of."

"I guess so."

"You must be. The *Haganah* began in the twenties, you remember."

"I didn't know that."

"Sure, 1920, I think it was. Most of its members were in the kibbutzim or moshavim. That's how I began — in 1935. When a counterattack or defensive action was needed, someone would call us, and we'd go do what had to be done. Then we'd come back. There was no full-time organization, that was the problem."

"And the *Palmach* was full-time?"

"Right. Though not in the beginning. As I started to tell you, one of the first camps was here — thirty-five men. Later it was expanded to 120 men, and was called Division Aleph. Yigal Allon was the commander. Dayan became commander of Division Beit. But, anyway, those of us who were in the Bilat camp, lived in the kibbutz, at least in the beginning. We went out on missions about half the month, then came back and did our kibbutz jobs the other half. The kibbutz supplied all our clothes, food — the necessities — when we were away. It was only a year or two later that the *Palmach* organization took over our upkeep, and we became full-time soldiers.... Just a minute."

Zakkai stood up, reached into his pocket, and took out the flashlight. Someone was coming from the direction of the dining hall.

"Benjy, what are you doing back?" Zakkai called. The soldier waved for Zakkai to take the light out of his face, but didn't answer. He had a mouth full of food.

"*Nu?*"

"I came back to give you a break," Benjy said, barely getting the words out.

"I thought at 10:00."

"Tonight at 9:00."

"Who said?"

"Meltzer."

"The lieutenant?"

"Yeah, Meltzer."

Zakkai shrugged, and handed Benjy the flashlight.

"Say, Zakkai, you forgot your cigarettes."

"Never mind. You keep them."

"No thanks. These make me sick."

Zakkai laughed, and Benjy gave him back the pack of cigarettes — the kibbutz brand, *Silon*. We walked off. Zakkai asked me if there was any place I wanted to go, and I told him that as long as we had time, I'd like to see where the other guards were stationed. I knew there were eight, but I didn't really know where they were, or what they did.

"Very simple. Why don't we go by way of the cowshed."

We turned around and took a short-cut over to the cowshed. On the way, Zakkai explained that there were five watchtowers strung in a semi-circle along the kibbutz's eastern perimeter, the one facing Jordan. The guards who manned these watchtowers were soldiers — usually reservists — and none of them particularly liked the assignment. It was safe enough, there was hardly ever any action, but it was boring. To keep from falling asleep, they shifted towers every hour "and they complain — it seems to keep them awake."

Zakkai chuckled to himself, and then stopped to point out the watchtower fifty yards or so from the cowshed. The tower was about fifty feet off the ground, a turret with windows, and you could see the silhouette of the guard sitting in it, his machine-gun facing Jordan.

"How about the kibbutz members?" I asked. "Do they ever do guard duty in the towers?"

"Usually not. Usually just at the front gate. It depends on the number of reservists available, the number of kibbutzniks available — things like that." Zakkai shifted the Uzi to his right shoulder, and we continued walking around the cowshed, towards the last row of apartments which sat next to the kibbutz perimeter. "Every male kibbutznik is supposed to be on night-watch duty one week every eight months or so, but you've got to be flexible. Take my son, Ami. He's a tank captain, away on reserves maybe eight weeks a year. Well, when he's home, we don't like to put him on guard duty. It's too much. You've got to be flexible."

"I see."

We passed the rear entrance of the kibbutz, the one that led down to the banana and olive groves. Again, some fifty yards to the east, there was a turret with a guard and machine-gun. Further down in the banana groves, Zakkai said, there were ambush patrols. They waited there all night, every night, for *Al Fatah* to try to come across the Yarmuk and plant mines in the fields. The occasional flares you saw in the sky were fired by our soldiers, and they lit up the entire valley below. Any terrorists who were sneaking across would be seen and "receive a taste of honey."

"How often do they make it across?" I asked, remembering the kibbutznik who two months ago was blown apart by a mine on the water spigot.

"Rarely. We can't afford to let them make it."

Zakkai sat down on a dirt mound near the last row of apartments. He pointed over his shoulder to the apartment where Baruch and Ofra lived. "See over there?"

"Yes."

"Almost had a bad accident three years ago. Shortly after the Six-Day War." Zakkai leaned back on the dirt mound and cupped his hands under his head. "Just lucky those bastards don't know what they're doing. They would have caused real damage. Sixteen kilos of TNT they put next to that house. That's right, they snuck right up here, and tried to blow up that apartment. But instead of putting the TNT under the apartment, and using the right-sized wick, they put it off to the side — about eight meters — and used a wick two meters long. So the stuff never went off. The wick blew out. The night-watchman found it early in the morning. Very lucky."

"Oh, we were specialists. A special division of the *Palmach*. Very interesting work."

We were back at the front gate, and Zakkai had just removed the Uzi from his shoulder, and sprawled out on the bench.

"You couldn't do the kind of work I did," he continued, "unless you looked like an Arab. You had to have Egyptian or Yemenese or Iraqi blood. And you had to have some fluency with the language. Otherwise, it would have been too hard to train you. Too difficult to make you blend in. And a spy who doesn't blend in, is no spy at all."

This blending process, he went on, was something you had to learn. If you had a special accent such as he did — Yemenese — you had to learn to cover it up. This took time, because any slip-up "could cause you problems." Then, depending upon where you were assigned, you had to steep yourself in the culture — local politics, local customs. Every detail was important. You had to learn, for instance, what to say in a barbershop: if a barber, say, in Damascus, asked you how you liked your haircut, you told him he had hands made by God. Or, if you were paying a restaurant bill in Amman, you had to know — according to the clothes you were wearing — just how much money to bring out of your wallet. You couldn't afford to make mistakes.

No, he didn't care to tell me what happened if you made mistakes. I could use my own imagination. Suffice it to say, that you weren't heard from again. Later, a tombstone with your name on it, was put up on Mount Herzl and it said "Fell behind enemy lines." That was all. That was enough.

What did he do? "Oh the usual things," he answered. "Same things spies do everywhere: gather information. For instance, when Abdullah — Hussein's grandfather — was changed from an Emir to a King in Amman, in 1946, we went to see what was going on; what was being said. That sort of thing. Or, let's say the *Palmach* wanted to blow up a police station. We had to find out how many guards were there, when and where they came, and how high the wall was — all kinds of details. The British wouldn't allow a Jew to go near the place, but Arabs could wander about freely. So we went with our robes and headdresses, and we inspected the police station, and we brought back what information was needed.

"The same thing with the illegal ships from Europe. No Jew could get near certain spots to see if they were safe, but as Arabs we saw everything. The night the ship was supposed to arrive, we would sort of drift around the police stations, the army depots, and the landing spots. Then we'd telephone the information to our headquarters, and they'd know what to expect.

"This was all part of the *Aliya Beit* — the illegal smuggling of Jews from all over the world into Palestine — and it was a bit difficult at times. But it was also the thing that gave us the most pleasure — bringing in these Jews from all over. Those from Syria and Lebanon, we sneaked across at night. The usual procedure was for our representatives in Beirut and Damascus to have a group of Jews ready for us at a prearranged place, date, and time. Children, old people, everyone. Sometimes we'd even get a few Arabs who tried to sneak along — as infiltrators. But them you'd get rid of .... Yes, in the usual manner.

"Anyway, we would meet these groups on the Lebanese or Syrian side of the border, and we'd take them by truck to the border with Palestine. Then, we'd grease a few palms — you always carried enough money for these occasions — and the Arab border officials would look the other way. Only once in awhile you had to get tough with them. But usually not. Usually it went smoothly. Then, what we'd do, is drive the people quickly to one of the border kibbutzim, before the British could catch us. We'd slip them into kibbutz clothes, and make them into instant kibbutzniks. Hardly any of them stayed very long, mind you; they usually went on in a week or so to the city or some settlement in the interior. But a few did stay. The best. Yes, the very best ..." Zakkai chuckled to himself. "But, of course, I am prejudiced. You see, my wife is one of them."

Victor

"Why *does* he want to come back?"

"You're asking me?"

"No, not you. Itzy."

Itzy, Zakkai's son, pretended to ignore the question. He climbed a few rungs higher on the ladder, and began picking the black olives at the top of the tree.

"Ask him again," Danit prodded.

David cupped his hands around his mouth. "Say, Itzy — Mister Artist — how about giving us the benefit of your wisdom?"

"Bug off."

"Come on, Itzy," Danit said coyly, "Be nice. He's only asking you a simple question."

"I gave him a simple answer."

"Please. I want to know."

Itzy was silent for a few seconds, and then said: "The whole thing is so damned obvious. Victor feels Bilat is his home. Why the hell can't you understand that?"

"How can he think it's *his* home, after what he said?"

"*What* did he say?" asked Itzy angrily. "I want for once to hear just what he said. I'm tired of all the damned rumors — Victor said *this*, Victor said *that*. Tell me what *you* heard him say."

David hesitated for a moment. "All right, personally, I heard nothing..."

"See!"

"Hold on a second! But if what everyone claims he said is true, then you've got to admit he's got no business coming back."

"David's right."

"The hell he is. Isn't this a democracy here? Can't a man say he likes China or Cuba or Russia, and still live here?"

"Not now he can't," David said. "Not with the Russians dragging their damned missiles up to our throats. Not now."

There was a short silence, and Danit turned to me: "What do you think, Michael? You've just been sitting there, very quiet. Do you think Victor should be allowed to come back?"

Everyone turned to me as if I were some sort of referee, and I thought for a moment what I would tell them. I agreed with Itzy, at least from what I had heard, but I had never met Victor, nor did I really know what had happened. And from what I could gather, Victor's return — or rather, his request for permission to return — was an issue almost as emotionally loaded as Egypt's recent violation of the cease-fire.

Ironically, the two had happened at almost the same time. Only a few days before the violations were announced, the *Masceeroot* had received a letter from Victor. According to Bierman, who read the letter, Victor had finished his poultry-raising course in England, and was coming back to Israel. He, Victor, was aware that there was some hard feeling in the kibbutz against him ("A real clairvoyant," commented Hannah), but he was anxious to come back and clear it up. His stay in England — he wrote — had convinced him that he needed a country, and neither South Africa, where he was born, nor England, where his family lived, felt like his country: Israel was *his* country. And Bilat, he felt, was his home in Israel.

"*Nu*, Michael," Danit repeated, "how do you feel about it?"

"Well, from what I know, he ought to be given a chance to come back and at least state his case. That, I think..." I stopped short. Someone was shaking my ladder.

"What's going on here?" Charna demanded to know. "Why aren't you people working?"

"I've already filled my four boxes," Itzy quipped.

"Never mind the wise-cracks. Today is no day for fooling around." She pointed to the army half-truck and four soldiers who had been watching over our olive-picking crew since 4:00 A. M. "We want to finish these trees and get out of here."

"Yes, ma'am."

"Don't ma'am me, Itzy. You want to fool around, and waste your time talking politics, do it later. Not in the olive groves. Now, let's get a move on it!"

"There are two things I have never liked — cops and reporters." Victor said this matter-of-factly, as if he were commenting on the weather; still he agreed to talk with me, but outside the dining hall, where "there are not so many ears listening to us."

He was not at all what I expected, this Victor. I had pictured a younger man, an angrier man — not this pale, fortyish school-teacher, who looked at me suspiciously from under those thick, metal-rimmed eyeglasses. He seemed very timid, almost scared, and I was sure that had it not been for the warm introduction that Linda had just given me, he would have refused to see me.

When we were outside the dining hall, he said that he wanted to go sit by the pool. Hardly anyone would be there at this hour, and that was just as well: nobody needed to know that he was speaking to reporters. And, if he "had any sense," he wouldn't talk to me at all, because that very afternoon he was having a meeting with the *Masceeroot* to discuss the possibilities of his return to Bilat. Quite frankly, he was worried about it. Formally he was still a member, but from what Linda had told him, some people were slandering him behind his back, and he feared the situation had gotten out of hand. He didn't know whether they would allow him to return.

"The whole thing is sort of vague to me," I said. "All I know for sure is that your coming back has stirred up a lot of feeling. But I don't really know why."

He looked at me suspiciously from under those thick eyeglasses, and asked what it was I wanted to know.

"Anything. Anything and everything that will give me an idea of what is going on."

He took his eyeglasses off, massaged his eyes with the back of his pale hand, and then, in a calm, almost detached voice, he began talking about himself.

From the early 1950's to 1963 he had been a leading member of the South African Congress of Democrats — a political party that was attempting to "alter the racist, exploitative nature of the South African state." As chairman of the Transvaal region, he wrote and spoke frequently, and consequently he was often tailed by the secret police. Then, in 1959, after the Sharpesville massacre, he was jailed for several months — on trumped-up charges — and his family, a wife and four children, were harassed by the police. When he was released from prison, he was deprived of his civil liberties. (He couldn't attend public gatherings, or leave Johannesburg without permission.) Eventually, he lost his job, and his wife divorced him and left for England. Still, he remained in Johannesburg and continued to work covertly with the Congress of Democrats, even after it was banned in 1961. He wrote, he spoke at clandestine meetings, and he organized. But, in 1962, the police again caught up with him, and he was jailed until 1963, when he agreed to leave the country.

"I came to Israel, then, more or less as a refugee. I hadn't been a practicing Jew in South Africa, nor was I by any stretch of the imagination a Zionist. I came to Israel because it was the one place I was sure I could get in, and I chose kibbutz life because it was — maybe still is — vaguely socialist. But I wanted no part of politics. I was through with it. I wanted only one thing, a chance to begin again."

Victor put on his eyeglasses, and looked around at a group of soldiers and high school students who had just jumped into the pool. He waved to one or two of them, then took off the glasses, and resumed: "Within a year or two after I came to Bilat, I began to feel like this was my home. I began to feel like a kibbutznik. Perhaps it was the shift to manual labor — I had never worked with my hands before — or perhaps it was just the lovely simplicity of life in a kibbutz. In any case, I came to love it here, and I applied for membership and they accepted me. This was in 1965."

"It wasn't until two years later, just after the Six-Day War, that I began to have some...some misunderstandings here. I have thought about it a great deal, and you know, I am convinced now that it wasn't I who changed, but they. My politics haven't changed at all since I came to Israel, nor has my rather persistent tendency to speak out whenever I hear someone say something foolish, or worse, bigoted. In this, I haven't changed one iota: but *they* have.

"Take, for example, what happened with the literature I used to receive in the mail. Soviet periodicals, Chinese periodicals, even American propaganda like *Time* and *Life:* I received all of them, right from the beginning, and nobody ever said anything against it. In fact, they were grateful. I used to put them in the clubroom for others to read, and the chap who was in charge of reading material thanked me profusely. Where else could they have obtained such materials at no cost?

"However, after the Six-Day War, this no longer seemed to be their attitude. People started to talk about my receiving communist propaganda, and instead of being grateful that I shared this literature, some of them said that I was deliberately trying to propagandize the kibbutz. Can you imagine such rot? *I* trying to propagandize *them?*" Victor shook his head slowly, and cupped his hands over his ears. He was no longer detached, but confused and even angry.

"What happened during the Six-Day War? I heard vague rumors of things you said, things you did."

"From whom?" he interrupted. "Who has been saying things? What have they been saying?"

I told him I could give no names, only some of the comments if he wanted to hear them. He did. So I told him something Hannah had said (though Bierman disputed it) — namely, that during the war, as the kibbutzniks stood on the roofs watching the Israeli tanks going up the Golan, Victor had said the Israelis deserved to be killed up there, for conquering Syrian territory.

"What?" he blurted out. "I don't believe it!" His jaw hung open, and he looked at me, startled. "I don't believe it. Linda told me they were saying some things...some rotten things, but nothing like this. No, not like this." He ran his thin hands through his sparse sandy hair, then looked at me closely.

"But I'm glad you told me. Now I know better what I'm up against. I hadn't realized things had gotten that bad here. I hadn't realized how anti-democratic they've really become. It's a little like the American McCarthy era. . . .Yes, that's what it's like."

He closed his eyes tightly, then slowly opened them. I asked him again if he would tell me what "misunderstandings" he had with the other kibbutzniks during the Six-Day War, and he said all right, he would let me know "what really happened."

He had been against the June war — completely, unreservedly against it — from the very moment he could see that it was going to break out. That had been in the spring of '67, when it became obvious from the hawkish speeches that Eshkol and certain cabinet members were making, that Israel was once again looking to start a war with Nasser.

"What?"

Yes, he continued, start a war with Nasser. It had been Israel's objective for almost fifteen years to topple Nasser. We hadn't done it in the Sinai War, but we were still determined to do it. Thus, when we threatened Syria in the Spring of '67 and Nasser then came to

Syria's aid — as he had to — we decided to get Nasser once and for all. We lied to the Americans about the number of Egyptian troops in Sinai, so that they would not oppose our going to war against them. That is what really happened, and that is why he was against the war. Nasser's regime may not have been a genuine socialist regime, but it was the most progressive in the area, and he was against toppling it.

"I don't believe it," I blurted out. It was my turn to be startled.

"It's all documented."

"I can't imagine it. The blocking of the Straits of Tiran, the movement of Egyptian troops into Sinai..."

"All documented. I don't want to debate it."

I looked at him closely. He's a madman, I thought. In my wildest revolutionary imagination, I had never doubted that Nasser wanted that war with Israel. In fact, only a few of the most doctrinaire Marxists at my university had talked this way, and them I had dismissed as bad propagandists. Don't tell me this Victor is one of *them?*

"Look," Victor repeated, "it makes no sense even discussing it. It was documented right there for anyone who wanted to see it, but nobody did. Nobody did, and I saw no point in telling them about it." He paused and ran his hands through his hair again. Then, contemplatively: "Wait, maybe with one or two of the younger people I did actually discuss it. Yes, prior to the war, I probably did discuss it with a couple of people."

"How did they react?"

"They didn't agree. We argued, and they didn't agree."

"And that was all that happened?"

Victor stared at me a bit suspiciously. No, he said, that wasn't all that happened. He had gotten into a couple of debates with some of the older kibbutzniks at the time Jerusalem was conquered. There had been great merrymaking in Bilat when it was announced on the radio that Israeli soldiers were inside the walls of the Old City, and had captured the Wailing Wall. Everyone drank to it, but he couldn't. How could an old wall left from Roman times justify the killing of people and conquering of territory?

"But mostly," Victor went on, "if I look back on it, my arguments with some of the people here took place *after* the war. That's when they started making their most outlandish comments, and I was quite unable to stay quiet. I remember once with Sadie, in the *Lool*. I suppose you know I worked there. Well, anyway, I did, and Sadie — if you've ever heard her — has a way of saying whatever nonsense passes through her brain, if you can call it that. She was listening to the news broadcast one time, and she started carrying on about the Arab barbarians; how they are such primitive, cruel people, and how they wouldn't leave the peace-loving Israelis alone. It was a bit much, and I told her so. I told her something to the effect that they will leave us alone, when we stop occupying their territory. Well, that did it. She went flying into a tantrum, ran to the *Masceeroot*, and told them I said we had robbed Arab lands, and the Arabs were right. Actually, I hadn't put it that way, but I wasn't about to try and defend myself. Not *then*. After all, I had fled from a fascist state in South Africa, and I didn't come to a so-called free society to have to defend myself again. So, I said nothing. I let Sadie say what she wanted to the *Masceeroot*, or to anybody else, and I expected — naively, perhaps — that they would take it for what it was."

"I don't see why you expected that, considering your pro-Arab..."

"I beg your pardon. I never said I was pro-Arab. I am not pro-Arab, nor am I anti-Israel. I only maintain, as I have always maintained, that we must live in peace with our neighbors, and not try to expand our territory according to some ancient Greater Israel scheme. That is all."

"Anyway, let me put it this way: in light of your views about the war, I don't see why you assumed nobody would be angry with you, or hold it against you."

"Look, I never assumed that *nobody* would. Some did. I could see that, and it was beginning to make me very uncomfortable. But, look, all I really assume, all I really hope, is that most people here understand that I am a citizen of this country, a member of this kibbutz, and that as a productive member of this society, I am entitled to see things, and say things, as I wish."

"Then why did you leave and go to England?"

Victor put his eyeglasses back on, stood up, and motioned for us to leave. "I saw that the political climate was becoming more conservative — and quite frankly, I didn't know at the time whether or not I wanted to stay here and fight it. I was confused, and needed to get away and think about it. England was an ideal place because my brother lives there, my children are there, and I figured I could spend a year studying poultry farming in one of the agricultural universities. The kibbutz did not vote me permission to go, but I felt I had to go anyway. Other members have left the kibbutz without permission and have come back later with no problems. I expected I could do the same. In fact, I never expected to have this problem now. You see, I love this kibbutz. I felt this even more strongly in England, how dear Israel is to me. Israel is my homeland, and Bilat is my home. I have lived here for seven years, most of my friends are here, and I love it more than any place I have ever been, or can hope to be. I am going to fight with everything I have to convince them of this, and I think I can. I think I will win."

"No, I don't think he has a chance." Rafael leaned back on the bench, and tilted his head up toward the night.

"Why not?"

"Take a look in front of you." He nodded at the large crowd that was filing into the dining hall for the *asifa* — the meeting in which Victor's future would be decided. "You ever see so many people come to an *asifa* before?"

"So?"

"So, that tells you something: they've come to get him. All those years he was here mouthing off, they listened to him and wished they could throw him out. They didn't, then. But now they will."

"You don't sound much like you want him back here, yourself."

"Me? I don't give a damn. He talks nonsense, but hell, a man has a right to talk nonsense if he wants to."

"Assuming the kibbutz is a democracy. Assuming it can *afford* to be a democracy now."

"Of course, it's a democracy." Rafael chuckled, and pointed to Saul, the shoe-man, who was walking into the dining hall with his St. Bernard dog. "See! Even the animals here get a chance to vote."

We followed the dog into the meeting, which was now packed with almost all of the three hundred kibbutzniks. There were no chairs left — only a few footstools along the far end of the wall — and the room vibrated with conversation. Rafael went out to the back patio where the outside T. V. set was located, and brought back two chairs. He then went into the kitchen and scrounged up a couple of oranges, and a platter of cookies. "All right," he said, finally sitting down, "Now we're ready for the main event."

He was just in time. Drora, the kibbutz secretary, was walking briskly up to the front of the dining hall, where the microphone stood alone, like an exclamation point on the bare Formica table.

"Catch Golda," Rafael mumbled. "Very serious tonight. Very solemn. I don't like it."

Drora tapped on the mouthpiece, and the room fell silent.

"Members of Bilat," she began deliberately, "Comrades. I am sure I do not need to tell you that we have before us tonight an issue of paramount concern. A member of our kibbutz, one Victor Lieberman, has left our fold and now wishes to return. The circumstances of his absence, and of his return, have not been altogether clear, and for that reason, the *Masceeroot* committee saw fit to speak with him prior to this meeting. Victor is not with us tonight. We felt that the best possible exchange of opinions might be impeded if he were here, and so he is awaiting our response outside the kibbutz. . ." Drora paused, and waited for a straggle of late-comers to slip in the rear door and become quiet.

She cleared her throat, and again in that deep, somber voice, she resumed. Three days ago, she said, the *Masceeroot* committee spent several hours "clearing the air" with Victor. They had informed him of the intense criticism against him here in Bilat, including the opinions of some people that he was "a member of the *Rakah* wing of the Communist Party." He denied this. True, he had received literature from *Rakah*, but he insisted that he was not now, nor had he ever been a member of the party. The committee felt he was honest in his disavowal.

Then the question came up why he wanted to return to Bilat if there was intense criticism against him. He told the committee that when he left Bilat a year ago, he hadn't realized the extent of his attachment to the kibbutz; nor was he aware of his loyalties to Israel. He came to realize these things while in England, where he sensed himself to be, in his words, "an Israeli in someone else's country." The committee again felt that he was sincere in his statement of his feelings. Nobody of course, could be sure that Victor had changed — only time would reveal that — but in the meantime, it was the opinion of the committee that Victor ought to be given another chance to prove himself: he should be permitted to come back.

"Well, I'll be damned," muttered Rafael, as Drora wound up her short speech. The audience was stirring now, and Drora tapped on the microphone attempting to quiet them down.

"May I have your attention please...Comrades...Comrades of Bilat. We have the *Masceeroot* committee's recommendation before us now..." She rapped with her fist on the table. "May I have your attention please...Thank you. The recommendation is before us. However, before voting on the issue, there no doubt are those who wish to express their opinions. So, please come forward. Let's get on with this."

Heads turned to see who would break the ice, but nobody came. Drora tapped nervously on the microphone — ten seconds, twenty seconds, thirty...and then, in the center of the dining hall, a chair banged against the table, and a man stood up. Bierman.

"Here come the fireworks," whispered Rafael. "Bierman will demolish him."

Everyone watched as Bierman strode up to the microphone, chest thrust forward, proud lion's head steady, a prophet about to deliver. He blew loudly into the microphone to make sure it was ready, and then began.

"Comrades! Let us come quickly to the point. We have heard the recommendation of the *Masceeroot*. We have heard that after meeting several hours with Victor, they are satisfied that he has changed and become one of us. He has joined our family. We all know that at one time Victor was not part of our family. He criticized, he accused — and always as an outsider. A man has a right to his own opinions, a right to speak them openly — we all believe in a free exchange of opinions, but the exchange must be made among members of the same family..."

"Here goes," mumbled Rafael.

"A member of *Rakah* is not one of our family. But the committee tells us Victor is not a *Rakahnik*. A man who does not believe in Israel, is not one of our family. But the committee tells us Victor believes in Israel. Victor has changed. He left Israel, left Bilat and wandered away; and in these wanderings, he has discovered where his home is. His home is here. He has returned. And I say, just as the

Masceeroot committee has said, that we cannot deny him. We must believe him. We must allow him to return."

"Well, I'll be damned," repeated Rafael, chomping on a cookie. "I never expected that."

Bierman returned to his seat, and Drora looked over a flurry of hands, momentarily calculating who to call on next. She pointed to Nimrod, and the sunburned gardener rose slowly, and walked to the microphone.

"I don't understand," he began hesitantly, "I simply cannot comprehend why the *Masceeroot*, why Bierman, think that the kibbutz must become a home for wayward boys." There was an immediate chortle of approval from the audience, and Nimrod, deadpan, waited for them to stop.

He hadn't meant to be funny, he said. Seriously, why should Bilat, at this difficult time, try to accommodate itself to problem children? Maybe if he were a son of the kibbutz, yes; then there would be no choice. But why go looking for troubles? Everyone was perfectly aware that Victor had made many enemies here, and that he, himself, was not very happy. It was not possible to forget what had happened — the arguments, the criticism — and if Victor was foolish enough to think that these things could be forgotten, at least the kibbutz ought not delude itself. If Victor had really changed — though this was debatable — another kibbutz would be glad to receive him. But not Bilat. Let him begin again elsewhere.

And Nimrod went back to his seat. The audience stirred again, this time — it seemed — more happily. The tide was visibly turning.

The next two speakers — the muscle-bound flutist from the cowshed, and a woman who worked in the laundry — agreed with Nimrod. Bygones could not be bygones, they said. And furthermore, it was highly doubtful whether Victor had changed. It did not matter that he was not a *Rakahnik*, or that he now considered himself a Zionist. A man did not change his political colors overnight. Especially Victor. Let him go elsewhere.

"You see," said Rafael, "I told you they came to get him."

"You think he's finished now?"

"No more predictions."

The next speaker was Reuben Ben-Zvi, an intellectual young man who worked in the bananas, and was born in Bilat. He generally seemed rather calm and self-assured, but now, as he stood before us, he fidgeted with the microphone, and had trouble finding words. It soon became apparent why: he had been a friend of Victor's.

"His only real buddy in the kibbutz," Rafael commented.

Nevertheless, Reuben told the audience, he had not come up to speak simply because he was Victor's friend. There were more important issues at stake than friendship — namely, the right of a man, any man, to hold beliefs that were contrary to those of the majority. Was this or was this not a democracy? That was the question. He, personally, did not agree with Victor, but he still supported his right to hold whatever beliefs he wanted. That was what he had learned here in Bilat as a schoolboy, and that is what he still believed. The kibbutz would be making an awful mistake if they rejected him. It would be going against its most cherished values. And this he would hate to see it do.

"What do you mean?" shouted a woman from the far end of the room. I couldn't see who it was. Drora called for her to come to the microphone: "If you have something to say, say it to all of us. Up here, Sadie, come up here and say it."

Sadie rose and walked quickly to the front of the dining hall, speaking to herself, and other kibbutzniks, as she made her way up there. "What do you mean, Reuben?" she shouted, from the side of the Formica table.

"Use the microphone, please," Drora interrupted her. "Then you won't have to shout."

Sadie glanced at Drora, but ignored her. "Most cherished values, you say! Going against our most cherished values! My God, how can you be so blind?" She hesitated, choking on her anger. "Is communism our most cherished value? Is that what we came from Europe to build here? Communists! Don't you tell *me*, Reuben Ben-Zvi. . ." She choked again.

"Use the microphone, Sadie. For God's sake, use the microphone." Sadie obeyed this time.

"Thirty-five years I have lived here now," she yelled into the microphone. "Thirty-five years ago I came here, chased out of Poland because I was a Zionist, because — they said — I was a communist. I hate communism. I won't live under communism. I won't, I tell you. . ." Her small, wiry body was shaking now in anger.

"If you tell me Victor must come back, I tell you...I tell you I won't let him. I did not spend thirty-five years making this my home, to have some *chutzpan*, some smart-aleck, tell me Bilat is no good, Israel is no good. I have gone through too much because of my beliefs to be harassed in my own home. I won't allow it. I won't let him come back. Not as long as I am here. I swear it."

Her small body bent over the microphone, and Drora went to assist her. The audience was hushed. Slowly, painfully, Drora escorted her back to her seat. Then, she returned to the microphone and called for any further comments.

But nobody came forward. They seemed numbed by Sadie's harangue, and called for Drora to get on with the vote.

"He hasn't got a chance now," Rafael whispered. "Sadie finished him off."

Drora tapped on the microphone. "If there are no more comments, then let us proceed with voting." She called two men to come forward and help with the tabulations. It would be a hand vote. "All right, all those in favor of Victor's return, please raise your right hands."

A large flurry of hands went up, and the tabulators counted.

"Damn," mumbled Rafael, "more than I thought."

"All those opposed?" Another flurry of hands, and the tabulators again counted.

"Abstentions?" The largest number yet, and the two men spent several minutes tallying them. Then they went over and conferred with Drora.

The kibbutz secretary tapped a final time on the microphone, and the dining hall was still. "Comrades!" she boomed out. "It is decided. 75 for, 91 against, 121 abstentions. Victor Lieberman is no longer a member of Bilat."

The Last Thing

It was the last thing they told you. Everything else, you heard about before that. The love life, the Arab threat, the children, the history — they all were told to you early and openly, with no intimation that you were invading their privacy. But this last thing, the thing that probably had molded them more than anything else, they always held back until they finally felt you were becoming one of them. And then they revealed it to you; the men themselves revealed it, and at last you felt you knew what the war meant to them, and why these men, these people, were what they were.

"If you have never been in a war, you will not understand," Edo had told me when I was in Bilat the year before, and asked him about his role in the Six-Day War. "Nor will you understand if you have never fought a war on your own soil. And finally, I am sure you will not understand, if you are not an Israeli because we are the only people who are fighting a war for survival. If we lose, we will no longer have a country, we will no longer be a people. You would have to become one of us to understand what this means."

"So you don't want to talk about it?" I asked.

"No. Nobody will talk to you about it."

And he was right. Not even after I was in Bilat for the second time, and had been a volunteer for a couple of months, would any of the men tell me about the war. There was always a brush-off, sometimes polite and sometimes not so polite, but always with the same result: no conversation. At one point, somewhere around the end of my second month in the kibbutz, I mentioned this to Lea, and she said she would do something about it. In fact, her neighbor's son, Shimon, had been in the Six-Day War, and he had a story which "ought to be told." His tank squadron had been ambushed by the Egyptians near the Canal, and virtually the entire unit was destroyed. He had been given up for dead, until several days after the war when they found him semi-conscious in his tank, among the corpses of his friends. It was terrible, yes, but people needed to know about these things, especially in America, and she would go fetch him.

Shimon came, obviously embarrassed. I had seen him around, a curly-haired tank of a kid, who couldn't have been more than twenty-one, and who was often filthy from spraying the banana trees. He was usually alone, rarely smiled, and now that he stood there listening to Lea, I could see he had a slight twitch over his left eye. "Michael has been here before," Lea told him. "He wrote a magazine article about us, and now is doing a book." Shimon glanced at her, his eye twitched, and he looked down at the floor. "He would like to know something of what happened during the war, something of what you experienced, so that the American readers will have some idea..."

"I'm sorry," Shimon interrupted, "I can't help him. Maybe somone else can. *I* experienced nothing." And with that, he excused himself and left.

"You know, I'm glad he told you. Very glad." Bierman smiled warmly at me, and then at Hannah. "A couple of months ago, Uzi wouldn't have opened up in front of you. He wouldn't have trusted...or let us just say, he wouldn't have felt you were part of the family. Now he does. I can see he does, and it makes me glad."

Uzi, who was now in the bathroom shaving himself, had just told me about his accident on the Canal. It was the first time I had heard about it, and I realized from the hushed, almost confessional way he was telling it, that I was being let in on something of a family secret.

Uzi had missed the war by a matter of weeks. He wasn't quite old enough, so he spent those days in Bilat, "bringing meals to the old men in the trenches." However, shortly after the war, he completed his basic training, and was sent as a tank driver to the Canal.

"The first year I was there, from the beginning right to the end of '68, it was quiet. Not a shot was fired. The Egyptians were only three hundred meters away and we used to yell to them in the few words of Arabic we knew, and they'd answer in the few words of Hebrew they knew. Friendly things like good morning, good evening, how are you? We got to know a few of them by name, and vice versa, so that if someone were missing for awhile, they might yell over, 'Where's Yacob? In Tel Aviv?' And we'd answer. Maybe not the truth, but still we'd answer. In fact, sometimes we even used to swim in the Canal, or fish in it. So did they. We were better swimmers, but they were better fishermen. Or maybe, the fish were on their side. I don't know. Anyway, it was all very friendly — nothing like what happened later."

Then Nasser began his "war of attrition." The fishing and swimming were over. They, the Israelis, had to spend most of their time in the bunkers, as the Egyptians employed the Soviet technique of saturation bombing. Yes, the Soviets were there. You could pick up their voices on the radio, and you could hear them directing the attacks. They were good, all right; they knew what they were doing.

Without them, the Egyptian artillery wasn't worth a damn. The Egyptians would just let it fire at the first noise they heard — no aim, no strategy. But the Soviets were teaching them something. There was no doubt about it.

Had he ever been afraid? No, he answered, not really afraid. Just sort of frozen. You don't think. You know that you're involved in something serious, but you don't think about it. You just go about your business, and hope it goes all right. The only time you do any thinking is, maybe, after something happens, after someone gets hurt.

He remembered how one night he in the Patton tank, and another group in an armored car, went out on patrol. Usually, on such inspection patrols, the tank goes first, then the armored car. But, as they passed through one marshy area, they decided to send the car slightly ahead. It was a mistake. The car went over a series of mines, and everyone was blown to bits. "After something like that, you think about it. You feel awful. You keep wishing you had gone through first in the tank. Then nothing would have happened. They would still be alive."

How had he gotten wounded? Uzi hesitated, and Bierman looked at him reassuringly. "Well, all right, I suppose you know about it anyway. It was on the Canal, last August. August '69. I was acting as an artillery spotter. It wasn't my usual job — usually I was in the Patton — but the regular spotter had just been hit badly. They needed someone to take his place. So I volunteered. You know how it works, right? The artillery is located a couple of kilometers back, and you, the spotter, are right up near the Canal watching where the shells hit. You phone back the corrections. It's a dangerous job. Lots of casualties among the spotters. You're out in the open, and it just takes one close shell, and you've had it. That's what happened to me. A shell hit a dozen or so meters in front of me, and I caught a piece of shrapnel in the groin. I didn't know exactly where at the time, but later in the hospital I found out. I thought it would be the end of my sex life. It looked that way for a while, but now I'm all right."

"Perfectly all right," assured Hannah.

"But, for a while it was touch and go. I'm very lucky. Other guys have it worse. They're scarred for life. Very bad."

"Like Danny," said Hannah. "Your friend in the Patton." Then to me: "Uzi told us about it a week or so ago. It was an awful thing." She looked back at Uzi, and I could see he didn't want to go into it. But Hannah told him I should know these things, and he said all right; he'd make it brief.

Danny was a buddy of his, also a driver in a Patton tank. Shortly before his own accident, he had lent Danny his gold wrist watch. It was about 3:00 A. M., and Uzi had just finished guard-duty. Danny was going on. He needed a watch, so Uzi lent it to him.

"Well, that night his tank caught a direct hit. The other man in the tank was burned to death, and Danny was rushed to the hospital. They didn't think he'd live. He had burns all over the front part of his body, and they thought it would kill him. But it didn't. He survived. I didn't see Danny after that for a year or so until last week. He came over to my table at the club — at the base where I've been reassigned. He was reassigned too. At first, I didn't recognize him. His face was burned so badly, you could hardly tell it was him. He said next month they are sending him to America for plastic surgery. I tried to make believe I didn't see anything so wrong; that really, he looked all right. We laughed, we made jokes, I tried not to be so shocked, and he tried, too. Then, just before he left, he told me how good it was to meet me. He had wanted for a long time to thank me for the watch. It was the only spot on the front part of his body that hadn't been burned. He showed me his wrist. 'Here's your watch,' he said."

"Nobody wants to talk about it anymore. It just makes you sick." Rafael shook his head in disgust, and toweled his hair. We had just come out of the pool, which was now filled with dozens of kids and their parents. It was *Shabat* — my last *Shabat* in the kibbutz.

"Right after the war," Rafael went on, "it was different. People wanted to talk, hear what had happened, get it off their chests. Now they try to forget it. Pretend it isn't going on. It's the only way you can go on enjoying life." He paused, and pointed to a squat, bearded man who was tossing a red and yellow beach ball back and forth with two children. "Jason. Do you know him?"

"Only to say hello."

"Drives the kibbutz truck. A terrific guy. One of the best. Well, he nearly got killed a couple of months ago on the Canal. His squad was ambushed — two or three dead, another six wounded. Only he got out unharmed."

"He told you about it?"

"No, he didn't tell me. But you find out. Believe me, you find out. Then you keep it to yourself. It's no good to go around chatting about these things."

Rafael stood up, and suggested we leave. He had something he wanted to show me, as long as we were on this "miserable subject." We put on our sandals, and started back to the apartment. But instead of taking the direct route, Rafael wanted to go by the main kibbutz gate. There was something near there that I ought to see.

"You know," he continued, as we left the pool area, "it seems strange now, but I'll make a little confession to you — something I haven't told anyone before..." He hesitated for a moment, and looked away at the datepalm trees which were now heavy with brown near-ripe dates.

It made him a little embarrassed, he said, when he thought back on it, but it's the way he used to be...before the war. He was younger then, more adventuresome maybe, and he never knew what war was like. Like a fool, he used to long for action, for fighting. Every time his reserve duty came around he got excited. He'd get into that crisp uniform with the three stripes on the sleeve — he was a sergeant — and go off enthusiastically to his post. He loved the army in those days, and he was always hoping for the chance to meet up with the Arabs and give them a taste of his machine-gun. But back then, there was hardly ever any fighting: a little near Syria, a little more near Jordan in the Negev, but nothing much. The closest he, personally, ever came to action, besides the training maneuvers, was war movies. The John Wayne kind. He and his army buddies used to go to the American films all the time. It was sort of a joke. Here he was on reserve duty, and he'd spend all his free time at war movies. But why not? Back then, he used to love them. A guy would get hit in his tank, or get shot out of an airplane, and he'd yell whoopie! It was terrific. He was a real kid. He knew nothing.

Just outside the front gate, we came to a slightly mangled datepalm tree that grew along the road.

"Looks like it was hit by a mortar," I said.

"Katyusha. See the hole?" He kicked a large mound of dirt that was a yard or so in front of the tree. "Remember it. I'll tell you more about it when we get to the apartment."

"Why the suspense?"

"No suspense. Just keep your pants on. I want you to see something else before I tell you about it."

We left the datepalm trees and headed towards the apartment. Rafael was silent for a moment, and then he began talking again about the war. He was no longer quite so descriptive, quite so casual. The war had been horrible, he said flatly. The taking of the Golan, the conquest of Sinai, the "recapture" of Jerusalem, all the glory that was now theirs, hadn't been worth it. Eight hundred men dead, many of his buddies among them. No, it hadn't been worth it. He knew. He had been in the first group that conquered the Old City of Jerusalem. He had stood there at the Wailing Wall, and no, hell no, it hadn't been worth it at all.

Then, later, when he came back to Bilat and heard about Hanoch and Mota, it was even worse. No matter how you felt about the kibbutz, no matter how often you had talked against it and called it a *kolkhoz*, still these were your friends — yes, even your family. And you felt it. You felt the loss and you realized how you and all the other men had changed. Maybe not at first. This took time. But eventually you saw it. Young boys like David ben-Alon and Shimon Panoff were no longer the same. They had gone away as kids and they came back as tough men — too tough. Panoff, the curly-haired kid who worked in the bananas, was the worst. He had been given up for dead in the Sinai. Then, almost by chance, they found him. He was frozen — emotionally frozen — and now, three years later, he still hadn't really snapped out of it. His nerves were shot. You just had to look at him to see it.

"And, so what do they say about us now?" Rafael asked angrily. "Militarists! War-lovers! That's what they say about us, isn't it? That's what all those New Left Arab sympathizers call us. Militarists!" Rafael's face tightened. He pushed open the front door of his apartment, and knocked over a chair. He didn't bother to pick it up.

"At one time, yes, I loved the uniform, loved the war movies, and wanted to see action. But now? I hate it. More than anything in the world, I hate this war. I don't want to see another minute of fighting in my life. Nobody does. We're sick of it. We who have seen war up close, hate it more than all those stupid kids in England and America who walked with anti-war signs on their shoulders. So what do they call us? Militarists!" Rafael stopped, bent down and picked up the chair, then went over to the closet. He began looking for something, but evidently couldn't find it. So he went on talking, his voice somewhat calmer now.

"Militarists, they call us. It's absurd. I'll tell you who the real militarists are. The Germans! Those are the people who loved our victory, and who still love our victory. That's right, thirty years ago they tried to wipe us out, and today we are their heroes. Did you see the headlines in the German newspapers after the War? No? Well, you should have. 'Israelis Do It Again!,' 'Victors in Six Days!' Things like that. And do you know why? Because we are fighting the dark-skinned Arabs. Never mind that half of us Israelis have dark skins; to the Germans *we* are now the Aryans. I tell you, the whole world is sick. Thirty years ago we were vermin, and now we are supermen." Rafael shook his head, and smiled to himself. "Yes, thirty years ago they made war and we made business. Now we make war, and they make business. So we are their heroes!"

He disappeared momentarily into the closet, and then threw out a folded blue blanket. It landed in the middle of the room. Then, he yanked out a piece of metal, maybe a foot and a half long, and carried it over to the blanket, and dropped it down heavily. It was a bomb fragment.

"Remember the hole?" he asked.

"The Katyusha shell?"

"Most of it. God knows where the rest of it went."

"You found it?"

"I was almost killed by it."

"*What?*"

"The night Hassan was hit. Remember? Well, I was coming back from Tiberias in the truck. I had gone to pick up a load of watermelons..."

"You never told me about this."

"Like I explained before, it's better not to mouth it up about these things. Anyway, the Katyusha hit down fifty meters behind me. I saw the flash, heard the noise, and drove like hell for the first safe spot. I was lucky. Not a scratch. A few seconds later, and I would have been a slice of watermelon myself." Rafael kicked the piece of shrapnel, and chuckled. "A slice of watermelon. Remember that: Rafael Cohen, the nasty Israeli militarist, was almost a slice of watermelon."

"There had to be war. There was no other way. Once Nasser ordered the U. N. troops out of Sharm-el-Sheikh, and U Thant went along with him, we knew we would have to fight. There was no other choice..." Baruch stopped, and called good-night to his two daughters who Ofra was just taking back to the children's houses.

"Why don't I take along Ilan, too," Ofra said.

Ilan was sitting on a cushion to the side of Baruch and me. He folded his arms stubbornly across his chest. "No!" he answered. "I'll go with daddy."

"I'll take him in a little while," confirmed Baruch.

Ofra nodded, and went off with the two girls.

"Actually," Baruch continued, "I knew there would be war before that. Several days before. The Straits of Tiran were closed on May 23rd, and sometime around the 14th or 15th I had been called up to my reserve unit..."

"Below the Golan?"

"Right. A few kilometers from Kibbutz Hulata. Exactly where, I'm not allowed to tell you. Near Hulata is close enough. Anyway, sometime in mid-May I received my notification to show up promptly at my post near Hulata. Our entire battalion had been called up. We all assembled in this one place, and then, a day or so later, we dispersed to our positions — our bunkers, which were right below the first slope of the Golan. We did not have a great deal of equipment — as I told you, we are an infantry battalion — but what we did have, we quickly dug in; protected from the Syrian artillery above. We used the kibbutz bulldozers to do it. By then, the men of that kibbutz were also away, so they weren't using them. They gave them to us...."

"Did you give them back, daddy?" Ilan interrupted.

Baruch laughed. "Yes, we gave them back. The kibbutz only lent them to us."

"Bulldozers are very expensive," Ilan said seriously.

"Right. Very expensive. We gave them back...."

Baruch paused; he seemed to have lost his train of thought. I reminded him that he and his battalion had just dug in, and I asked what had happened next. "Nothing," he answered. "Absolutely nothing." They had just sat around and waited. Three weeks like that, listening to the radio, reading the newspapers, trying to keep calm, and all the time knowing that the war was coming, any day coming.

"When it finally came," Baruch said, "we first heard about it over the radio. Just like anyone else in Tel Aviv or Haifa. There wasn't a shot fired in our area that first day, and if we didn't have the radio we wouldn't have thought anything was going on...."

"Didn't you hear the Israeli jets heading for Syria?"

"No. Nothing. Just the radio. The wonderful radio. But who could believe it? The Egyptian Air Force destroyed on the ground. The Syrian and Jordanian Air Forces completely demolished. Even *we* found that hard to believe. Though of course, we knew it had to turn out that way. There was no other way...."

For his battalion, it began on the second day, June 6th. The Syrian Army, perched above them, opened fire with everything they had — tanks, cannons, Katyushas. The whole area shook. He and his men didn't dare go outside and return the fire, because they had no equipment with which to fight back, and besides, they were in a very poor position. So they stayed inside and took it ("At such times, it doesn't pay to be a hero."), and waited for instructions from Tel Aviv.

But Tel Aviv was uncertain. Should they take the Golan or should they leave it alone? They couldn't decide. On June 7th, his battalion was ordered to attack the following morning. But then the orders were reversed: no attack. They'd leave the Golan alone. The entire battalion would be sent elsewhere. There were even rumors that the war was already over, and they would be sent home.

Yet, no sooner had these rumors begun to sink in, when Tel Aviv again reversed itself: the attack was on again, this time for the morning of June 9th. Naturally, the men were happy that they were getting the chance to take the Golan after all. ("The Syrians had never tasted the full force of the Israeli Army.") But what the hell was going on in Tel Aviv? Why all this switching around?

Later they found out. At first Moshe Dayan had called off the attack because he feared that even with all the softening up which the Israeli Air Force had done to the Syrian positions, there would still be several thousand casualties. It didn't seem worth it. However, once the attack was called off, there came an immediate protest from the kibbutzim that sat right underneath the Golan. For years they had been taking a terrible beating from the Syrian artillery. A delegation of kibbutzniks went to the government and threatened that they would abandon the kibbutzim altogether, if the Golan were not taken. So the attack was called on again.

"On June 10th, at 9:00 A. M., our battalion was loaded into trucks and driven to a thickly wooded area near the border. It was a few kilometers to the south of our bunkers. There, the Golan rose straight up — at about a 45 degree angle — and we could see the first string of Syrian positions. About three hundred meters above us, and very silent. We had no way of knowing whether our air force had destroyed them, or whether they were sitting there, waiting for us. We had to assume the worst.

"We began the climb slowly — in small units, of course. A unit to check for mines, a unit to cover them, and so on. You just don't send eight hundred men rushing up the hill, like in the American war movies. Everyone has a specific job, and the entire battalion functions according to plan. Our plan was to make it up to the first string of Syrian positions before nightfall — if possible....if we weren't pinned down by their artillery.

"As it turned out, we made it up there in just a little over an hour. Our only problem was an occasional mortar shell from further up on the Golan. The first line of defense had been abandoned — completely abandoned. We couldn't believe it. We knew they were poor fighters, cowardly fighters, but we at least expected some kind of resistance. I mean, what army in the world sits directly above you, and then runs in fear? It was hard to imagine.

"The strategy of this — if you can call it that — we discovered on the second leg of our climb. This was another three hundred meters straight up, and we had to assume, from the previous mortar fire, that they were dug in there with all their artillery ready. This, too, overestimated the Syrians. The strategy, evidently, was to catch us up there, when we would be a little tired. But it failed, because almost all of them had again taken off. Only a few units remained, some with artillery, some with machine-guns, and they attempted to hold us back.

"For us, this was the most costly part of the attack. The Syrians didn't need more than a couple of machine-guns to challenge our entire battalion — not from those positions. All they had to do was sit still and wait for us to move. For our part, there was no choice. We had to keep going at them, even though we knew they would hurt us. It was a miserable couple of hours. Stop and go all the time, machine-gun fire all around us. Very bad. There was no time to think about casualties. Later we found out that more than fifty men had been hit; a third of them critically. It was a bad time for us. A very bad time...."

Baruch stopped, and shook his head slowly. Then, without saying anything, he went into the pantry and came back with a platter of fruit. He tossed me an apple, and behind his back he flipped Ilan an orange. The boy dropped it, and it rolled underneath the sofa. "Ah hah!" he said jokingly. "Caught you napping, didn't I?"

"I want to hear about the fort," Ilan answered, ignoring the orange.

"Listen to him!" Baruch said to me. "My commander-in-chief wants to hear about the fort. All right, but first find the orange."

"And tell about the pilot...." Ilan whispered loudly, looking under the sofa for the orange.

"Sssh! Sit still now, and listen!"

All right, Baruch said, the Syrian fort — that pigsty of a Syrian fort. He was surprised they hadn't smelled it five kilometers away. It was that bad. Actually, according to aerial photographs taken of the area prior to the war, it was supposed to be the most important ammunition depot between Israel and Kuneitra. Very heavily armed. But, when they got there, instead of meeting any resistance, they found that the tanks and artillery (all Soviet equipment) had either been abandoned, or destroyed by the Israeli Air Force.

All that remained was the squalid cement fortress which smelled the way that Arab buildings sometimes smell. The bathrooms were next to the mess halls. The rooms were like cages — no beds, no windows. And the soldier's uniforms, still hanging from nails on the wall, were filthy and torn. The only ones who lived at all like human beings were the officers, and they obviously had been the first to run. Almost all the casualties (they had found several dozen corpses) were privates, men from nearby villages who were probably wretchedly poor.

"The whole thing was disgusting to us. Disgusting and pitiful. We knew that the Arab soldiers were treated like pigs, but until you see something like that you do not *really* believe it...."

"I believe it," interrupted Ilan.

"Nobody asked you" Baruch held his hands over Ilan's mouth for a moment. "We had originally intended to make that fortress our temporary base, but one glimpse of it — one whiff of it — was enough to make us change our plans. We decided to find another spot. By then, our army had control of the entire Golan, right up to Kuneitra, and it was just a matter of mopping up a little. Taking prisoners, flushing out the snipers — that sort of thing. We decided to go fifteen kilometers north to K'ala, where we knew there was another abandoned army post — a much smaller one, and hopefully, a cleaner one. We radioed for transportation, and then some hours later, we were picked up by Egged buses — just like the ones you see in Tel Aviv — and we were taken to K'ala, where we stayed for the next few days. We kept the buses with us, and used them to make prisoner roundups.

"These roundups were very pathetic, but still we had to do it. We knew that many of the soldiers were hiding out in their villages. Once they saw that their officers had abandoned them, they got rid of their uniforms and went home. We had no way of knowing whether they were armed or not, but in any case, we weren't about to let Syrian soldiers escape so easily.

"Altogether, we took about a hundred prisoners. The usual procedure was to search every house in the village, and if we found any young men, we asked to see their papers. If they had no obvious reason for being there in the village, we took them. That was the sad part. The wives and mothers begged us not to take them. Once we tied the men up and put them in the bus, these women came running after us, screaming and crying. They were terrified by what we might do to the men. And no wonder! They knew very well what the Syrian Army did to our men; how they were tortured in prison.

That is, if they ever got there, if they weren't butchered by the Syrian Army or the villagers, themselves, somewhere on the way. That's right *butchered!* Two of our pilots shot down over Kuneitra — You know how we found them? — tied to the front gate of an Army fort, disemboweled, and with their genitals in their mouth.

"So, no wonder the women were terrified. If they are barbarians, why shouldn't we be? And you know, I tell you honestly, even though we would never do a thing like that, when we found our pilots that way, we wanted to do something....anything to retaliate. But we didn't. To our credit, we didn't. In fact, except for a few prisoners who gave us a hard time, we never laid a hand on them. We just tied them up and brought them back to K'aia, where we questioned them, and later released them. Almost all of them wound up going back to their homes before we did."

And that was the end of it, Baruch said. After the prisoner roundup, they returned to their original base near Hulata, disposed of their weapons, and returned home. Only the officers stayed longer — for a celebration. There were about twenty-five officers in the battalion, and those with wives arranged for them to be brought to the camp. Then they threw an all-night victory party, and afterwards, they all went on a three-day holiday together — a kind of victory tour.

"Officially, nobody was permitted to travel so soon to the conquered territories, but as officers they let us through. We had about eight command cars, and as a joke, we mounted Syrian flags on the front antennas. We traveled everywhere — the Golan, the West Bank, Jerusalem, Gaza — and each night we had another victory party, and slept out under the stars. It was beautiful. For Ofra and I, who had never been out of this country, it was like a trip to Europe. Very beautiful.

"After this, we returned to Bilat, and I went back to work in the olive groves. The harvest was just about to begin, and there was a lot of work to do. However, as a lieutenant, I had to go to the funerals of all the men killed from my platoon — eleven of them. They were all buried in the same spot, Afula, because it is fairly close to the Golan. I had to make a speech about each of them, and then answer questions from the parents about how their son had died, and whether he had fought bravely. Particularly the Oriental Jews wanted to know that; for them, it is very important that their son fought with honor. And what could I say? Of course they had been brave. Of course they had fought with honor. I do not say this just because I am an Israeli, but because it is true: every man who went up the Golan had to be brave."

A Prediction

September 3, 1970

It was my last evening in Bilat, and Bierman, who had just finished telling me how disappointed he was that I would not stay until the end of the month for *Rosh Hashanah* now announced that he had a prediction to make. It was something he had been meaning to say to me for several weeks, and now, sad to say, he could hold off no longer.

"You may not like to hear this," he began, "because nobody likes to have predictions made about them, especially when they are young like you, and especially when the predictions are true. But I will tell you anyway, and when you are back in America writing your book, you can remember that Bierman told it to you. You can even put it in the book, and pretend it is your own idea."

"*Nu*, Bierman!" Hannah coached. "Stop talking like a lawyer, and say what you have to say."

Bierman smiled, and moved over on the sofa, so that he was sitting right next to me. Then, slowly, almost confidentially, he said: "You remember a few weeks ago, Michael, when Golda announced that we were going to begin the cease-fire with Egypt? You and I watched it on television down there" — he pointed out the window to shelter 7 — "and then we came back here and talked. You remember what you said?"

"Yes....yes, of course." I recalled how disappointed and angry I had been that America had goaded Israel into accepting the cease-fire, and I said — what almost everyone else was saying then — that it would not last. Egypt would break it, and then Israel would have to go in and destroy the missile sites at a heavy cost.

"Right. Exactly right. And I might add, not a bad prediction, except for the fact that we will not be able to go destroy them. For the time being, we will have to live with them. But that is not what interests me right now. What interests me is you — you and us. You, the American Jew, who is becoming...finally becoming, one of us."

"What are you talking, Bierman? He's *already become* one of us."

Bierman laughed. "All right, already become one of us. It's not just Hannah and I who know this, but everyone in the kibbutz. You have changed, Michael."

"Yes, I know."

"I knew you would," added Hannah.

"I am very happy about this," Bierman continued, "and yes, even a little relieved. I'll make a small confession to you; Hannah can tell you that it's true. When you first came here last spring, Michael, you remember we spent that long evening together, and you told us about yourself — your parents, your revolutionary ideas, your Arab friends, and all the rest. You remember that, don't you?"

"Yes."

"You were not one of us then, my friend. A Jew, yes, a Diaspora Jew with his feet in the air, yes — *that* you were. But one of us, no. Not then. And what did I say to Hannah after you left. You know what I said? I told her I was worried about you."

"That's what he said," confirmed Hannah.

"I told her you were too much a *luftmensch*, a man of the air, to change overnight. You see, it's a strange thing about these Diaspora *luftmenschen*. They've been in the air so long, they think they can fly. They forget that their place is on the ground, here in Israel. I was worried that you wouldn't stay here long enough to see this. But now I am no longer worried."

"Nor am I, " added Hannah.

"No, Michael, you can go on saying that you are still unsure, still need time to think it over. I am no longer worried about you. Go back to America, go anyplace you want and write your book. Then you will come back to Israel. I am sure of it. I am sure that next year at this time, next *Rosh Hashanah*, you will be here with us."

"Maybe sooner," said Hannah.

"Never mind sooner. *Rosh Hashanah* is soon enough. He will need time to pack his suitcases. Won't you, Michael?" He placed his heavy hand on my shoulder, and looked at me squarely. "Won't you?"

"Yes....I think so," I answered. "I will need time."